The Outcast Dead

By Paul Slade

ISBN: 9798857162194

Contact:

paul@planetslade.com.

This edition – the book's first in paperback – is an expanded and updated version of the Kindle e-book I published in 2013.

For my parents.

"Almapa"

Table of contents

Guide to illustrations.

Unless otherwise noted, all pics are by Paul Slade.

<u>Book One</u>
The Borough.

The original "Touch 4 Love" sign in 2013.

Introduction

"Where to, mate?" the cabbie asked as I settled in my seat.

"To London's outlaw borough," I thought. To the sanctuary sought by every runaway Roman slave; to the Liberty of the Clink where London's own jurisdiction is left far behind. To the home of bawds, killers and cutpurses throughout our capital's dark history. To the city's dumping ground for its desperate and its despised; to the streets where Victorian industrialists placed their filthiest factories; to the site of London's wildest acid house parties of the 1990s.

Where to? "To Shakespeare's London," I thought. To the site where he and his friends built the original Globe theatre with stolen timbers; to the taverns and brothels where he found his models for John Falstaff and Doll Tearsheet. To the broiling nightlife of bear pits and dogfights, where the young Bard himself was dragged into court for threatening another man's life. To the home of so much great London theatre today.

Where to? "To Shard City," I thought. To the latest tumour spawned by London's financial district, where Renzo Piano's jagged office block is now the tallest building between Guangzhou and Chicago. To the equally soulless developments coming in its wake. To a place of female power, now overshadowed by the biggest prick in Europe; to a giant shiv waved in the face of London's poor.

Where to? "To a host of unquiet graves," I thought. To the site where London's paupers were buried in unconsecrated ground; to a cemetery built for the Bishop of Winchester's licensed whores but later annexed for outcast burials of every kind. To graves which were routinely emptied after only a few months to make room for the newly dead; to the shallow pits where victims of London's plague epidemics were hastily consigned. To a burial ground where the city's most notorious gang of corpse-snatchers knew they'd always find easy meat.

Where to? "To a modern shrine," I thought. To the spot where

—

a shamanic local writer leads monthly vigils to honour its humble dead; to a site which now attracts 50,000 visitors a year. To a pair of gates which Britain's sex workers have made a memorial to their own; to perhaps the only place in Britain where the murdered women of Ipswich, Bradford and Nottingham are given their due. To the display of a thousand fluttering white ribbons carrying the names of three centuries' dead; to a patch of wasteland made beautiful by an invisible gardener. To one of London's most neglected, yet most potent landmarks.

"Where to?" he asked again. "Redcross Way," I replied. "It's in Southwark."

These remains of a Roman mausoleum were discovered on the site right next to Cross Bones. (Pic: Museum of London.)

1: Roman Southwark

Southwark got its first brothels when the invading Roman army arrived in 43 AD.

The Iron Age settlement once sited there had long since been abandoned, leaving nothing but a patch of swampy ground on the south bank of the Thames. General Aulus Plautius marched his troops straight here from their landing point on the Kent coast, a distance of about 63 miles, meeting little or no resistance along the way. Forced to halt by the Thames, they camped opposite what is now Cheapside, where a network of tracks branched out towards every corner of the island.

It was there, on the river's north bank, that Britain's defenders had chosen to make their stand. Plautius ordered his engineers to build a platoon bridge at the relatively narrow, shallow spot where Southwark Bridge now stands and this was quickly done. The Romans made short work of the British fighters waiting at Cheapside, replaced their original pontoon bridge with a permanent wooden structure and set about expanding their Southwark camp into something more like a small town.

"At the bridgehead, they established their commissariat and stores, because Southwark - and not London - would have been their resistance base if the campaign had gone wrong," Ephraim Burford writes in his 1976 book *The Bishop's Brothels*. "At least a cohort must have been stationed there and at that period a cohort comprised between 600 and 1,000 men, to which must be added the supporting establishment and the camp followers. There would have been at least 2,000 people in that settlement at any one time." [1]

Those camp followers included a good number of prostitutes – meretrix was the Roman term - who set up shop in the new timber and thatch buildings provided just off the military highway. Any army camp of that size would have produced ample demand for the women's services and this grew further once the Romans had established landing docks nearby to disembark new soldiers and unload supplies.

Within seven years of arrival, the Romans had already pushed their British frontier all the way to a diagonal line between the Humber and Severn estuaries - now marked by the old Fosse Way. It was also around this time that Roman merchants first built a town on the Thames' north bank, surrounding it with defensive earthworks and christening the place Londinium. Tacitus, the Roman historian, tells us that the Londinium of 61AD was already "much frequented by merchants and trading vessels".

By 75AD, Southwark had grown into a large suburb, snaking out a string of taverns along the access roads to its south. Throughout the Roman occupation, these were the busiest roads in the country, lined all the way to the coast with grog shops and inns, each one with a resident meretrix on duty. As its population grew, Southwark shipped in female slaves from all over the empire to keep its brothels staffed. Evidence of busy landing docks and slave markets from this period has been found all along the Thames' north bank opposite Southwark at sites such as Queenhithe, the Tower and Billingsgate. [2]

A steady supply of new women was essential to replace the many who Southwark simply worked to death. "Once sold, these slaves had no rights whatsoever," Burford says. "Each one would spend the rest of her life on her back, day and night, submitting to every sexual vagary forced upon her by exigent men, until she died. If she were not lucky enough to be bought by some admirer for his personal pleasures, she would die of exhaustion or disease by the age of 30."

Disease was a problem for the Roman army too, if only because it didn't want its men so clap-ridden they could no longer fight. In an age when condoms and penicillin were still centuries away, however, there was nothing much their commanders could do to combat venereal disease but order every soldier to give his balls a good scrub every now and again. The only other precaution available was to ensure that any woman who was obviously diseased be banned from further sex work, and that responsibility fell to a band of civic officials called the aediles.

Every Roman city had a team of these men, who were charged with keeping a register of all the town's licensed sex workers. They financed this operation by collecting a fee and taxes from every woman registered and from every brothel-keeper too. Once she'd got a licence, the woman could choose a name to work under, tell the aedile what type of clients she planned to serve and then hang up a shingle outside displaying her prices. The licence gave her a measure of protection under Roman law, but in return she had to succumb to the aedile's regular health inspections and agree never to dress in a way which concealed her profession. Although local pimps and procurers were free to become Roman citizens, that privilege was not extended to the women themselves. [3]

Southwark's busy brothels soon produced a satellite trade of rough-arse taverns, sleazy gambling joints and every other form of low-life entertainment. These, in turn, pulled petty thieves, gangsters, killers and conmen to the area, partly for the opportunities it offered them and partly because they felt safer there than in respectable Londinium itself. Runaway slaves and other fugitives flocked to Southwark too. "The very nature of the surrounding land - marshy, dank and uninhabited - made it a natural hiding place and refuge," Burford writes. "It was regarded as part of the pomerium of London. This was a swathe of 'no man's land' outside the walls of Roman cities, which was deliberately left clear so that approaching enemies could quickly be spotted and dealt with."

In placing their brothels outside the city wall, with a river segregating them from more respectable neighbourhoods, the Romans were following a familiar pattern from home. Rome's own red light district, the Trastevere, was sited just across the Tiber from the city itself and named to reflect precisely that fact: Trastevere translates as "on the other side of the Tiber".

There were other amusements on offer in Southwark too - perhaps including an arena for the Roman games. Archaeologists have found evidence of a female gladiator's funeral feast in what's now Great Dover Street, and the grave goods buried with this woman suggest she was a worshipper of Isis. Another team of archaeologists found a Roman jug inscribed "London, at the Temple of Isis" in the Thames riverbed near what's now Southwark Cathedral, which Burford believes was used in the regular "days of drinking" her worship required. [4]

By 150AD, the Romans' army base had moved to a new home in London's north-west suburbs, leaving Southwark's brothels to serve a civilian clientele instead. Burford describes their new customers as "freedmen, petty traders, travellers, lower officials, even slaves - and, of course, criminal elements using whorehouses for nefarious purposes."

Rome's soldiers had dominated Southwark for little more than a century, but even in that short time, they laid down the pattern of everything we'd see in the borough for the next two millennia: licensed prostitution, frantic commerce, boozy travellers, disease, low-life entertainment and a dual status as both London's sanctuary and its dumping ground. All these elements will surface again and again as we proceed through Southwark's history, and all their seeds were planted by Roman hands.

John Constable speaking at Cross Bones in 2012.

2: Arriving at the Vigil

The cabbie dropped me off where Redcross Way meets the far wider and busier Southwark Street. A broad Victorian railway bridge passes overhead exactly where these two roads meet, casting everything beneath it into permanent shadow. Redcross Way's narrow entrance - just wide enough for a single car - is topped by a brick archway helping to support the bridge and flanked by two banks of coloured lights blinking forlornly through the gloom. [6]

It was a cold, foggy evening in October 2012, already dark, and that month's vigil at the gates of Cross Bones was due to start at 7:00pm. I had about ten minutes to spare as I entered Redcross Way and I could see a dozen or so winter-coated pilgrims already huddled round the gates, waiting for something to happen. They were mostly women, mostly middle-class and looked like the sort of respectable crowd you might find at a *Guardian* newspaper event or an upmarket crafts fair. Behind them, the Shard thrust skyward, its tip sheathed in fog. [7]

People began decorating this old burial ground's gates with candles, ribbons and other offerings in October 1998, when John Constable led the first of his Halloween processions to the site. Constable himself had discovered the gates only two years earlier when, consumed in a frenzied night's writing at his home nearby, he realised he was no longer alone. He'd been writing that night in his persona as John Crow, a trickster poet figure who first appeared in Constable's 1995 Edinburgh Fringe show *I Was An Alien Sex God*. "When I wrote as John Crow, I was writing in a slightly different persona and going places I wouldn't normally go," he told me a few days after the October vigil. "By about 11:00 o'clock that night, I was in full spate as John Crow, this sort of slightly rogue prophet holding forth. And then..."

And then he sensed another presence in the room. "It was as if a fleshed-out, fully-formed character walked into the room and started telling me her history, in my head, in verse," Constable told me. "I was quite scared by it. I thought I'd pushed the boat out a bit too far that night and we weren't coming back. So I started writing it all down." [8, 9]

The medieval prostitutes who worked the streets of Southwark had the Bishop of Winchester as their landlord and hence were nicknamed Winchester Geese. These were the women first consigned to Cross Bones and Constable quickly came to think of his visitor as a voice for them and all the others buried there. What else could he do but name her in their honour: she was the Goose. He'd read some of the Winchester Geese's history while researching Southwark for another project, but never heard it told in such urgent and vivid terms as he did that night.

"It was things I knew, but they seemed to be coming out in a much more radical form," he later wrote. "With this narrator, with her own voice. The Cross Bones graveyard reference - 'And well we know how the carrion crow / doth feast in our Cross Bones graveyard' - was like the hidden part of the jigsaw. I was seeing all these visions of places and, for that, when I wrote it down, the vision was of a graveyard - but I was thinking pirates, really. I pictured the Goose with a knife in her garter in case one of her johns got out of order. Later, I thought it was as if she'd deliberately kept one card hidden to impress me." [10]

Most people didn't know Cross Bones existed in 1996 and Constable is adamant he'd never heard of it either. But he's content to let others interpret his experience however they will. My own suggestion was that he must have already known about Cross Bones long before the Goose's visit, but that the information had since slipped so far to the back of his mind that he no longer knew he possessed it. Surely the Goose was simply a product of his own brain, teased into an altered state by the John Crow process, finding a way to haul the burial ground's name back into his conscious awareness?

"I can't say I'd never unconsciously seen some little footnote in a paper," he replied. "Whether that's true or not, I just don't know. What I know is that it presented itself to me that night as a completely unknown thing. When I wrote those lines, I saw it almost as the Goose trying to scare me. And I was scared: it was a frightening night."

What's undeniable is that *something* happened that night and whether we call it a ghostly vision, a resurfaced memory or a drug experience, Constable's life would never be the same again. The two birds - Goose and Crow - laced their wings together the moment they met, they've flown in tandem ever since and many changes in the concrete, tangible world around us have directly followed from that.

By now it was the small hours of the morning, but the Goose hadn't finished with Constable yet. As her fragments of poetry accumulated, he realised they were building towards a verse journey through the streets of Southwark, with the Goose leading John Crow through the Borough's dark history. It was obvious what he had to do next. "By now, it was after midnight and this was a rough area, but I felt completely fearless," Constable told me. "Maybe it was the Goose saying to me 'Don't worry, dearie: we're the scariest thing on the street tonight'. So we went on this long walk."

Southwark in 1996 was a far more dangerous place than it is today. In those days, taxi drivers often refused go there after dark and the police warned residents against showing their cash in the street. Redevelopment of the area had hardly begun, and its poorly lit alleyways still led through a maze of derelict warehouses and Dickensian railway arches, in neighbourhoods which Victorian reformers had reckoned among the worst in London.

Progressing first through the local history sites Constable did know - the Cathedral, Chaucer's Tabard Inn, the site of Shakespeare's original Globe Theatre - the Goose eventually led him up from Marshalsea Road, under the trees towards a fenced patch of anonymous waste ground in Redcross Way. "I remember walking up there having a very particular, perhaps a Blakean, sense of eternity," Constable said. "That was the place where I felt 'I'm John Crow, walking in eternity – now'.

"We ended up at the gates of Cross Bones. I didn't know what they were, but it seemed like there were these voices coming through - they started singing. There were lots of cans rattling, papers blowing. There were all these sounds that were making me very jumpy. And somehow, out of that, *John Crow's Riddle* almost sang itself there at the gate. I was kind of singing it, but not knowing where it came from. So I wrote more at the gates and I carried on walking and I came home and I wrote more. Finally, I went to sleep at dawn."

I knew the bare bones of this story already as I entered Redcross Way on that October night, taking in the crowd outside the gates, the office workers arriving at the Boot & Flogger pub directly

---

opposite and the two old charity schools which lay ahead of me towards the Union Street corner. I'd been here five or six times before and watched the vertical bars of the tall, locked gates become more and more crammed with offerings of all kinds: costume jewellery, crocheted flowers, dreamcatchers, poems, scraps of ribbon from a child's dressing-up box, a silk stocking. All those objects were still in place, plus a thousand more besides. [11]

I didn't know it at the time, but that night's event was to be the 101st vigil held at Cross Bones and the last one its celebrants planned before taking a break from the custom. Perhaps that's why they'd made a special effort to decorate the gates, hanging a long string of red and gold bunting showing Our Lady of Guadalupe along the top of the gates and a truly beautiful quilted portrait of Santa Muerte next to the graffitied wooden fence. A row of flickering candles in glass jars ran along the gates' base, next to a child's cheap bracelet, a bird-shaped wicker basket and a bottle of Gordon's gin. Through the bars behind the Santa Muerte quilt, I could see Cross Bones Mary, the battered Madonna statue standing guard just inside the site entrance. [12]

The crowd had grown to about 50 people by 6:55pm, when a tall, white-haired man wearing a long velvet cloak and beads round his neck strolled up. John Crow had arrived and we were ready to begin.

Cross Bones in song

The Winchester Geese, by Stuart Forester (2010).
"Say a prayer for all your sins / Cross your bones and take to wing / A pauper's grave is all that waits / And you'll be turned from Heaven's gates." I discovered this acclaimed Hull folksinger's mournful account of the tale on a YouTube video filmed in Southwark's Bermondsey Square. That's since vanished, but the studio version on his *Pennies for Gold* album survives.

Winchester Geese, by The Unbending Trees (2010).
Hungary's answer to Low pare it right down to a slow, whispered mediation of harp and vocals alone here. "No-one knows about them / No-one cares about them / The Winchester Geese / Men could make them fly by / Men could make them fall down / Just as they please." Filmed in a studio rehearsal, but – as far as I'm aware – never released on disc.

A Rose for a Winchester Goose, by John Crow (2011).
John Constable's shamanic alter ego recorded this slow, gentle ballad with acoustic guitar, harmonica and female backing vocals. It tells the story of a sea captain called Tom Bones, who leaves his true love working in a Bankside brothel while he goes off to roam the oceans. Their story begins as a straightforward love song, but turns sour when Bones returns home. Hear it for yourself on Reverbnation.com.

Crossbones Graveyard, by Pillarcat (2011).
This driving, bass-led instrumental is very much a showcase for the band's rhythm section, with background colouring added by some subtle horns and flashes of wibbly synth. The result is both catchy and enjoyable. Find it on their 2012 album *Weave*.

Lullaby and Leave This City, by Gaggle (2012).
The all-female choir performed both these songs at the Cross Bones gates during the June 2012 ceremony there. The first was chosen for its chorus ("Will you take good care of me?") and the second because, as the choir's Katy Wilkinson put it, "it's about having nowhere else to go". In their album versions, both songs feature shrill and sometimes jarring electronic music, set against moments of childlike, delicate

beauty. Available on: *From the Mouth of the Cave*.

Winchester Geese, by Cherry Choke (2013).
Leicester psych-rock outfit tear it up onstage with this number from their *In the Arms of Venus* LP. Highlights include the powerhouse drums and a couple of admirably stinging guitar solos. I caught a reference to "resurrection men" in one verse, but beyond that the lyrics are a mystery to me.

A quilted portrait of Santa Muerte on the Cross Bones gates.

3: Laying Siege

The Roman Empire ended its persecution of Christians in about 313AD, a century or so before its soldiers abandoned Britain altogether. Christianity here slowly grew in numbers and visibility throughout the fourth century, but was still very much a minority faith when the Romans went home in 410AD. Most Britons continued worshipping the old pagan gods, who seemed to serve them perfectly well.

The historian Mary Boast believes that the disruption following Rome's withdrawal may have pushed crowded, anarchic Southwark to the point where it became unsafe for civilian occupation. Presumably, that means the various local warlords were fighting to see who could gain control of the area, whose bridge access alone made it well worth having. Any lingering residents risked becoming collateral damage, so only those with no other choice would have stuck around.

Evidence from this era is very scarce, but it does seem that Southwark had been at least partially tamed by about 550AD, when the seven Saxon kingdoms known as the Heptarchy began their 200-year rule. The Saxons were an oral rather than a written culture, but we do have references to bustling wharves and trading docks along the Thames during their time. By 850AD, Christianity had tightened its grip enough for the Bishop of Winchester - later canonised as St Swithin - to build a monastery at Southwark, near the southern end of the bridge. This building later became the nunnery of St Mary Overie, the first in a string of transformations which made it more and more important to the borough's life as time went on.

In 871AD, the invading Vikings took occupation of London, giving the brothels that still flourished in Southwark a whole new clientele. "The Danes would certainly have had regard for the maintenance of any institutions of pleasurable convenience on Bankside during the lulls in the fighting," Burford writes. "The customers' nationality did not concern the whores or their masters. It was the cash that counted."

From the women's own point of view, the new clients were something of an improvement. John of Wallingford's *Chronicle*, written in the 13th century, describes the Danish mercenaries stationed in East Anglia when London was over-run. "[They] caused much trouble to the natives of the land," he writes. "For they were wont, after the fashion of their country, to comb their hair every day, to bathe every Saturday, to change their garments often and set off their persons with many such frivolous devices. In this manner, they laid siege to the virtue of married women and persuaded even the daughters of the nobles to be their concubines."

The Danish occupation of London ended in 886AD, leaving King Alfred with the job of rebuilding the city they'd sacked. It was his renewal of the dilapidated wooden wharves and bank reinforcements in Southwark which gave the area its modern name. Alfred's "Suthringa Geweorche" (Surrey Works), became "Sudweca" (South Works) and finally "Southwark". [13]

By the year 1000AD, there was already a Saxon mint in Southwark, suggesting again that some order had been restored. As a recognised borough - that is to say, a fortified town in its own right - Southwark remained independent from London, with the right to make its own laws. There were other boroughs scattered around London too, but Southwark had a military importance to the city which put it in a category of its own. It became known not merely as a borough, but *the* Borough - a nickname Londoners still use for the area today.

Southwark's people took their independence seriously, and none more so than Godwin, Earl of Wessex, who owned a lot of property in the town. In 1052, he mounted a challenge against King Edward the Confessor, anchoring his ships off Bankside in a show of force. But the *Anglo Saxon Chronicle* tells us that "his band continually diminished the longer he stayed" and it's thought that's because they were unable to resist slipping off to Southwark's nearby brothels. The rebellion succeeded in forcing Edward to end Godwin's exile abroad, but got no further than that.

One of Godwin's beefs with Edward had been the Normans' increasing influence in the English court, which culminated in William the Conqueror's invasion of 1066. William's cavalry chased the remnants of King Harold's fleeing army all the way to London, where the city's fortifications forced them to turn back. Frustrated, the invaders burnt the churches and inns along Borough High Street, but seem to have left the riverside brothels untouched. Like the Vikings before them, perhaps they felt these establishments were too good to waste. [14]

One account has it that William himself owned brothels in Rouen, a business venture that carried no hint of stigma at the time. European royalty and nobles in every country thought nothing of renting property on their land to brothel-keepers and were happy to openly take the income this produced. The other major landlord of that era was the Christian Church, which did exactly the same thing. But raking in the cash these rents provided did not stop the bishops simultaneously condemning anyone whose sexual morality they found wanting.

"It was the Norman Conquest that really cemented the power of the church in England," the BBC website says. "The medieval period in Britain is really a story of how Christianity came to dominate the lives of the ordinary people. From the cradle to the grave, and every stage in between, the Church could be your ally or your foe - and ultimately your passport to heaven or hell." [15]

Marriage then had little to do with romantic notions of love, but was a hard-headed calculation between two families who each believed they had something to gain from the union. It was understood that young men must be permitted to sow their wild oats, but essential this didn't endanger the family's plans. "If you were a young buck or a nobleman - an alderman's son, say - you couldn't have a sexual relationship with your social equals for the simple reason that it would cause a scandal if it came out," the Southwark historian Patricia Dark told me.

"Obviously, if you got married, that would be fine. But if you get married to the girl next door because you've knocked her up, you probably aren't going to be generating any advantage for your family. Whereas, if you take your hormones off to Southwark and deal with your needs that way, you still have the freedom to enact a better marriage. Whenever possible, you're trying to marry up." [16]

Two hundred years of more or less unbroken warfare had created thousands of widows and orphans in the English countryside and devastated much of the farmland they needed to survive. The conscription and slaughter of the Crusades, which began in 1096, hit rural areas far harder than the towns too, because the noblemen leading this charge to the Holy Land used farm workers from their own estates to drag along as cannon fodder. Many of the women left behind in England's villages had no option but to trudge into the nearest large town, hoping to eke out a living there however they could - and for many that meant just one thing. "Women of doubtful virtue abounded," Walter de Hemingburghe wrote after visiting a medieval fair. "The price was a packet of lace needles."

There would never again be enough legitimate work for the hordes of poor women flooding into urban areas. Southwark's brothels were where many women in this position finished up and the Church's new dominance there meant it would rule every aspect of their lives. [17]

Jen Cooper at the Cross Bones gates with a photo of her late son Gary.

4: Samhain at the Gates

We come now to the tricky question of what name I should use for the man who officiated at the Cross Bones vigil that October. Was it John Constable running things that evening or John Crow? Constable's own answer can be found in Dr Adrian Harris's 2010 paper *Honouring the Outcast Dead*. "A newcomer to Cross Bones, apparently a little unsure about which John had shown her around the graveyard, asked if his name was John Crow," Harris writes. "'Yes,' he said and added with a smile, 'especially here'." So: John Crow it is. [18]

Greeting a few familiar faces in the crowd, Crow picked up three or four of the candles waiting at the base of the gates and handed them out among the crowd. The women he'd chosen clutched the candles reverently to their chests, the light dancing on their faces from below. Suddenly, our gathering looked like a carol service and that proved quite an appropriate image for the ceremony that followed.

Two of the evening's helpers shrugged into yellow high-visibility vests and shuffled us all a few steps forward out of the narrow road to form a close-packed congregation around Crow and the gates behind him. These were the Goose Samurai, he explained, and the yellow "no parking" lines which now separated us from Redcross Way could be viewed either as a simple marker to keep us safe from traffic or, more mystically, as the boundary of our ritual's "liminal zone". The Goose Samurai themselves preferred a more playful term: "Please keep within the Lines of Death," they reminded us every time a car approached.

On the dot of 7:00pm, Crow rang a tiny bell to mark the beginning of the ceremony. He told us a little about the history of the site and the ideas behind tonight's event, explaining that each month's vigil had a slightly different theme. I smiled when he mentioned in passing that every July's vigil was dedicated to Isis, thinking what a pleasing echo this made of the ancient Roman worship I'd been reading about. Often, the vigil's theme is a seasonal one, drawn from the pagan calendar, and tonight we were to celebrate Samhain ("sou-wain"), an old Gaelic festival marking the end of the harvest season and the beginning of winter.

Jen Cooper, another of the helpers, handed round a bundle of black cardboard leaves, about six inches long, cut carefully into shape and with a handwritten message added in silver marker pen. On one side, mine read, "The Goose and the Crow bring you the Samhain gift of…". Flipping it over to complete the message, I found "…open pathways". These, Jen explained, could be kept as our own souvenirs of the evening, added to the gates as an offering to Cross Bones' dead, or passed to someone else in the crowd as a gesture of goodwill. I kept mine and have it still. [19]

As we settled into the ceremony, an atmosphere of quiet respect spread through the crowd and one which even the sillier "new age" aspects of the proceedings could not dispel. As Crow began telling us about the type of people condemned to a Cross Bones burial, for example, it suddenly felt very wrong that I should still be wearing my cap, so I found myself removing it and spent the rest of the evening bare-headed.

Crow dotted two or three songs throughout the ceremony, performing them with an acoustic guitar and encouraging us all to sing along. That's a big ask for a thoroughly repressed white Englishman of my generation, but even when it came to *Hoof & Horn's* hippyish insistence that we are all "one with the Goddess", I did my best to join in. I was quite emphatically *not* there to mock what was going on and, once I persuaded myself to surrender a little, I had to admit the evening was rather moving. Twenty minutes in, I found myself so swept along by the ceremony that I was reaching forward to touch the gates and chanting along with the best of them.

At the heart of every Cross Bones vigil are the long white ribbons distributed to everyone attending, each with a name, a date of death and an address or occupation inked on to it by hand. These are drawn from a list of about 150 names which Constable compiled from the St Saviour's Parish burial register, selecting those individuals whose circumstances marked them as likely candidates for a pauper's grave. The parish records don't distinguish between the various different graveyards in St Saviour's, so this is the best hope we have of putting a name to most of Cross Bones' dead. "The truth is, the vast

---

majority of people, we don't even know their names," Constable told some visitors at the gates in 2006. "These names are really symbolic of all the people who are buried here." [20]

"It's a tricky thing, because people like absolute certainty," he added when I questioned him about the ribbons later. "I went to the Metropolitan Archives and found two microfiche rolls full of names from the 18th and early 19th centuries. My guide was really just professions and addresses. Somebody from the workhouse, somebody found dead in the street, all that kind of stuff. Someone with an address like Redcross Way, or Union Street or one of those neighbouring streets. And jobs - the sort of good, honest, working-class job that might still indicate you're likely to end up at Cross Bones. I think the most we ever tied on the gates was 123 names at one of the Halloween vigils."

The ribbon Jennifer handed me at the October vigil was labelled "3rd November, 1838. Eliza Hennacey, Gravel Lane, aged 4 months". When everyone in the crowd had taken one, Crow asked us each to read our own ribbon's details aloud, overlapping or taking turns as we pleased, and then to step forward and tie it on the gates. He asked the veterans there to take a lead and about half the rest of the crowd followed suit, the names and dates spilling out to fill the night air around us. [21, 22]

When a moment's silence opened up, I read out Eliza's name, trying to give my tone a touch of extra poignancy when I reached her age, then knotted her ribbon tightly round a bare spot on the gate's upright bars. All around me, others were doing the same. Crow turned to face the gates and recited some Japanese verses beneath our jumbled chorus of names, dates and ages. A slight sense of absurdity seemed to strike him at this point and he said something about the vigils including some elements which seem thrown in almost at random, but that being just the way they've evolved over the years. [23]

After another song - I believe it was *John Crow's Riddle* - we turned to future plans for Cross Bones and the City of London's new interest in Southwark. With the £450m Shard development now completed so close to Cross Bones, Crow explained, pressure to build here could only increase. Our own concerns about the site came in a long historical tradition, he added, calling forward another Cross Bones helper to illustrate this. She read aloud from an 1883 letter to *The Times* protesting at plans to use Cross Bones as a building site even then. In the letter, Lord Brabazon, chairman of the Metropolitan Public Gardens Association, called on the authorities "to save this ground from such desecration and to retain it as an open space for the use and enjoyment of the people". [24]

In an ideal world, that's what the Friends of Cross Bones would like too, with the site turned into a public park and given over to the local residents. In our later interview, though, Constable acknowledged that some development there is probably inevitable and the most realistic strategy is to insist that this incorporates a small memorial garden to acknowledge Cross Bones' significance. "Clearly, the land is worth millions," he told me. "To tell Transport for London, 'You can't develop any of it' would be insane. But at the same time, it cannot be simply about the financial value of the land - it needs to take account of what that land means to people." [25]

Back at the gates, Crow took us through a little more of the site's history, then asked if anyone there would like to step forward and perform a song or poem of their own. The first to oblige was a woman in woolly hat and glasses who looked rather like a put-upon librarian. She read her own poem about coming to the Cross Bones site every time she felt lost for some reason and the way it helped her celebrate a wild side to her personality which found no outlet elsewhere. Next up was a painfully shy young man called Sergai with long black hair and a black beard, who borrowed Crow's guitar to sing a few verses which he said had occurred to him that very moment. He sang and played very quietly for a minute or two, then dissolved in a cloud of self-consciousness, handed back the guitar and melted into the crowd again. "That just came from the moment, didn't it?" Crow said as we clapped. "That's lovely."

Crow gave us one more of his own songs then, after about an hour of ceremony, it was time to wrap things up. We shuffled even closer in, those at the front almost burying their faces in the be-ribboned gates, and Crow led us in a couple of final chants, one dedicated to the Goose herself and one to the gates' role as an improvised shrine. As we repeated each line, Jen circled behind us, drizzling gin on the ground to bind us all inside the ritual's sacred space. The gin's juniper scent infused the air like incense as we chanted the ceremony's final words:

"Here lay your hearts, your flowers,
Your book of hours,
Your fingers, your thumbs,
Your 'Miss you, Mum's,
Here hang your hopes, your dreams,
Your 'Might have beens',
Your locks, your keys,
Your mysteries. " [26]

As our scrum round the gates broke off into knots of two or three, Jennifer passed the goose-shaped wicker basket round for donations to help defray the cost of the evening. The taller guys present were drafted to untie the Guadalupe bunting so it could be safely stored for another day, one or two of us took the opportunity to buy a copy of Constable's *Southwark Mysteries* paperback and, amid many hugs, people started to drift away. As I turned back up Redcross Way towards the Tube, I heard a final voice from the gates behind me. "Someone finish off the gin," it said. [27]

Why was Cross Bones left unconsecrated?

One question no-one can quite answer about Cross Bones is why St Saviour's vestry would have refused to consecrate one of its official parish burial grounds. Even if we assume the parish took a dim view of sex workers, it seems a little rough to consign the blameless paupers buried there to the same treatment.

The Museum oLondon's report offers a possible explanation. "This is probably due to the land being held on a lease from the Bishop of Winchester," the report says. "It was customary to consecrate only freehold land." St Saviour's *did* consecrate the local workhouse's leased burial ground, but Southwark historian Patricia Dark confirmed this practice would have been the exception rather than the rule. [28]

"It was very unusual, because you have a fundamental tension between the fact that it's consecrated and the fact that it will one day revert to someone else," she told me. "With Cross Bones, it could be that they just decided, 'Well, this is going to be used as a graveyard and nothing but a graveyard, so it's consecrated in all but name'."

Dark thinks it's also possible that Cross Bones had been consecrated once, long before St Saviour's Parish took an interest in the site - perhaps by the Bishop of Winchester himself when he still had charge of the surrounding Liberty. If so, no record of this ceremony has survived, but that's not to say St Saviour's wasn't aware of it at the time.

A third possibility is that St Saviour's first leased Cross Bones during one of the periodic spikes in Southwark's death rate and was simply too busy shoving fresh corpses into the ground to worry about niceties like consecration. This is lent some support by sources claiming St Saviour's first took out the Cross Bones lease in 1665, the year of the Great Plague. In circumstance like that, who could blame the churchwardens for choosing to believe the Bishop must have consecrated his Liberty's burial ground at some point or another and just get on with the emergency at hand?

"It's one of those things that nobody quite knows, so everyone's being a little bit cagey on it," Dark told me. "But I do find it weird that the parish would be burying people on ground they knew for certain wasn't consecrated."

It's also worth asking whether the people who buried their loved ones at Cross Bones cared whether it was consecrated ground or

---

not. The Reformation of the 1530s, which transformed England into a Protestant country, had erased the Catholic concept of Limbo and any notion that your place of burial influenced your soul's destination. But how far that doctrinal change filtered through to the hearts of Southwark's common folk is another matter.

"Popular or uneducated perceptions were in many respects out of line with official teachings," Reading University's Professor Ralph Houlbrooke told me. "The post-Reformation Protestant church insisted that where a body was buried had no influence whatsoever on the fate of the soul. But many of the poor and less well-educated may well have thought it unlucky to be buried in unconsecrated ground." [29, 30]

"There's always been a lot of shame around people not being given the burial they would have hoped for," adds Southwark Cathedral's Dean Andrew Nunn. "Think of the way we talk about paupers' graves and things like that - people being buried by the local council - there is some shame attached to that. If Cross Bones were known to be unconsecrated ground, there would be a feeling of shame to it – [the idea that] shameful people deserve a shameful burial."

Whatever their theological fears about a burial at Cross Bones, however, most of the families facing that prospect would have other worries higher on their list. "It is likely their overwhelming priority was the cost of burial," Professor Jeremy Boulton of Newcastle University explained. "A pauper burial, wherever it took place, was done at parish expense. Those interred had to accept a lower quality interment in exchange for not paying burial fees." [31]

The short answer to Cross Bones' unconsecrated status, then, seems to be that no-one in authority cared enough about the people buried there to bother changing it. The families themselves had no clout to protest and would in any case have feared that consecrating the site might lead to higher fees. "Burial location was determined far more by social status than by religious or spiritual concerns," Boulton reminded me. [32]

Dean Andrew Nunn of Southwark Cathedral.

5: Birth of the Liberty

England started the 12th century with a new King, when Henry I seized the throne from his older brother William Rufus in 1100. Both men were sons of William the Conqueror, whose 1086 Domesday Book survey of the kingdom mentions St Saviour's dock as a working harbour and credits the area with at least 40 households and a large church on the site of what's now Southwark Cathedral. The Icelandic saga *Heimskringla* refers to a place across the river from London called Suthvirki, which it says was "a very considerable trading place" in the 11th century.

Most of Southwark - or Suthvirki - was then owned by Bishop Odo of Bayeux, William the Conqueror's brother. Shortly before Henry took the throne, Odo passed his Southwark estates to the Abbot at Bermondsey Priory. That change came in 1090 and was signed into law by Henry when he granted the priory jurisdiction over "the hide of Southwark". This meant neither London nor the county of Surrey had any authority over Southwark and created what was later known as a "Liberty" - an area ruled only by its *hlāford*, an Old English word which translates roughly as "lord of the manor".

"All justice came from the King," the Southwark historian Patricia Dark told me. "The person who was ultimately responsible for courts and taxes and fines and fees - and who ultimately got them - was the King. But the King can do whatever he wants and one way to either reward a faithful follower or to make somebody into a faithful follower was to give them the rights of justice for a certain geographical area. It could be a county, it could be the area immediately round your manor, it could be a whole bunch of different manors."

In creating a Liberty, the King would retain the right to try major civil cases and very serious criminal offences such as murder in his own courts, but delegate everything else. "Quite a lot of the fines and fees would go into the coffers of whoever held the rights," Dark explained. "So if you were the King, you had a vested interest in saying, 'If it's a really, really big civil case, then I want that money to go into my purse, not yours'."

Another gap in the Liberty's power was the right to try clergymen. Even the King didn't have this power, which the Church insisted on retaining for itself, so he was in no position to delegate it to the Liberty either. "Technically, if you were a priest, you could not be tried under the King's justice," Dark told me. "You were not a subject of the King so much as you were a subject of the Church." It followed that members of the clergy who committed a crime must be tried in the Church's own ecclesiastical courts. This underlines the point that even an Abbot or a Bishop relied on secular authority in running his Liberty, not on religious power. In this respect, they were just one more earthly lord of the manor like any other. [33]

For the Abbot, Odo's gift brought the opportunity to collect rent from Southwark's residents and fines from those who broke his rules. But it also carried the troublesome duty of policing this turbulent part of London. The King's courts would step in where an exceptionally serious charge such as murder was involved, but otherwise whatever happened in Southwark was the Abbot's problem - and perhaps that's why he decided not to hang on to the area for long. In 1107, he leased the Liberty's 70 acres of Bankside real estate between Southwark Bridge and what's now Tate Modern to the Bishop of Winchester, William Giffard, at an annual rent of £8.

This area included all of Southwark's biggest brothels plus its most violent, crime-ridden pubs - and the Abbot made it clear that taking over responsibility for keeping order there was part of the deal. Unlike the priory at that time, which had started rebuilding only in 1082, Giffard's bishopric had the staff and organisation needed to set up a proper administration at Southwark with all the courts, bureaucrats and enforcers that required. "It was the responsibility of the hlaford to administer correction to the 'light-tayled huswives of the bank' for the sins of fornication and whoredom, as well as overseeing the 'light' houses themselves," Burford writes. "And Bishop Giffard had now become the hlaford." [34]

It's important to understand that bishops in medieval England were not just churchmen, but politicians and statesmen too. Winchester was one of the oldest, richest and most important dioceses in the country at this time, which ensured its bishop a great deal of influence. "In the very early part of the medieval period, Winchester was actually the most important city in England for the simple reason that's where the Royal Treasury was," Dark told me. "When William Rufus died in the New Forest, the first thing Henry I - as he became - did was to ride hell for leather to Winchester and claim the Treasury, which contained the crown." [35]

Winchester is only 60 miles from London, but even that might be two days' journey in the 12th century. By taking on the Southwark estates, Giffard was planting his bishopric's flag in the nation's capital and ensuring it a useful source of income there too. Not only that, but the Liberty's Thames-side frontage gave anyone living there an easy commute by river from the steps at Stoney Street to the King's Westminster court.

Giffard was succeeded as Bishop of Winchester in 1129 by Henry de Blois, who immediately decreed that heavy new penalties must be imposed on any woman found working in the Bankside brothels while infected with "the filthy disease". He certainly had some kind of venereal disease in mind, but we don't know which one. [36]

At some point in the 1140s, de Blois tightened his grip on Southwark by purchasing the leased land outright and beginning work on a new bishop's palace there, which he called Winchester House. Because he bought the Liberty's land in his official capacity, it would pass down to be managed by each new Bishop of Winchester in turn. Just like a modern corporation, the bishopric itself was effectively immortal and that ensured the arrangement could remain stable for centuries to come. De Blois had helped his brother Stephen take the English throne in 1135 and remained a major player even after Henry II became monarch in 1154. "Winchester House would have been his pile in London and it allowed him to keep a finger on the political pulse," Dark told me. "He was somebody powerful enough that even Henry II couldn't oppose him."

As the Liberty's ruling authority, de Blois was entitled to collect rents and licence fees from all the individual brothel owners along the Bankside, as well as fines from anyone found guilty in the courts he maintained to police these establishments. His new palace was sited neatly between the church that became Southwark Cathedral and the notorious Clink prison where offenders were consigned. Tucked cosily between these symbols of his godly authority on one side and his secular responsibilities on the other, de Blois surveyed his domain. [37]

The official name for this area was the Liberty of Winchester, but its sarcastic residents dubbed it the Liberty of the Clink instead. The prostitutes who filled its streets were quickly nicknamed "Winchester Geese" to reflect the Bishop's role as their new lord and master. The Bankside brothels themselves came to be called "stews" either after the carp ponds on the Bishop's estate (which were known as "stew ponds" for their role in supplying food) or as a corruption of "estuwes", the Norman French word for "stove". It's thought that the stoves lent this name first to the bath-house sweating tubs they heated, then to the bath-houses themselves and finally to the brothels which bath-houses were always assumed to contain. It followed that the brothel-keeper was known as a "stew-holder", even when - as was often the case in Southwark - his establishment offered no bathing facilities at all. [38]

In 1161, Henry II decided he needed to beef up the rules imposed by custom on Bankside for over a century and signed into law his *Ordinances Touching the Government of the Stewholders in Southwark Under the Direction of the Bishop of Winchester*. Soldiers returning from the Crusades were bringing all kinds of new STDs and other infections back with them to England and Henry knew from his own brothels in France just how much disease and disorder such establishments could spread if not properly policed. It was time to crack the whip.

Southwark's customary rules, the proclamation explains, "of late were broken to the great displeasure of God and great hurt unto the lord and utter undoing to all his poor tenants there dwelling and also to the great multiplication of horrible sin with the single women, who ought to have their own going and coming at their own liberty, as it appears by the old customs". Henry's new ordinance set out 39 rules for running the brothels on Bankside, formalising the understanding of established custom and practice there into cold print. The regime these rules imposed - its rights as well as its penalties - gave Southwark's brothels what amounted to royal recognition, giving them a special status and protection they would enjoy for the next four centuries.

Henry's rules fell into seven broad categories. Here's a taste of what he included:

Protecting the "Single Women"

- Amount of rent a woman could be expected to pay for her chamber within the brothel set at 14 pence per week. She must be allowed to enter and leave at will.
- Quarterly police searches to ensure no women were imprisoned in a brothel. If found, such prisoners to be escorted out of the Liberty, and hence beyond the stew-holder's reach.
- Any loan from the stew-holder of more than six shillings and eightpence to be declared void by the Bishop's court – the idea being to avoid women being enslaved by the running up of unpayable debts.

Protecting the Customers

- Customers refusing to pay their bills must no longer be imprisoned on the premises or have their belongings confiscated. Disputes of this kind to be settled by the Bishop's court instead.
- No stew-holder to allow any woman to operate from his premises if he knows she is either pregnant or has "the burning sickness" (probably gonorrhoea).

Protecting the Church

- On religious holidays, the stews could open only between the hours of noon and 2:00pm. (Evidently, there was a lunchtime trade to be catered for.)
- All sex workers to remain outside the Liberty from 8:00am till 11:00am and from 1:00pm till 5:00pm on holy days.
- No nun was to be accepted for work in a brothel without the Bishop's permission. Burford thinks growing poverty among nuns may have been tempting them into prostitution at this time.

Protecting Other Businesses

- Each stew's support staff limited to the stew-holder, his wife, one washerwoman and one male ostler (who often doubled as a bouncer). This seems designed to prevent any brothel expanding into a full tavern - or perhaps simply to prevent any single brothel growing too large.
- No woman at the stews to engage in spinning or carding during her

breaks. These trades were governed by powerful guilds, which didn't want the competition.

- No stew-holder to sell food or drink from the brothel's premises. Again, this seems designed to protect the surrounding taverns.

Protecting Society

- All "single women" to identify themselves by wearing some agreed garment indicating their trade. Aprons were banned, as these were then seen as the mark of a respectable woman.
- No soliciting at the brothel's entrance by pulling at passing men's coats or any other item of clothing. No stew-holder's wife to entice any man into the house against his will.
- All stews in the Liberty to close between sunset and dawn on any day when the King's Parliament or Council is sitting at Westminster. This was to ensure legislators didn't slip off to the brothels when they should have been working. [39]
- No stew-holder to employ an ostler on a contract of more than six months. Big, tough men were always in demand as bouncers in Southwark's brothels, but the King wanted to ensure they were available to the army instead.
- Each woman's final customer of the day must be allowed to stay overnight. This was designed to minimise night-time river traffic, when brothel customers returning to the north bank might otherwise have helped to conceal thieves or political plotters making the same journey.

Fighting Corruption

- Any constable failing to report a breach of these rules to the court to be imprisoned till he has paid whatever fine the Bishop imposes.
- No constable or bailiff to accept bail personally for a prisoner's release. Instead, the bail must be collected by the Bishop's court.
- No bailiff to allow an offender bail without the court's authorisation.

General Administration

- No-one to bring any claim involving more than 40 shillings (£2) to the Bishop's court. The King would want to reserve bigger, more lucrative cases for himself.

- All stew-holders to register new women arriving to work there with the Bishop's officials.
- Constables to search every brothel once a week for miscellaneous infringements.

Many of these rules seem quite enlightened - particularly those designed to protect the women themselves from sexual slavery. By paying the Bishop's court its licence fee, the stew-holder and his workers were placing their business on a legal footing. Keeping that legal status meant obeying the Bishop's rules - or at least not flouting them too openly - but it also gave the women a chance to take complaints against the stew-holders or their johns to a court that recognised they themselves had some rights. "In my work, the Goose regards the Bishop as her protector," Constable reminded me. In *The Southwark Mysteries*, he puts it like this:

"I was born a Goose of Southwark,
By the Grace of Mary Overie,
Whose Bishop gives me licence,
To sin within the Liberty."

It's worth remembering here that writing down a rule is always a lot easier than enforcing it, and that the Bishop's constables and bailiffs would often have been willing to turn a blind eye if the bribe a stew-holder offered them was big enough to outweigh the risk. In some cases - such as the stricture against big loans - the woman herself may well have been complicit in breaking the very rules laid down to protect her. Where else was she supposed to go for desperately needed money except to the stew-holder? And if the Liberty's court disregarded her debt, then so what? The stew-holder could always threaten to beat it out of her instead, or simply throw her out on the street to starve. The number of women driven into sex work was always greater than the number of chambers available to them in Southwark's licensed brothels, so a replacement would not be hard to find.

All too often, the fines levied against a brothel would ultimately have come from the women working there anyway. All the power was on the stew-holder's side in this relationship, giving him plenty of ways to extort extra money from them by whatever violent or bullying means he chose. The women were left with no choice but to work harder than ever to replace their lost income and where was the incentive to report an infringement when that was the most likely result?

Some offences imposed a penalty of fines on both the woman and the stew-holder involved, but added a second physical punishment for the woman. Where an unregistered prostitute was discovered on the premises, for example, the stew-holder could be fined as much as 40 shillings (£2). But the woman herself was assumed to be complicit too and subject not only to a fine of up to 20 shillings, but also to a session in the cucking stool and expulsion from the Liberty. The cucking stool was a refinement on the ducking stool we've all seen in depictions of witch trials. But instead of dunking the offender in a village pond, the cucking stool dipped her in raw sewage, and the prescribed penalty in this case was three full immersions. Even if she survived that - which couldn't be taken for granted – she'd be thrown out of the only part of London which offered her livelihood any measure of legal protection.

Breaking another rule's ban on taking a lover of her own could earn the woman a session in the cucking stool too - one immersion in this case - plus three weeks in prison, a fine of six shillings and eightpence and expulsion from Southwark. Naturally, there's no penalty involved for the man she chooses, even though he may well have been her pimp or the stew-holder himself. Causing a disturbance outside the brothel could land her in prison too, that penalty being set at three days jail plus, once again, a fine of six shillings and eightpence.

The 1161 rules set their biggest fine of all at 200 shillings (£10), which was used to ensure any dispute involving more than 40 shillings went direct to the King's court instead of the Bishop's. To get an idea of what a vast sum £10 was at that time, remember that it would have been enough for a woman to rent her own working chamber in a Southwark brothel for over three years (at the going rate of 14 pence per week). In the 12th century, even the wealthiest baron in England had an annual income of less than £700 and you could run the average castle for only £16 a year. [40]

Further down the tariff was a batch of £5 fines aimed at fighting corruption. These would be imposed on stew-holders who impeded a constable's search of their premises and officials who

---

allowed bail without the court's permission. "Keeping clandestine whores was another way to fiddle extra money and no doubt the constable could always be squared," Burford writes. "That offences were concealed by venal officials is clear from the regulation, which made such activities punishable by a spell in prison for the official concerned."

The measure he has in mind there allowed the Bishop's court to imprison any official who knowingly concealed an offence and to keep him there till whatever fine the court imposed had been fully paid. The bigger the fine, the longer the jail sentence would be, and that gave the court what amounted to an open-ended power. This Draconian measure suggests that corruption was both so widespread and so lucrative that only the severest penalties stood a chance of denting it. [41]

Other £5 fines were added to the rules later, levied for allowing a prostitute to work on your premises when you knew she had a venereal disease or for employing an old soldier recently returned from overseas (and hence assumed to be carrying an STD himself). This tells us how great the fear of such disease was and how little the doctors of the time were able to do to combat it.

It's also instructive to look at which offences carried the lowest fines, these presumably being the crimes which the authorities thought they should make some token effort to suppress, but which no-one much cared about one way or the other. The fine for accepting a nun without the Bishop's OK, for example, was set at just one shilling (12 pence), which meant the stew-holder had to collect only a single week's rent from the new recruit to get himself back in profit. A stew-holder who stopped one of his workers leaving the premises when she wanted to do so faced a fine of just three shillings and fourpence, as did any brothel customer who caused trouble. Contrast that with the treatment dished out to the women themselves for the same offence: three days in prison, plus a fine of six shillings and eightpence.

We can see from surviving records of the Bishop's courts - known in the jargon as courts leet - that some minor offences were simply impossible to enforce. One example would be the rules governing a woman's behaviour as she waited for business in the brothel's entrance, which allowed her to do nothing more than sit there quietly and look enticing. "She was not allowed to solicit custom by cries or gestures or to grab the potential customer by his gown,"

Burford writes. "That this rule was a non-starter is evidenced by the great number of cases that came up before the courts leet for centuries afterwards." The fine in this case was 20 shillings which, when collected so regularly, must have given the courts a very useful source of steady income.

The first stone version of London Bridge - not Tower Bridge but London Bridge - opened in 1209, leading directly from what's now Monument into Borough High Street and making it easier than ever for Londoners to reach Bankside. Southwark was unable to satisfy Londoners' appetites on its own, however, and a second zone of legalised prostitution was opened just outside the city walls at Farringdon in about 1240. That street, halfway between Smithfield and the Old Bailey, was quickly dubbed Cock Lane, a name it still carries on the London map today. Near Cock Lane - and also just outside the city walls - Chancery Lane and Fetter Lane had brothels of their own. [42, 43]

We have deeds from this era showing that many of the properties known to operate as brothels in all three of these streets were owned by the Parish of St Mary Overie - a piece of Southwark real estate which included both the Bishop of Winchester's palace and the whole Liberty of the Clink. Burford thinks the London city authorities must have deliberately engineered things this way to give the Liberty jurisdiction over the new red light districts and so ensure the 1161 rules were applied there too.

The idea was evidently to confine prostitution to certain designated areas outside the city walls so that London itself could be kept free of the trade. Brothels within the designated areas - the biggest of which was Bankside itself, of course - were happily tolerated providing that order there was more or less maintained. By 1287, even the Dean and Chapter of St Paul's Cathedral owned property in Cock Lane which they knew perfectly well was let out as a brothel.

At this point, Europe was still entirely Catholic and that allowed the 13th century Church a certain pragmatism where human frailty was concerned. Prostitution was seen as a necessary evil, which gave society a vital safety valve and protected other women from rape. The theologian Thomas Aquinas, who lived from 1225 to 1274, compared a town's red light district to the cesspool in a palace. "Take away the cesspool and the palace will become an unclean and evil-smelling place," he wrote. That comparison may have been unflattering to the women working in Southwark's stews, but at least it acknowledged they were playing a useful role in society.

"There were even religious people who advocated for prostitutes' rights as labourers," Melissa Ditmore adds in her 2005 *Encyclopedia of Prostitution and Sex Work*. "Thomas of Chobham, for example, dedicated four chapters of his early 13th century manual to prostitutes and argued, among other things, that they deserved to be paid for their labour just like any other worker." [44]

That atmosphere of easy tolerance and the sensibly pragmatic laws it produced were soon to face a severe test. Disease was coming to London and it would hit Southwark particularly hard.

Slaves in all but name and old before their time

Southwark's medieval prostitutes were trapped in slavery just as surely as the Roman captives who'd come before them. Burford cites research showing that, even in Bankside's most upmarket brothels, each woman was expected to service as many as 12 men a night. In the mid-priced establishments, a nightly 30 men per girl was about average, he adds, and in the cheapest places of all even more. [45]

"Within three or four years, the girl would be worn out," he writes. "With the lack of hygiene and sanitation, all diseases were a hazard. If she caught VD, she would be thrown out. She might perhaps get some sort of treatment from the Lock Hospital, but that was a mixed blessing, because cross-infection through ignorant treatment was frequent." [46]

This raises the question of what such women did when their charms began to fade and the stew-house no longer wanted them. A fortunate few might find besotted clients prepared to marry them, just as Pope Innocent III had suggested good Christian men should do. The most entrepreneurial might decide to set up as madams, using the lessons of their own hard-won experience to run a stable of fresh young talent. For most, though, the only options were to switch to the life of a solo street prostitute - an interim measure at best - or put up with becoming a servant to the same stew-house women they'd once worked alongside. Often, this meant a lifetime labouring in the brothel's laundry or kitchen.

The smartest such women would have gathered enough knowledge of midwifery, contraception and folk remedies to make themselves indispensable on those grounds and so ensure they were still treated with a measure of respect. But no stew-house required more than one or two such "wise women" on the staff, which hardly made a dent in the hundreds of exhausted girls Bankside spat out every year.

In this place of healing where the
Wild Feminine is honoured and
celebrated for all that she is
whore and virgin, mother and lover
maiden and crone, creator and destroyer
we will remember and offer prayers
for the murdered women of Ipswich
and honour them as women

FOR ALL THAT THEY WERE
AND COULD HAVE BEEN

Tania ⚜ Gemma ⚜ Anneli ⚜ Paula ⚜ Netty

This Cross Bones plaque pays tribute to five Ipswich sex workers murdered in 2006.

6: Say Their Names

On the morning after the Cross Bones vigil, I gathered a few offerings of my own for the gates and prepared to set off for Redcross Way again.

I'd gone along the previous evening expecting one of the site's routine monthly ceremonies, planning to return with my gifts when the full Halloween ritual came round in a week's time. Instead, I'd arrived at the gates to discover a flyer announcing that evening's proceedings would fold both October ceremonies into one. "This is our 101st consecutive vigil and will feature elements from the Halloween of Crossbones ritual drama (1998-2010), including the names of the dead," it explained.

I asked Constable later why they'd decided to do this and he replied that everyone simply needed a rest. "We did 13 Halloweens and we might do another cycle of them sometime," he told me. "But it was quite good to do 13 and then have a break, because it was an awful lot of work to do them. When we stopped, we moved some of those Halloween elements to the 23rd of October."

It was that first Halloween procession in 1998 which began the tradition of decorating Cross Bones' gates with all the ribbons, costume jewellery and lace they've sported ever since. A few days after the 1998 procession, the first of the site's homemade plaques appeared too. "A plaque has mysteriously appeared commemorating the Southwark prostitutes who were buried in unconsecrated, forgotten graves," the *South London Press* reported. "Playwright John Constable, who has long campaigned for the working women of olde Southwark to be remembered, is delighted. He first spotted the carved wooden plaque on a wall in Redcross Way." [47]

Constable takes up this story in *The Southwark Mysteries*. "The plaque, adorned with varnished flowers, was widely believed to be the work of a local working girl called Emily," he writes. "It read: 'To fix in time this site, the Crossbones Graveyard where the Whores

---

50

and Paupers of the Southwark Liberty, in graves unconsecrated, lay resting. Where now, at Millennial turning, the Whores and Paupers and our Friends return, incarnate, in ritual, with tributes and offerings, to honour, to remember'."

Like many of the plaques that have since appeared at Cross Bones, this one didn't last long. "As the Halloween of Crossbones evolved into an annual event, a succession of home-made plaques regularly appeared," Constable writes. "Each was eventually vandalised, or perhaps removed by the site owners, to be replaced by a new plaque - until, in 2005, Southwark's 'Cleaner, Greener, Safer' fund paid for the official brass plaque and ivy planters which now adorn the gate." That official plaque, which has remained safely fixed to the centre of the gates ever since, carries this wording:

> *"Cross Bones Graveyard. In medieval times, this was an unconsecrated graveyard for prostitutes or 'Winchester Geese'. By the 18th century, it had become a paupers' burial ground, which closed in 1853. Here, local people have created a memorial shrine. The Outcast Dead. RIP."*

Constable's group, the Friends of Cross Bones, had put the site forward for one of Southwark Council's official blue plaques four years running by the time the brass one appeared, but always lost out to more prestigious sites in the Borough. "One year we were up against Shakespeare's Rose Theatre," he told me. "They're an international trust and they were getting votes from all over the world. Once we got the brass plaque, we thought that's actually better in some ways."

Several other home-made plaques have joined the brass one on the gate since, the most touching of which are the laminated cardboard ones memorialising the street prostitutes murdered in Britain today. They're a sobering reminder of how little has changed for women pursuing this most dangerous of trades and of how casually such woman are murdered and thrown away. Here's just a few examples:

> *"Gemma, Anneli, Paula, Netty, Tania: In this place of healing where the Wild Feminine is honoured and*

celebrated for all that she is - whore and virgin, mother and lover, maiden and crone, creator and destroyer - we will remember and offer prayers for the murdered women of Ipswich and honour them as women. For all that they were and could have been." (48)

"Suzanne, Susan, Shelley: In this place of healing, we shall remember and offer prayers for the murdered woman of Bradford and honour them as women. For all that they were and could have been. RIP."

"In memory of all the women who died whilst working in the oldest profession, who the rest of society chose not to remember: Jane, Caroline, Rachel (2000), Tracey (2001), Sarah, Tina (2002), Fiona (2003), Hashley, Deborah, Tracey (2004), Samantha, Ellen, Sam (2005), Emma, Zoey, Michelle (2006), Caroline, Julie (2007), Sonia (2008), Miss P (2009), Kim, Ann, Joanne, to name a few. It's not just another day! It's not just another Death! In memory of all the workers never forgotten."

Everything I'd read about the Cross Bones Halloween ceremonies suggested that was where the gates' most colourful supporters gathered, so I was sorry I'd missed the chance to take part in one myself. "Political activists, evangelical Christians, locals, rough sleepers, actors, former addicts and passing tourists as well as the regular pagans and sex workers turn up," the *Financial Times'* Kesewa Hennessy wrote after her own Halloween visit to the gates in 2008. (49)

That year's event had begun, as they always did, in the basement bar of the Hop Cellars in Southwark Street. Katherine Angel of *The Independent* was there too, waiting nervously at the back of the room as Constable swept in wearing his long black cloak and announced they were ready to begin. (50)

"A priestess started things off, leading us in a meditative moment of humming," Angel writes. "A single note was held, surprisingly tunefully, by the crowd. I felt a space open up in the room.

52

My ears, my whiskers, perked up; I was suddenly alert and curious. A witch broke into a rap. [...] Someone then asked us to close our eyes and think of the dead. To think of past pain, past loss, past regret - and let these go. We each read out a word: light, compassion, generosity - things to wish for and cherish.

"Constable then took over, adopting his persona of John Crow, his 'trickster-shaman'. Actress Michelle Watson became the Goose, a prostitute on the Bankside, a wise and sassy creature radiating erotic scorn. Together, Crow and the Goose performed, in verse and song, sections of Constable's poetry, bringing to life the women refused burial on consecrated ground by the very Church that licensed their practice. The Crossbones campaign celebrates a strong, elemental and witchy female sexuality. This is the language Crossbones speaks most eloquently through the 'Whores d'Ouvres' of the Halloween event: two women in basques who schooled us in the spiritual potential of our pelvic floors. We held hands with our neighbours, breathed and moved our hips in unison - a lesson in spiritual burlesque." [51]

Dr Adrian Harris of Winchester University adds a few more details in his own account of a Halloween ritual at the Hop Cellars. "The performances consisted of songs and poems from *The Southwark Mysteries* and a demonstration of Tantric breathing from Jahnet de Light and her Whores d'Ouvres," he writes. "Many people, especially the women, were in fancy dress. But instead of the usual 'trick or treat' ghouls, they sported the Elizabethan costume of the commoners - just the kind of garb that would have been worn by the 'Winchester Geese'. The large basement room was decorated with flowers and two altars; one for our own beloved dead was designated as an 'Altar to the Ancestors'. The other was dedicated to the prostitutes of Crossbones. This latter altar was laden with suitable offerings: chocolate, cigars and a bottle of gin."

Constable confirmed these accounts when I asked him what I'd missed by not being able to attend a full Halloween ritual. "With the Halloween ones, we went as close as I would go to doing a proper magic ritual," he told me. "I've always said we do a kind of magic at the gates, but it's the sort of magic you can do in the open. That's the thing about the vigils: we only do stuff there that anyone, whether they're a pagan, a Christian or a happy atheist can participate in without feeling weird about it. So the vigils are very much shaped by that.

"The Halloween ceremony obviously pushed that envelope a bit. When we did it at Halloween, we'd have a Samhain ritual to greet the New Year and people would bring photos of their own dead. Then we'd have performances from selected poems in *The Southwark Mysteries* and the third element would be the Goose's tantric teachings. We'd always have a tantric sex worker, who would lead a simple workshop. Everybody kept their clothes on, but it was interesting. People would be holding hands and inwardly squeezing their pelvic muscles and all of that. We'd end with a procession to the gates, where we'd read the names and tie the ribbons."

Introducing too many of the Halloween ritual's freakier elements into the mainstream monthly vigils, he added, would risk putting off anyone who found the gates' memorial role interesting but ran a mile from anything that smelt of new age twaddle. People like me, in other words - and perhaps like many of those crowded round the gates with me on that October evening too.

"I like the fact that we get all sorts there," Constable told me. "There's a couple of ladies well into their eighties who come a couple of times a year - churchgoers, not the sort of people you would expect there at all. And that's what I love. We are genuinely an eclectic group of people, of all kinds. The thing with the vigils is you can just turn up and fully participate without needing some sort of initiation into it."

You'd think rapping witches and a spot of pelvic squeezing would be enough for anyone attending the Halloween ceremony, but some insist matters don't stop there. In the *Londonist's* October 2012 podcast, Quentin Woolf interviewed Constable and a Dulwich activist called Ingrid Beazley together on location at the Cross Bones gates. "We were sitting on the floor and we were handed a little round mirror," Beazley told him of one Hop Cellars ceremony she'd attended. "And on the mirror was engraved: 'You are Beautiful'. It was for the women and we were supposed to look at our fannies with it."

Woolf moved on before Constable had a chance to comment on this in the recording itself, but the memory still rankled when I interviewed him a year later. "I remember it well - it was a male sex worker who handed out the mirrors," he told me. "But she remembered him saying, 'It's for women to look at their fannies with' and I don't remember that at all. I remember him saying, 'You look at yourself in it' - your face. Which makes a lot more sense."

All this information was buzzing through my head as I sorted through my own offerings on the kitchen table. The Altar to the Ancestors which Harris describes sounded a lot like the Day of the Dead shrines I'd seen in Mexico and Texas, so that's where I started my trawl. I'd been collecting Day of the Dead calacas for years - tiny clay figurines with skulls for heads and skeleton bodies, each dressed to embody a certain job or personality type: the priest, the tycoon, the drunkard, the gambler and so on.

Picking through my collection, I chose a street urchin hawking newspapers and a smartly-dressed businessman with a briefcase. The first figure, I thought, could represent both my own trade and the humble folk of Southwark's past, while the second stood in for the City traders whose shiny office blocks now threatened to crush Cross Bones underfoot. Somewhere in Texas, I'd bought a cheap necklace of 16 clay beads on a nylon string, each shaped and painted like a skull, which had been languishing in a drawer ever since. Now, at last, I knew where it belonged.

To these items, I added a small plastic doll of Lois Lane I'd somehow acquired. Clad in green micro-skirt, black knee-length leather boots and with a large "city-gal" handbag slung jauntily over her shoulder, she had just the feisty sex appeal needed to do the Goose justice. A few days earlier, I'd bought two plastic miniatures of Gordon's gin to use as Cross Bones offerings, so they went in the bag too.

The final item returned me to my Day of the Dead souvenirs, where I found a small picture frame made from beaten tin, which Mexican mourners would typically use to display the photo of a departed loved one on their family shrine. Like the necklace, this frame had been something I'd failed to find a home for ever since bringing it back to England, but now its true purpose was clear. It was as if the necklace and the frame had been waiting all this time - ten years or more - until it finally dawned on me that they belonged on the Cross Bones gates.

I knew just which picture to put in the frame too. Nasra Ismail was a Somali-born sex worker murdered near King's Cross in March 2004, whose case I'd written about on my website. I fixed a photocopy of her picture into the tin frame, added her name and date of death, then threaded wire through the frame's corners to tie it on with.

Down at Redcross Way, I fixed Ismail's portrait to the gate's vertical bars, knotted the necklace into place a few feet to the right and wedged Lois into the knot of a convenient ribbon. The two Day of the Dead figures went just inside the gate, where the bars allowed me to reach through and place them among the burnt-out candles and debris littering the makeshift altar there. I photographed everything, then waited for a quiet moment by the Union Street corner before lobbing the two plastic miniatures of gin over the eight-foot wall into what I knew was the centre of the graves themselves. Someone will find them there one day - a tramp, a site worker, a Cross Bones volunteer - and when they do, they're very welcome to have a drink on me.

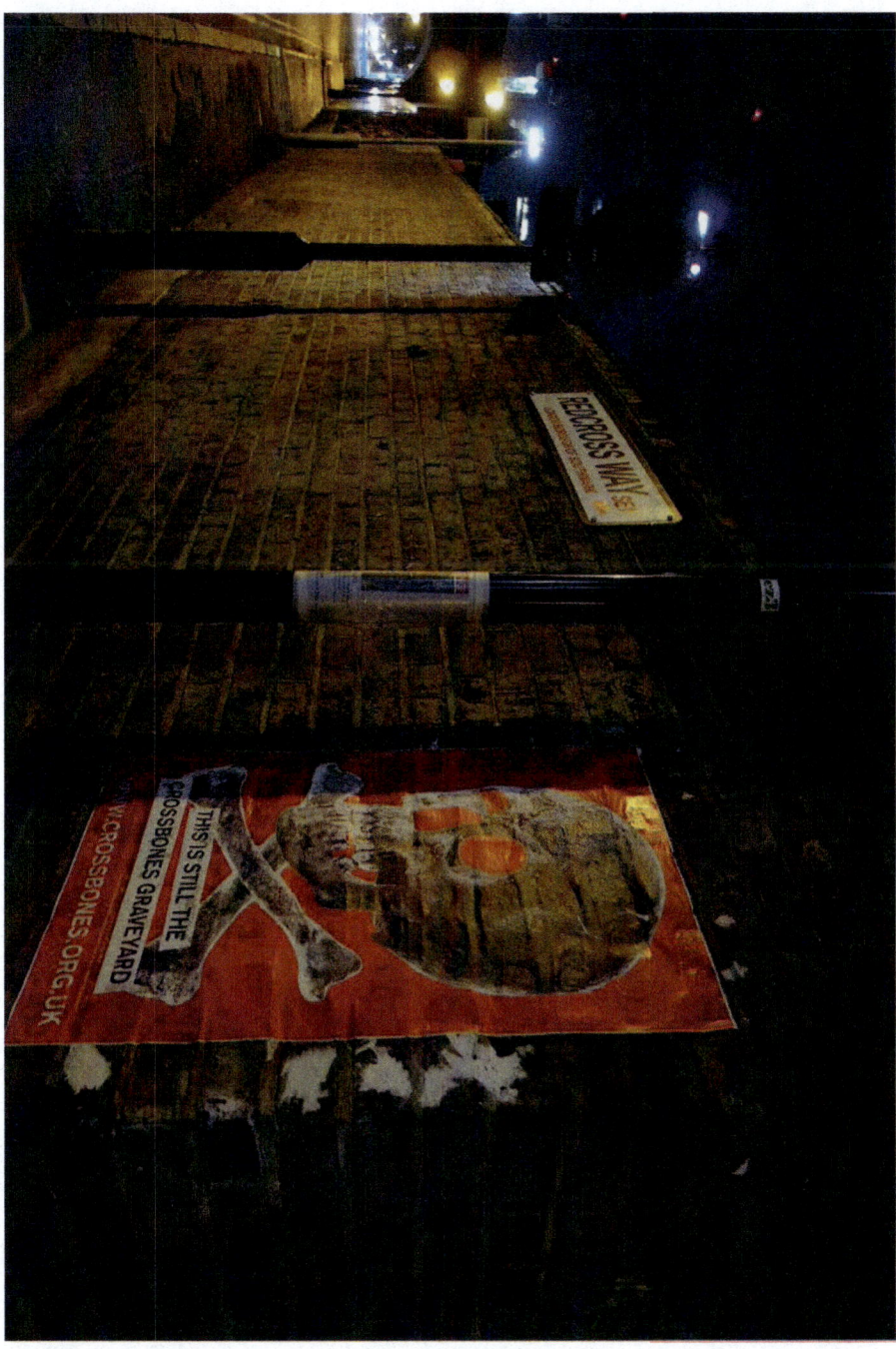

Redcross Way by night.

7: The Black Death

John of Gaddesden, an English doctor writing in the early 14th century, had some advice for women on how to protect themselves against venereal disease. Immediately after sex with any suspect man, he said, the woman should jump up and down, run backwards down the stairs, and inhale some pepper to make herself sneeze. Next, she should tickle her vagina with a feather dipped in vinegar to flush infected sperm out of her body, then wash her genitals thoroughly in a concoction of roses and herbs boiled in vinegar. [52]

It's hard to imagine anyone actually following this advice - let alone one of the women in Southwark's stews. It would unsettle the customers for a start, and running backwards downstairs sounds like an excellent way to break your neck. Other doctors writing at about the same time had equally eccentric remedies of their own, but at least everyone now recognised that diseases such as gonorrhoea were spread by sexual intercourse. That in itself was a big step forward. [53]

The filthy state of Southwark in those days ensured other diseases were quick to spread there too. The Borough's streets were still unpaved and there were no sewers. Residents who were out and about relieved their bladder (and bowels) in any quiet alleyway, while stay-at-homes emptied their brimming chamber pots out the nearest window. Once again, the informal street names coined by the locals give us a clue to what their lives were like. The area's sex trade gave it place names like Codpiece Lane, Cuckold Court and Sluts' Hole, while the sheer amount of filth in its streets christened Dirty Lane, Foul Lane and Pissing Lane. [54, 55]

All this made Southwark an ideal breeding ground for the bubonic plague, which hit London in 1348. "Historians estimate that the Black Death killed half the population of 14th century England," Stephen Smith says in his 2004 book *Underground London*. "If anything, the devastation in London was even worse. The transmission of the disease was encouraged by the narrow, busy and filthy streets, crowded houses and noisome sanitary conditions. The toll among Londoners has been variously put at between 50,000 and 100,000."

A year into this plague, Edward III urged London's borough authorities to combat the infection by cleaning up their streets, but was told all the street cleaners were already dead. The more people died, the fewer were left to dispose of their remains and the faster infection spread. "London burial grounds were soon full to overflowing and new ones were hastily dug," Smith says. "The biggest was in Southwark, where some 200 corpses were interred every day." Another of these new grounds, opened just across the river from Southwark in East Smithfield, managed to stuff 2,400 bodies into its small plot by placing them five deep in long trenches rather than using individual graves. Measures like this were the only way to get each new wave of corpses buried before the next consignment arrived.

Older bodies were dug up again with indecent despatch to make more space in the ground. All over London, disinterred bones were thrown into the graveyard's charnel house. This was either a vault beneath the church itself or a small building on the grounds, where "clean" bones - those from which all the flesh had rotted away - could be consigned. In calmer times, these bones would be treated with great reverence, perhaps even prayed over by the priest, but when the pressure on graveyards hit these heights, speed was all that mattered. [56]

"Burial arrangements could break down during epidemics," writes Reading University's Professor Ralph Houlbrooke. "The Black Death compelled urban communities in particular to find new burial space quickly." There's no evidence that Cross Bones itself was used for burials this early, but it may well have been a later outbreak of plague in London which forced St Saviour's parish to requisition the site. [57]

In 1349, Edward III suspended Parliament to let MPs escape London for the relative safety of the British countryside. Anyone else rich enough to flee the capital got out too. Southwark's brothels seem to have remained open throughout the plague years, however, despite official warnings that casual copulation with multiple partners increased the risk of infection. Henry Knighton, a 14th century historian who lived through the Black Death, says the stews were actually busier than ever during the plague years. Many male

Londoners adopted an attitude of fatalistic abandon, thinking it was all but certain they'd catch the plague anyway, so why not do so while enjoying the charms of Bankside? At least that guaranteed you a little pleasure before you died.

In the spring of 1350, the death toll in London started to abate at last and Edward turned his attention to the anarchy that now prevailed in Southwark. Many of the Bishop's officials had fled during the plague years, leaving the Bankside brothels and their surrounding taverns more lawless than ever.

Anyone committing a crime inside the city walls knew they had only to get across London Bridge to claim sanctuary and the welcome they now found there was warmer than ever. "Those who have committed manslaughter, robberies and diverse other felonies are privily departing into the town of Southwark, where they cannot be attached by the ministers of the City and there are openly received, " said the King in an address to London's people. "And so, for default of due punishment [they] are emboldened to commit more such felonies."

If those felonies had been limited to Southwark alone, Edward might have found them easier to bear. By now, though, Southwark's thugs had grown so bold that gangs of 200 or more youths would periodically burst over the bridge into London, rob the passers-by there, loot the shops and then dash back across the river to safety. Only London had the men and resources needed to restore law and order in Southwark, but no-one who lived there was willing to call them in if it meant surrendering their borough's treasured independence. The result was an uneasy stand-off.

As far as London itself was concerned, the authorities concentrated on preventing prostitution within the city walls and on ensuring that the women working designated areas like Cock Lane wore the proper clothing. In 1351, the City of London passed an ordinance saying "lewd or common women" must wear a striped hood to identify themselves as such and refrain from beautifying their clothes with any fur trim or fancy lining.

Any woman not of noble birth could be described as "common" in that sense and this sloppy wording made the ordinance such a wide one that it seemed to cover almost every female in the city. London's proud womenfolk weren't going to have men dictating what they could wear, so most simply ignored the ordinance and challenged any constable to arrest them if he dared. When Edward III put his own authority behind this law three years later, he was careful to specify it applied only to London's "common whores". The striped hoods and lack of decorative trim, his proclamation declared, would "set a deformed mark on foulness to make it appear more odious".

Some prostitutes continued to live inside the city walls but commuted to Cock Lane or the Liberty to earn their daily crust - perhaps finding somewhere to change on the way. But it wasn't long before they were banned from even lodging in the city and subject to very heavy penalties for doing so. A 1383 ordinance required any offender caught in London to have her head shaved and be carted through the streets in a special wagon while minstrels played all around her to attract a crowd. On arrival at the nearest prison, she'd be placed in a pillory and publicly whipped.

"The ineffectuality of all this punishment is evident in the ordinances themselves, which provide for repeated offences and increased penalties," Burford says. Offenders caught a second time, for example, would serve ten days in jail on top of all the other penalties, while a third offence got you ten days' prison and permanent expulsion from London. A woman in this final category would be taken to one of the city gates, where she'd be roughly thrown outside. If the authorities had been able to trace her origins to Bankside - as was often the case - she'd be escorted back there and warned to stay put.

In 1393, these rules were tightened once again, saying no prostitute must "go about or lodge" in London or its suburbs, but "keep themselves in the places thereto assigned, that is to say, the stews on the other side of the Thames and in Cock Lane". Offenders could face all the penalties detailed above and have their identifying hood confiscated too. Replacing this garment was an expensive business, but the woman could not move back to the relative safety of licensed sex work till she'd done so. Many must have run the most terrifying risks as a result.

We know there were at least two murders in the stews at around this time, because both are mentioned in the Bishop of Winchester's court rolls for 1378. One was carried out by William Chepington of Northamptonshire, who killed a Scarborough man called John Drenge at the Cardinal's Hat, one of the biggest brothels on Bankside. In the same year, an unnamed Flemish man was hanged for another murder in the stews. [58]

Dutch people - then known as Flemings - had first come to Southwark as mercenaries in William the Conqueror's army, so their relationship with the native English population was sometimes thorny. Many Flemings were talented entrepreneurs and the stews they ran on Bankside operated with an efficiency and cleanliness that put their homegrown competitors to shame. We can judge their popularity by the fact that so many English prostitutes chose to work under the Dutch name Petronella to indicate they were both fashionable and highly skilled.

The Dutch madams may have been popular with punters, but their success did not go down well with their resentful English competitors. When Wat Tyler's tax rebels arrived in Southwark in June 1381, one of their first targets was the Rose, a Dutch-operated brothel owned by William Walworth, the Lord Mayor of London. Until then, Tyler's men had attacked only formal symbols of the King's authority, such as prisons and the Inns of Court, so you have to wonder if it was Southwark's English stew-holders who suggested they burn the Rose.

"It's likely that the rebels destroyed the brothel not from outraged morality, but from hostility to the foreigners, specifically the Flemish," says Derek Brewer in his 1978 book *Chaucer and his World*. Having sacked these premises, which stood near London Bridge, the rioters then went on a day-long rampage, killing up to 160 Flemish people as they moved west through the Liberty. [59]

Many Southwark folk seem to have joined in the mayhem simply for a chance to eliminate a rival business. "[They] beheaded without judgement or trial all the Flemings they found," one contemporary report tells us. "Mounds of corpses were to be seen in the streets and various spots were littered with the headless bodies of the slain. In this way, they passed the entire day, bent only on the massacre of the Flemings." [60]

A few months after these riots, all the brothels attacked were back in business again. Surviving 1381 tax records from Southwark show seven men listed as stew-holders in the Borough, all with addresses in the Bishop's Liberty. "They evidently represent the proprietors of the Bankside stew-houses," says Martha Carlin in her 1996 book *Medieval Southwark*. "All were married men, with both male and female servants; none had children aged 15 or older living at home." [61]

The seven stew-holding couples listed, together with the tax assessed as due from each pair, are:

- *Walter Shirborn & wife Christian: Six shilling & eightpence.*
- *Robert Power & wife Agnes: Four shillings.*
- *Yevan Wallchman & wife Isabella: Four shillings.*
- *John David & wife Isabella: Four shillings & eightpence.*
- *Robert [illegible] & wife Isabella: Four shillings & sixpence.*
- *Richard Bailif & wife Margery: Four shillings & sixpence.*
- *William Brounes & wife Joan: [Figure missing]*

The average tax payable per individual householder in Southwark that year was just one shilling, against an average of over five shillings for the couples above. That means the stew-holders were being taxed at two and a half times the rate of their neighbours and presumably that their earnings were that much higher too. But how much of that money actually found its way to the women who earned it?

Of the 137 unmarried woman identified in the Southwark return, Carlin found a dozen who she believes worked as prostitutes. These were not the women who worked in the Bankside stews, who'd be lumped in as "servants" with the families above, but freelancers operating from the precinct of St Thomas' Hospital and therefore outside the Liberty's rule. "These women probably were independent or 'private' prostitutes, working from lodgings rather than from public brothels," Carlin writes. "Their residence within the hospital precinct presumably shielded them from any interference by the officers."

Even among this relatively privileged group, only three of the 12 women paid assessments above the Southwark-wide average of one shilling - and seven paid well under that. Their average assessment was only ninepence halfpenny - just over a third of what even the poorest stew-holder paid - and the richest of them just one shilling and fourpence. Once again, it's reasonable to assume that a much lower tax bill means a much lower income too.

Whoever else was getting rich from the Bankside stews, then, it sure wasn't the women who worked there. The eminent men who owned brothels like the Cardinal's Hat, the Boar's Head and the

---

rebuilt Rose did very nicely from renting them out to stew-holders, some of whom were able to start building family dynasties on the profits. These families certainly weren't in their landlords' class, either for income or status, but they still managed to rake in a great deal more money than most other businesses in Southwark could provide. The women whose sheer bloody resilience kept the whole show on the road had to make do with its scraps. [62]

Prostitution in Southwark was still officially licensed only in the Liberty's designated Bankside area, but the seven establishments there couldn't hope to satisfy total demand. At some point in the 1380s, local businessmen made a concerted effort to establish a new red light district in Southwark's St Olave's Parish, which lies west along the river from Bankside. The site they chose was not in the Liberty, but part of a manor still owned by the King himself, so opening unsanctioned brothels there was a risky business.

The men who owned the five new St Olave ventures included John Mokkyng, shown in the 1381 tax return as one of Southwark's richest men, and Robert Power, the Bankside stew-holder mentioned above, who now hoped to make his own step up into the landlord class.

We know this because both men are named in a 1390 petition from the people of Southwark complaining the St Olave stews had turned their neighbourhood into a war zone and urging King Richard II to shut them down. There had always been violence and disorder on Bankside too but, with neither the 1161 rules nor the Bishop's enforcers to keep a lid on things, St Olave's became a hellhole. "The petitioners charged that the place had become notorious, a breeder of quarrels and homicides and a resort of thieves, to the peril of local residents," Carlin writes. [63]

The petitioners added that the new brothels' customers included not only married men - who were hardly a novelty on Bankside either - but also "all manner of persons of religion, namely monks, canons, friars, parsons, vicars, priests". Married women and female servants, they said, were being kidnapped, imprisoned at St Olave's and forced into prostitution there. The alternative was a slit throat.

The King responded by demanding that all the landlords and stew-holders responsible for the five new brothels appear before him and his court at Westminster on July 4, 1390. One of the landlords, John Brenchesle, who seems to have run his own St Olave stew

---

personally, was sent to the Tower of London, as was John Osteler, his servant. Four others, all of whom were either stew-holder tenant-managers or their staff, went to the Fleet Prison for ten days. [64]

Efforts to police the stews at Southwark continued as the 15th century got underway and it's this period which gives us our earliest surviving records of real cases passing through the Liberty's courts. Many of these involved the sort of minor offences which keep an English magistrates' court busy today, like breaching the licensing laws, public drunkenness or fighting in the street. Other charges were far more serious, such as forcing a woman into sex work against her will.

Take the case of Elizabeth Butler, who was visiting a friend's London house in 1473, where she happened to meet a man called Thomas Boyd. Boyd offered her a job as a domestic servant at what he said was a Bankside inn, promising good pay and excellent working conditions. She accepted and went with him to Bankside, but quickly realised the building was actually a brothel and Boyd its manager. Far from the light housekeeping duties his offer had implied, Boyd's real plan was for Butler to join the building's stable of prostitutes. "He would have compelled me to do such things and service as other his servants done there," she later testified.

When Butler refused to play ball, Boyd claimed she owed him rent and took her to the Bishop of Winchester's court demanding a cash sum so large he knew she could never hope to pay it. The court found Butler guilty and jailed her when she admitted she had no money. That was exactly what Boyd had hoped would happen. He'd be happy to get Butler out of jail by cancelling her debt, he said - but only if she did what he wanted on Bankside.

Butler was stubborn and still she refused. After three weeks in the Bishop's Clink prison, she somehow managed to get a petition to the Bishop of Durham, pleading with him to get her case heard in the higher court of Chancery. She got as far as a hearing before London's City Chamberlain, but frustratingly that's where the records peter out.

There were other cases too. In April 1439, for example, a known procurer named Margaret Hathewyck was charged with supplying a young girl called Isabel Lane to a group of men from Lombardy. "Isabel was deflowered against her will for money paid to the said Margaret," the City Chamberlain's court rolls tell us. After the Lombards had finished with Isabel, Hathewyck delivered her to a

Bankside brothel "for immoral purposes with a certain gentleman on four occasions against her will". Hathewyck's name appears at about this time among the list of prisoners sent to the Clink, where she seems to have served a 20-year sentence.

The Bishop's court convened every four to six weeks and kept its records on parchments called pipe rolls. Eight examples from the 15th century have survived - all from the period 1446 to 1459 - and these show a steady tightening of the screw against corruption. By 1455, even the relatively minor offence of eating or drinking with the women they policed could land cops and bailiffs with a large fine.

There was a flurry of activity at the national level too, with three successive Kings - Henry IV, V and VI - each passing their own ordinances aimed at cleaning up the stews. First to bat was Henry IV, who extended the Lord Mayor of London's powers in 1406. For the first time, the City of London's own police could now arrest criminals in Southwark - an area previously beyond their jurisdiction - and drag them back across the river to Newgate for trial. All this achieved was to stoke the good folk of Southwark's customary resentment at interference from London. Any City constable brave enough to exercise his new powers in the Borough risked sparking a full-scale riot, as we can see from one incident soon after the 1406 change came in.

This involved a Frenchman who murdered a Southwark widow in her own bed, then fled to St George the Martyr's church in Borough High Street to claim sanctuary. London's authorities agreed not to arrest him on the condition that he leave England immediately, and sent a constable to St George's to escort him down to the south coast and make sure he caught the next boat out. But the outraged women of Southwark had other ideas. When the constable and his deputies came out of the church with their prisoner, they found a huge crowd waiting.

"The women of that same parish where he had done the cursed deed came out with stones and canal dung," one contemporary report tells us. "And they made an end of him in the High Street, notwithstanding the constable and the other men too. There was a great company of them and they had no mercy, no pity." With a reaction like that, you can see why even the bravest copper might think twice before throwing his weight about in Southwark. The new law was quietly shelved as a result. [65]

Henry V followed up with his own ordinance in 1417. He began by directing the Lord Mayor's attention to "the many grievances and abominations, damages and disturbances, murders and larcenies" carried out by "lewd men and women of evil life" in the Bankside stews. Quite what the poor old Mayor was supposed to do about it Henry didn't say - beyond a peremptory command to sort it out.

The King's own contribution was to ban London's City aldermen and other respectable citizens from letting out any building they owned to tenants "charged or indicted of an evil and vicious life". This was clearly aimed at the many churchmen, noblemen, officials and wealthy merchants who happily rented out their property to known stew-holders. There were only so many houses to be had in the Bankside's licensed area, so anyone lucky enough to own a building there could command premium rents if he let it be turned into a brothel. Outside the licensed area - in Borough High Street, say - landlords could argue they were accepting more risk by taking an illegal stew-holder on and insist the rent must be set higher to reflect this. Few other businesses in Southwark pulled in enough cash to match the rent stew-holders could offer.

All this added up to a powerful financial incentive for landlords to accept stew-holders as their tenants and that's what the King's ordinance was up against. It must have been simple enough to arrange your affairs to circumvent the new law - perhaps by renting your building out through a middleman - and like Henry IV's measures before it, the ban had little effect in practice.

It was Parliament's turn to step in next and it decided to concentrate on a different problem. By the time Henry VI came to the throne in 1422, the Bankside stews were at the peak of their profitability and the money flooding in allowed many stew-holders to buy themselves freehold property elsewhere in Southwark. Some used these additional properties to open inns or taverns which doubled as illegal brothels in Borough High Street, but that was only the beginning of the trouble their new riches brought.

In order to serve on a 15th century jury, you had to be a property-owner, which was taken as evidence you had a stake in society and so could be trusted to treat your responsibilities in court seriously. This gave the newly propertied stew-holders a whole new opportunity for corruption. By hiring out their services to the highest bidder, stew-holders on the jury could deliver whatever verdict their paymasters required.

The stews at this time were dominated by a handful of powerful families, creating a network of useful connections which every stew-holder could draw on when he needed to fix a court case. The Gardiners, for example, were involved in running three of the Bankside's 18 brothels: the Lion, the Hart's Horn and the Boar's Head. John Sandes' name is found linked to both the Castle and the Unicorn, while jobbing managers like John Gray and Robert à Murray moved regularly from one establishment to the next. "The Gardiner family is so prominent that the conclusion is inevitable that they were a gang of brothleers, as also were the brothers David and Robert à Murray," Burford writes. "All seem to have been people of some substance and some of them seem to have been elected constables on occasion."

Most the time, bent jurors were engaged to ensure a guilty man walked free, but sometimes it worked the other way round. Among the examples Carlin quotes is that of Henry Saunder, who had been taken to the Bishop's court by a stew-holder called Thomas Dyconson. Saunder asked that his case be transferred to the higher court of Chancery because the Bishop's jury he faced was packed with stew-holders who were determined to falsely condemn him.

Another petitioner, Agnes Johnson, complained that she'd been falsely accused in the Bishop's court. Her accuser, she said, was both rich and the court bailiff's brother-in-law, which meant no juror would dare cross him and that she'd never get a fair trial. A third prisoner dragged before the court described the jurors there as "bawds and watermen, the which regard neither God nor their conscience". Only with these people in your corner, she complained, was there any hope of victory.

Parliament's answer to this was to pass a 1433 law barring Southwark stew-holders from serving on juries or accepting any other official post in the Borough. Three years later, MPs heard an urgent petition from a group of Southwark citizens complaining that illegal brothels were still operating along the length of Borough High Street. "Many women have been ravished and brought to evil living," the petition said. "Neighbours and strangers are oft-time robbed and murdered." Parliament responded by declaring once again that stew-houses must be restricted to the licensed area provided - but gave no clue as to how this might be achieved.

In 1460, Henry VI set up a commission of 20 respectable citizens from both Southwark and London to consider the Borough problem. Violence and thieving in Southwark had now reached such heights that its own people looked ready to accept some help from London at last. For their own part, the City authorities realised that shovelling wrongdoers across the river and hoping the Bishop's courts could keep order there was no answer at all.

Once, the fear of damnation had been enough to dampen some of the worst behaviour on Bankside, but now this ecclesiastical sanction was losing its power. "The impotence of the ministers and officers of the church was scarcely surprising," Burford writes. "The corruption and sexual licence of that body had bred such scepticism and contempt that even the constant threats of Hell no longer deterred those who sought some little sexual pleasure in this world."

Henry VI's commission recommended that the City of London send men into Southwark to remove any prostitutes or stew-holders found operating away from Bankside and if necessary imprison them. The King seemed sincere enough in his desire to clean up the Borough, but the War of the Roses deposed him just a few months after the commission's report, so he had little chance to act.

The new King, Edward IV, took a more relaxed view of the stews - perhaps because his own sexual habits left him little room to criticise what went on in Southwark. The only significant measure he took to regulate them was a 1479 royal proclamation that all the licensed Bankside stews should clearly identify themselves by painting their riverside walls entirely white. Each house had its own symbol painted like a pub sign on the same wall and - as often as not - a couple of bare-breasted woman shouting from a riverside window to attract boat-bound customers. [66]

By the end of the 1400s, there was an unbroken line of 18 white-faced buildings like these lining the Thames' southern bank all the way from London Bridge to what's now Tate Modern. Just five years later, every one of them was forcibly closed down in a 1505 crackdown launched by Henry VII. His action was prompted not by any desire to fight crime in Southwark, but by an unwelcome new guest which all the Bankside stews were now hosting. Syphilis had come to London.

Bankside's 18 brothels & their ruling families

Court records from the 16th century give us an intriguing glimpse of how the Bankside brothels were run. Stew-holders were fined pretty regularly for one offence or another and the fact that so many of the family names involved pop up again and again shows the web of connections between them.

The list below shows the 18 legal Bankside brothels trading in 1500. Each stood in its own large grounds, stretching back from the riverbank as far as Maiden Lane on their southern boundaries. Burford estimates that they probably employed about 350 women between them, or roughly a third of the 1,000-plus prostitutes he believes were working Southwark at this time. The rest relied on the many illegal Borough joints found in the High Street and beyond. [67]

Between them, the 18 licensed brothels formed an unbroken line along the river all the way from London Bridge to what's now Tate Modern and that's the east-west order I've given them here. [68]

The Castle: One of the two largest properties on Bankside (the other being the Unicorn). John Sandes' name is found linked to both establishments, suggesting he may well have been the stew-holders' leader.

The Gun: One of the six brothels never re-licensed after the 1505 closures. The others were the Swan, the Bull's Head, the Rose, the Bell and the Cardinal's Hat.

The Antelope: Managers included both David Arnold and John Gray, who's linked at other times to the Castle and the Elephant.

The Swan: Another of the six brothels refused a new licence after the 1505 closures. Not to be confused with the Swan Theatre in nearby Paris Gardens, which opened in 1595.

The Bull's Head: Like the other five brothels refused a new licence, the Bull's Head probably re-opened anyway. From that point on, they had to operate outside the law, with all the risk that implies.

The Hart: Run by Margery Curson, who was fined £1 in 1500 for "living without a husband". It was an offence for a single woman to

---

run a stew-house, but Margery went right on and did it anyway. She rented The Hart from the churchwardens of St Margaret's Parish.

The Elephant: Managed at various times by Edward Wharton and Robert à Murray, whose name is also found linked to The Barge and The Antelope. Robert's brother David was also involved in running the Bankside stews.

The Lion: At various times, both Richard Gardiner and Joan Gardiner are mentioned as running the Lion. On another occasion, Joan Gardiner is said to be managing the Hart's Horn.

The Hart's Horn: Represented at a 1505 hearing by Margaret Toogood. She's thought to be either the widow or the daughter of the Thomas Toogood pilloried for enticing women into prostitution in 1494.

The Bear: Re-opened for legal trade on August 29, 1506, under the management of Eleanor Kent.

The Rose: This is the brothel once owned by London Mayor William Walworth. By 1552, it was owned by Henry Polsted, who leased it to a manager called John Davison, who also ran the Unicorn at that time. [69]

The Barge: Re-opened for legal trade in June 1506, with Robert à Murray as its manager.

The Bell: Nothing known.

The Unicorn: The second of Bankside's two biggest establishments and again managed by John Sandes. See the Castle.

The Boar's Head: Run by first Agnes Gardiner and then by Annian Gardiner. Both were presumably related to the Gardiners who ran the Lion and the Hart's Horn. A manager called William Aldersley spoke for the Boar's Head at a 1505 hearing.

The Cross Keys: Managed in 1505 by Anna Ratclyffe.

The Fleur de Lys: Managed in 1505 by Joan Freeman and in 1664 by Robert Younger.

71

The Cardinal's Hat: Mentioned by Shakespeare in *Henry VI Part 1*. Gloucester uses this infamous brothel's name to taunt the Bishop of Winchester in Act I, Scene III. See chapter 11 for details.

The Invisible Gardener's pyramid as it is today.

8: The Invisible Gardener

About three weeks after the October vigil, I interviewed John Constable in a Borough café, then asked him if we could retrace his steps on the night he first met the Goose. As we turned north from Little Dorritt Court into Redcross Way itself, he talked me through it all. The same trees he'd passed under that night overshadowed us now, the same Victorian railway arch glowered ahead and the same century-smoothed kerbstones echoed our footsteps. [70]

On our left passed Octavia Hill's 1887 charity cottages and the gardens where a man named William Kirwan had strolled just before meeting his killers in 1892. To our right was the house once occupied by Victorian workhouse reformer Janet Johnson and then - just a few yards ahead now - Cross Bones itself. The sky was darkening into early evening and the closer we came to the burial ground's gates, the more John Constable seemed to morph into John Crow before my eyes. I began to see what he'd meant about the 21st century dropping away when you walked these streets. [71]

We paused at the gates so I could point out the handful of offerings I'd left there a few days earlier and examine the ramshackle fencing for any fresh graffiti. Constable produced a key, unlocked the site's access door, and led me inside – something I hadn't been sure he'd do till we actually got there. Until very recently, he told me, security at the site had been so loose that passers-by would sometimes find this door swinging open and pop in for their own casual tour. That's what a local resident I'll call PP did while showing an American visitor round Southwark in May 2004, later describing what they found on a south London message board: [72]

> *"Several diseased-looking dogs ran at us, barking loudly and frightening my guest. Then two men emerged from the old industrial building in the northeast part of the yard, both wearing dirty*

clothes and looking aggressive. One held a syringe. The other brandished a metal pipe and began telling us to 'f*** off' out of their 'f***ing yard'.

"The man with the syringe apologised for his friend, who he said was sick. He said that he and four or five friends were living in the sheds, that a couple of them had mental health problems and all had a drug habit. [...] He led us to the door of the large shed and we popped our heads in. After a few seconds, we withdrew for the smell of excrement was indescribable.

"In the room, I saw two women, one middle-aged and one younger, lying on what appeared to be piles of decomposing rubbish on the concrete floor. Our host explained that the older woman lived there and the younger one was 'waiting for gear'. [...] He explained there was no plumbing of any sort and they have to use the ground as a combined toilet, bathroom and kitchen.

"My guest has gone back to America to report that medieval conditions exist in 2004, a stone's throw from London Bridge. I have informed the council about this visit in the hope that something may be done." (73)

The area of Cross Bones he's discussing seems to be not the burial ground itself, but the concrete yard separating it from Southwark Street to the north. Whether it was PP's report that jabbed Southwark's police and council officers into action, I don't know, but soon afterwards the homeless people there were evicted and measures taken to ensure the door stayed locked. By 2012, what I could see of the yard showed only a bare surface and some overgrown foliage. (74)

To Transport for London's credit, it had continued to allow Constable and his team enough access to let them help keep the site tidy. On St George's Day 2007, when volunteers met to clear rubbish from the burial ground, Constable noticed that someone else had already been working there, clearing overgrown vegetation, assembling stones from the site into geometric sculptures and shaping the bushes into topiary. No-one had ever seen this mysterious figure in action, so Constable nicknamed him the Invisible Gardener. Some said this secret horticulturalist was a Network Rail employee, others that he'd once lived in a caravan inside the Cross Bones gates.

The Invisible Gardener finally introduced himself one Saturday in June 2007, when a lanky figure strolled up and shook Constable's hand at the Cross Bones gates. "He just came up to me," Constable recalls. "My partner Katy and I were walking past the north gate on Southwark Street when we were approached by the Gardener with the words, 'John Crow, I've been watching you'."

Constable didn't feel free to give me the Invisible Gardener's real name when I asked him, and all I was initially able to discover from other sources was that he'd been some sort of muse for the fashion designer Vivienne Westwood. The matter rested there till a PlanetSlade reader who knew I was working on Cross Bones sent me a 2009 piece in the *Independent* profiling Andy Hulme, who'd met Westwood when she employed him as her gardener and went on to design the floral catwalk set for her 1994 Erotic Zones show. Towards the end of this piece, Hulme shows the paper's Emma Townshend a photograph which anyone who knew Cross Bones was sure to recognise.

"It's a stark pyramid of brick in a wild open space, backed by railway bridges and a faraway glimpse of the Swiss Re building," she writes. "Straggly buddleias flourish in the Tarmac cracks. The pyramid is weighty and silent, giving shape to the neglected urban space. 'That's my garden,' he says." [75]

Armed with this information, I started Googling Hulme and discovered that his own Victorian country-gentleman look had inspired a whole menswear collection for Westwood in 2009, leading to profiles of him appearing in several national newspapers and a host of fashion mags. Every one of these articles uses the word "muse" to describe his relationship with Westwood - exactly the word my first informant had chosen. One also mentions his run-ins with the police as a youngster, confirming the rebel streak he'd need to conduct guerrilla gardening on Cross Bones' epic scale. The *Sunday Times'* profile coyly refers to him having a Southwark 'garden', carefully placing that final word in quotation marks to suggest a hidden significance. [76]

Final confirmation came when I contacted Hulme himself and -

slightly to my surprise - he said he was happy for me to use his name here. "The anonymity and secrecy around that garden was not something I sought," he told me. "However, when I exhibited some photos of it earlier this year I did present it as the work of an obsessed security guard, now vanished. It seemed like a better story."

Hulme did remarkable work at Cross Bones, creating a garden worthy of *Alice in Wonderland* or *The Prisoner's* Portmeirion. Here's what one lucky group of gate visitors saw when they turned up for the Summer Solstice vigil in June 2008:

"John Crow led the way through the secret doorway, a battered old building site door graffitied with the invitation to 'touch for love'. Stewards in reflective tabards (the goose samurai), guide the 50 celebrants round the safe pathways.

"Crow shows us the shrine of the lost and found, a circle of bricks surrounding a primitive stone cross with a red lantern at its centre. On the bricks are arranged a fragment of a jawbone, a plastic lizard, a broken pair of glasses, half a scissor, a green comb and a tangle of tiny coloured wires - objects found during a previous clean-up of the site by these informal friends of Cross Bones.

"And Crow shows us the knot-garden, ablaze with poppies, in the shape of an eternity sign - or, more precisely, a double-diamond <><> - walled with rubble cleared from the site. [This is] enclosed by broken bricks and concrete chunks retrieved by the Invisible Gardener and his trusty sidekick Sidney from the aftermath of a previous Museum of London excavation.

"One of the larger chunks, from a more recent structure on the site, clearly shows bones and the crown of a skull protruding from the concrete foundations that ripped them from their resting place. This evening, bathed in the light of the setting sun, the gardens are vividly stained with red and black poppies." [77]

As Constable led me round the burial ground that day in 2012, everything I'd read about the place took on new flesh. There was the white pyramid Hulme had shown Townshend, the apple tree he'd lovingly grafted with mistletoe and the bush he'd patiently clipped into the shape of a dagger-pierced heart. "It's like a sailor's tattoo," Constable had said when describing this bush back in the café and I could see now he was right. Elsewhere in the garden, there was a perfect topiary sculpture of a Scottie dog, a massive swing set constructed from old railway sleepers and so much more.

I could see all the sculptures, planting and topiary around me had been done with great care, but also that nothing there was manicured into such antiseptic tidiness that it risked losing its soul. The site still pulsed with ungovernable magic in those days, its power only enhanced by the imagination and outlaw creativity which people like Constable and Hulme had invested there. Struggling to conjure an image that summed up the place's spirit, I found myself thinking of the jaggedly beautiful albums Tom Waits produced in his "junkyard orchestra" period. If *Swordfishtrombones* was a garden, I decided, this is the garden it would be. [78]

A short history of the Clink

"The clink" has been a British slang term for any prison ever since the early 16th century and is still widely used in that sense on both sides of the Atlantic today. It's the Bishop of Winchester's notorious Southwark prison which gave us this long-standing term.

The Bishop would have had some sort of prison at his disposal ever since about 860AD, but at that time it was probably just a single cell in a priests' college. When he took over responsibility for policing the Liberty surrounding his Southwark palace in the 12th century, naturally a bigger prison was required.

He built the first version of the Clink on Maiden Lane, opposite what's now Sumner Street. It looked like a medieval castle's gatehouse - there's a Gatehouse Square on the site to this day - with circular towers at each corner and battlements topping the walls. Very soon, the Clink gained a reputation for brutality. "Unspeakable treatment became commonplace," says Jennifer Jones' Southwark history guide. "Entirely at the mercy of their keepers, prisoners were obliged to beg or prostitute themselves in order to provide the income necessary to improve their conditions by bribing the jailers."

In 1352 the law changed, allowing debtors to be imprisoned for the first time, and that increased the Clink's population a great deal, giving the staff even greater opportunity for corruption. A century later, when Bishop Henry Beaufort died, he left £400 in his will to be distributed to inmates at the Clink and other local prisons. This would have been worth perhaps £1m in today's money and Beaufort hoped the prisoners would use it to alleviate their misery.

Our first written record of this prison being called the Clink dates to 1503. Fifty years later, the Catholic Queen Mary I began imprisoning Protestant dissidents there and her successor, the Protestant Elizabeth I, did the same for Catholic heretics. Elizabeth jailed a lot of Protestant puritans in the Clink as well, where many of them starved to death.

Henry Barrowe and John Greenwood, both of whom served time in the Clink before being hanged at Tyburn in 1593, were founders of the puritans' Independent Church, whose congregation supplied many of the pilgrims who sailed to America on the *Mayflower's* 1620 voyage. Barrowe had originally come to the Clink only to visit Greenwood, but when the keepers realised who he was, they refused to let him out again.

The Clink was still known as a fearful place where prisoners were left to rot. Its main function for the next 100 years was to jail offenders from the nearby brothels, bear pits, theatres and taverns. By 1745, the building was in such terrible disrepair that its inmates had to be moved to a new site near Borough Market. The prison's name was transferred to its new premises too, which much later led to that whole street being named Clink Street. In 1780, the Gordon Riots burnt out the Clink and it never opened as a jail again. There's a prison museum on its site in Clink Street today, where it pulls in thousands of tourists.

In 2002, the legendary graffiti artist Banksy painted his *Chequebook Vandalism* piece on the Clink's outside wall. Southwark Council promptly painted over it and must be kicking themselves for doing so today. A Banksy mural removed from a wall in Wood Green, North London, fetched over £750,000 at auction in June 2013.

A passer-by stops to admire the gates' latest offerings.

9: Farewell to the Stews

Most historians agree that it was sailors returning from America after Christopher Columbus's voyage there in 1492 who first brought syphilis to Europe.

One of the first cities hit was Naples, where it gained its toehold during a war between Charles VIII of France and the city's own Alfonso II. Both men's armies included Spanish mercenaries who'd accompanied Columbus to the new world and were now infected. Alfonso's men amused themselves in the city's brothels as they waited for the fighting to begin, just as Charles's would do to celebrate their successful occupation of the city in February 1495. By the time the French army returned to Paris later that year, Naples was already awash with syphilis and its spread across Europe had begun. Soon it had spread throughout France, Switzerland and Germany, reaching Britain in 1497. [79, 80]

That was the year Cesare Borgia, then just 22, arrived in Naples to attend the coronation of its new King. His sexual adventures there produced a predicable result. "First a chancre appeared on his penis," Sarah Dunant explained in a recent article for the *Guardian*. "Then crippling pains throughout his body and a rash of itching, weeping pustules covering his face and torso. Over the next few years, [Borgia's personal physician] charted the unstoppable rise of a disease that had grown men screaming in agony as their flesh was eaten away, in some cases down to the bone." [81]

This was a world without condoms, penicillin or even the most basic standards of hygiene but people did travel, and this combination of circumstances ensured the infection continued to spread with Biblical ferocity. In 1498, British travellers took it to Calcutta and by 1500 it was all over the Scandinavian countries, Hungary, Greece, Poland and Russia. Africa, China and Japan escaped infection only till 1520 or so.

The death toll in Europe alone was counted in the millions -

some say five million, some say ten - and there are estimates that as many as 20% of Europeans were infected at the epidemic's peak. "I know of nothing of which I am so afraid," the artist Albrecht Durer wrote from Venice in 1506. "Nearly every man has it and it eats up so many that they die." [82, 83]

The one thing people knew about syphilis in these early years was that it spread through sex, which made it obvious that brothels were the single most important source of infection. Even a clean establishment would have been a serious threat to public health, but that threat was doubled by the primitive laundry arrangements prevailing at the time. One inspector checking a 15th century Paris brothel found sanitary towels there heavily stained with both blood and a green discharge suggesting gonhorroea. These were washed in what he called "a filthy tub" of sulphur or mercury solution, before being laid out on stoves to dry and then re-used. The procedure in Southwark probably wasn't much better.

Edinburgh was one of the first British cities to react to the epidemic, closing down its own brothels in 1497, but London dragged its feet till 1505. That was the year when, according to *Fabyan's Chronicle*: "The stews or common bordello beyond the water, for what hap or consideration I know not, was for a season inhibited and closed up. But it was not long ere they were set open again, albeit that where before were occupied 18 houses, from henceforth should be occupied but 12." The women evicted either found work in the even filthier illegal premises elsewhere in Southwark, or else fled across the river to set up shop there. *Cock Lorell's Bote,* a satirical ballad written in 1510, records their exodus:

"There came such a wind from Winchester,
That blew these women over the river,
In wherry, as I will you tell,
Some at St Katherine struck aground,
And many in Holborn were found.
Some at St Giles, I trow,
Also in Ave Maria Alley and at Westminster,
And some in Shoreditch drew thither."

The "wind from Winchester" of course was the syphilis infection responsible for closing the Liberty's brothels. Most of the districts mentioned, including St Katherine's Parish, Ave Maria Alley and Shoreditch, were then just outside London's City wall and so had spawned red light districts of their own where the Southwark women knew they'd find work. Westminster's demand was provided by its proximity to the King's palace and Holborn's by the Inns of Court, where many of London's barristers both lived and worked. It was only a few months till Southwark's licensed brothels were allowed to reopen, at which point most of the displaced women simply moved back across the river and resumed business as usual.

Some other European countries kept their own licensed brothels closed for years when syphilis first arrived, so why did London decide to abandon its precautions so quickly? One answer may lie in the same exodus *Cock Lorell's Bote* describes. Ever since Roman times the Thames had served as London's moat, protecting it from all the chaos that went on across the river in Southwark. Closing the Bankside brothels had amounted to an invitation for every sex worker in Southwark to cross that moat, and now they thronged round London's walls like a besieging army. Where once the thieving and violence spawned by street prostitution had been kept safely at arm's length, now it was at the City's very gates.

Richard Foxe, who was Bishop of Winchester at the time, must have been quick to remind King Henry VII of all this. The loss of licensing fees and fines from the Bankside brothels would have put a big dent in Foxe's income and yet done little to reduce the cost of policing his unruly domain. As England's Lord Privy Seal - one of the nation's five great Officers of State - Foxe would have had ample opportunity to lobby the King and bring his considerable influence to bear. And Henry had his own financial considerations to weigh too. In normal times, a good chunk of the money Bankside generated ultimately found its way into Henry's own coffers and his displeasure at losing this cash evidently outweighed any concerns about public health. [84]

By August 1506, 12 of the Bankside's 18 established brothels were trading legally again and producing fresh offences for the Bishop's Liberty courts to tackle. the Gun, the Swan, the Bull's Head, the Rose, the Bell and the Cardinal's Hat were still refused a licence, but it's not clear whether that's because they were thought to be the worst carriers of disease or simply because they'd failed to bribe their way back into favour. Most of them probably re-opened without a licence anyway, posing as an innocent inn or tavern but continuing their old trade in the shadows.

With the stews back in business and their licensing fees restored, the Bishop's forces concentrated on imposing draconian punishments for any woman who continued sex work when she knew she was infected. Offenders were arrested by the bailiff and his constables, fined a whopping £5 and forcibly expelled from Bankside. In France, the treatment such women received was even harsher. Some were simply executed for continuing to work as prostitutes in defiance of the anti-syphilis laws and others were soldered into an iron collar or whipped through the streets. [85]

In the days of the Crusades, it had been the death of so many male breadwinners in rural areas which drove women into prostitution, but now a second pressure was added too. The prototype "factories" which started to appear around 1500 had a devastating effect on the cottage industries many country women had relied on to survive. "Hundreds of thousands of the poorer women were thrown on to their own resources in an environment that had, as yet, no capacity to employ them," Burford writes. "By the time Henry VIII came to the throne in 1509, for countless thousands of women, the only remaining alternative was to peddle their bodies."

One of the new King's first moves to control prostitution came in 1513, when he commanded that any woman found soliciting among his soldiers must be branded on the face with a hot iron. Most likely, it was fear of syphilis that lay behind this proclamation, as Henry wanted his men fit enough to fight, not laid up in bed nursing their sores.

Six years later, he followed up this measure by ordering Cardinal Wolsey to purge Southwark of its "vagabonds and loose women". Wolsey duly dispatched City officials across the river, where the 54 people they arrested in Bankside brothels included John Williams (one of the King's own footmen), Will Borage (a yeoman of the King's guard) and David Glynne (a royal servant). This total's particularly impressive when you realise that Bankside's one small patch yielded as many arrests as all the rest of Southwark put together.

As with the Black Death of 200 years earlier, the fear of syphilis did little to dampen demand on Bankside. In 1519, John Skelton's morality play *Magnificence* was still able to refer to people who

---

"runneth straight to the stews" in depicting a London he knew his audience would recognise. Latin grammars dating from about 1520 show that middle-class schoolboys as young as seven were routinely taught to translate phrases such as "He lay with a harlot all night", "Thou art a strong harlot" and "She is bawd to a whore". It was taken for granted that, as soon as they reached puberty, these lads would be frequenting the Bankside brothels like every other red-blooded young man.

Ten years on from Wolsey's purge, Southwark remained as lawless as ever. In 1529, Bishop Foxe complained that the Borough gave him more trouble with criminals than anywhere else in his domain. The sneaky residents there, he said, were still "dicing and carding till past midnight and there picketh another's purse and doth resort them in and out at a back door". Later that year, the religious reformer Simon Fish smuggled his anti-clerical pamphlet *A Supplication for the Beggars* into England, attacking the Church for its hypocrisy on sexual ethics. "Who is she that will set her hand to work to get threepence a day and may have at least twenty pence a day to sleep with a friar, a monk or a priest?" he asked. The Catholic Church responded by declaring his pamphlet heretical.

The Reformation which would transform England into a Protestant country and move so much Church property over to the Crown was now very close. Henry VIII passed the first of his statutes breaking with Rome in 1532, continuing the process of separation with roughly one new statute every year for the remainder of that decade.

In 1535, laws were passed to ensure that taxes previously paid to Rome went to the English Crown instead and Thomas Cromwell, the King's chief minister, set about assessing the taxable value of all Church property. The first statute transferring this property's ownership to the Crown passed in 1536 and by 1540 that process was complete. Often, the King sold on his new property to private landlords, who he was confident would make more productive use of it than the Church had ever managed to do.

While all the Reformation's changes were going through, Henry VIII also found time to renew his assault on the Bankside brothels. In 1535, he ordered that the Southwark stews be "as far as is possible publicly and entirely suppressed" because they harboured "unclean persons unfit to associate with honest men". His admission there that it was never going to be possible to completely sweep prostitution away is a telling one. Like the illegal drug trade today, the Bankside stew-houses offered people at the very bottom of society the promise of cash they could never dream of getting from any other source. As Fish's pamphlet points out, that made the risks involved worth bearing no matter what obstacles the law put in your way.

For proof of this, we need look no further than Robert Allen, a Bankside stew-holder hanged at Tyburn in 1537. Allen began his working life as an ostler, caring for horses at a London tavern, but was sacked from that job after being charged with theft and what we'd today call grievous bodily harm. After a year in prison for failing to pay his debts, he found work in a Bankside brothel, where the boss promoted him to manager and he saved enough money to buy premises of his own.

He looked set for a prosperous old age till his vicious streak surfaced once again: he attacked a rival stew-holder and went to the gallows for it. Not the end he'd hoped for, I'm sure, but in a world where respectable work offered him nothing but hunger and endless drudgery, who's to say he made the wrong choice?

Henry VIII took another swipe at Bankside in 1546, this time giving his proclamation the full panoply of a royal trumpeter and a herald-at-arms. "Miserable and dissolute persons have been suffered to dwell in open places called the Stews and there, without punishment or correction, exercise their abominable and detestable sin," the herald announced. "There have of late increased such enormities as to invite vengeance of Almighty God and also to cause such great annoyance to the common wealth by enticing the youth to fleshly lusts. The brothel-keepers and their women must therefore, before the Easter coming, depart to their natural countries with their bags and baggage."

The phrase "natural countries" here means that Henry was ejecting not only the Bankside's foreign sex workers, but also any British ones from outside London, who were expected to return to whichever town they'd come from. The proclamation was made on April 13 and Easter Sunday that year fell on April 24, so they had just 11 days to pack up all their belongings and find a new home. In order to further hinder anyone who tried to continue operating on Bankside, Henry also banned bear-baiting on that side of the river, so depriving the stews' customers of one of their favourite interim diversions.

Most of those who moved out after the King's proclamation

probably expected to return once the fuss had died down a bit - just as they'd done in 1505. But the difference this time was that many of the former church properties the stew-houses occupied now belonged either to the Crown or to private landlords who were keen to develop Bankside for themselves. The new Protestant orthodoxy that now ruled the English Church took a less laissez-faire attitude to prostitution than the Catholic authorities had done, which also played its part in making it impossible for the Bankside stew-houses to re-establish themselves.

Henry VIII died in 1547, so he was cheated of the chance to see his proclamation's effects work through in practice. How much of this he'd planned and how much was merely an unforeseen side effect of his other policies, I don't know, but there's no doubt that the combined effect of his 1546 evictions and the Crown property seizures going through at the same time succeeded in changing Bankside where every other sanction had failed. "The closure of the Stews in 1546 seems to have rid Southwark of most, if not all, of its professional prostitutes," Carlin writes. "The parish register of St Saviour's records no burial of a 'single' or 'common' woman after February 1547."

By "professional prostitutes" there, Carlin means those who worked full-time on Bankside under the Bishop's rule. No-one doubts that the illegal brothels in Southwark remained as busy as ever after the licensed ones closed and now the red light districts north of the river were thriving too. This fact did not escape Edward VI's court preacher, Hugh Latimer, who preached a 1549 sermon on the subject to a congregation which included the new King. "My Lords, you have put down the Stews, but I pray you, how is that matter amended?" Latimer asked. "What availeth that you have merely changed the place and not taken the whoredom away? There is now in London more than ever there was on the Bank."

There were more changes for Southwark in 1550, when the King sold London's Lord Mayor and Sheriffs the power to "farm" the Crown's recently acquired Southwark lands in return for a hefty cash sum. This gave London the right to collect taxes in Southwark and granted the City some formal power over its outlaw borough at last.

London's authority still didn't extend to the twin Liberties of the Clink and Paris Gardens, which would not succumb to London rule for another six years. That final blow fell in 1556, when all of Southwark was absorbed into London as the city's 26th ward - known as Bridge Ward Without. Paris Gardens still formed the centre of London's low-life gambling industry and Edward VI had allowed bull-baiting and bear-baiting to creep back in on Bankside, but the Liberty and its licensed stews were no more.

"The women their breasts did show and lay out"

Puritan commentators of the 16th century were quick to condemn the slightly more revealing fashions middle-class women were then beginning to adopt. One way of doing this was to satirise such women by comparing their dress to that of a Bankside prostitute. In 1540, for example, the anti-papist poet Charles Bansley wrote: "For a Stewed strumpet cannot so soon / Set up a lewd light fashion / But every wanton jilt will like it well / And catch it up anon".

The Anatomy of Melancholy's Robert Burton (1577-1640), noted that the real working girls of his day went about with "their necks open almost to the kidneys". That was no more than necessary advertising in their case, but respectable women had no reason to go so far. In practice, the most skin a nice girl ever flashed at this time was probably the saucy glimpse of collarbone seen in William Scrots' 1546 portrait of the teenager who would become Elizabeth I.

That didn't stop the Kentish doctor John Hall attacking such women in his 1565 volume *The Court of Virtue*. Described as "a puritanical parody" of the cheerfully filthy ballads found in the 1558 best-seller *The Court of Venus*, Hall's work includes this verse: "The women their breasts did show and lay out / As well was it [seen] whose dugs were stout / Which usance at first came up from the Stewes / Which men's wives and daughters after did use."

Hall's contemporary readers would have recognised his description as a mixture of parody and propaganda, so we must be careful to take it with a pinch of salt too. I asked Susan North, a curator of fashion at London's Victoria & Albert Museum, to put this verse in some sort of context.

She thought it much more likely that the wives and daughters Hall mentions were trying to copy not the Bankside stews, but the aristocracy. Again, the Princess Elizabeth portrait mentioned above gives us our best idea of what this meant in practice - and even that look was pretty risky outside England's blue-blooded elite.

"This was perfectly acceptable within the aristocracy and the world of the court," North said of Elizabeth's 1546 décolletage. "But it's very difficult to determine if any middle-class women actually dressed this way. If they did, it's more probable that they were attempting to copy the revealing head-dresses and necklines of women's court dress. But it reinforced the claims of misogynistic moralists to accuse them of dressing like strumpets." [86]

Cross Bones' Shrine to the Suicides began with a single offering.

10: The Southwark Mysteries

"At one point, Jesus was admonished by St Peter for his swearing and responded, 'In the house of the harlot, man must master the language'. At another, Satan, played by a female actor, strapped on a huge red phallus before using it to beat his sidekick Beelzebub." [87]

That's an extract from the *Sunday Telegraph's* review of John Constable's verse drama *The Mystery Plays*, which made its debut at the twin venues of Shakespeare's Globe Theatre and Southwark Cathedral on April 23, 2000. First published as part of his *Southwark Mysteries* paperback, the play had found a triply significant date for its staging: not just Shakespeare's birthday and St George's Day but Easter Sunday too. Mark Rylance – then the Globe's artistic director - and the cathedral's Dean Colin Slee had both been drafted by Constable in his determination to make the event a reality.

"I wrote to Colin and told him about *The Southwark Mysteries*," Constable told me. "And he wrote back - quite guarded to begin with. Then I met Mark Rylance. They were very wary of me. Mark had just taken over at the Globe and I think he felt he had to be quite careful. He was representing an international trust, so he didn't necessarily want a local turning up and saying, 'I've had this vision and now you're going to do this play'. So we had a very rough ride to get there, but it did actually happen."

Constable saw his drama as a modern version of the traditional medieval mystery plays, complete with their warts-and-all acceptance of human imperfection and the carnival atmosphere in which they were staged. These plays had religious content at their heart, certainly, but scorned all attempts at piety and that gave Constable a perfect template for his own version. "It's a sort of left-handed form of Gnostic Christianity, which didn't come down through churches and priests, but through actors and whores," he told me. "There's a very strong sense in the whole work that, through songs, through sayings and jokes, very profane activities, something sacred is being revealed."

As the first production took shape, it was decided that its first, more controversial act should be staged at the Globe and its second at Southwark Cathedral. Rylance himself – now an Oscar winner, of course - was Constable's first choice to play John Crow, but declined the role as he already had far too much on his plate. Constable stepped in to play Crow himself and director Sarah Davey set about casting everyone else. Among the major roles, Roddy McDevitt signed on as Christ, Jacqueline Haigh as Satan and Di Sherlock as the Goose. Local volunteers and children from Southwark's schools were recruited as extras, spear-carriers and miscellaneous crowds.

The play begins with a group of Jubilee Line workers inadvertently raising the spirits of the Goose and John Crow while tunnelling at Cross Bones. Here's the production's own summary of what comes next:

> *"Satan appears to announce the Day of Judgement and to claim the Whore (Goose), the Heretic (Crow) and the other wicked souls of Bankside. He unleashes Oliver Cromwell and his Puritans, who are in the act of closing the theatre when Jesus appears, riding a bike and bearing a radical teaching of mutual forgiveness.*
>
> *"He recognises the Goose as Mary Magdalene, wrestling with Satan for her soul. John Crow is not so sure he wants to be forgiven, reminding Jesus of the abominations that have been carried out in his name. The first act ends with Jesus enacting a healing ritual, re-enacting his crucifixion on an operating table at Guy's Hospital.*
>
> *"The second act takes place in Southwark Cathedral, which has been taken over by Satan and his devils. They are in the process of inflicting horrible punishments on the Goose, Crow and the other lost souls. Their orgy of retribution is interrupted by Jesus bursting into the Cathedral. He challenges Satan for each of the lost souls, finding creative ways of forgiving them and embracing them into his Divinity."* [88]

Constable kept up a constant to and fro with Slee as rehearsals got under way. The Dean was a fierce defender of the project against all outsiders, but never hesitated to let Constable and the rest know when he felt their plans went a step too far. Not all his notes were accepted by any means, but Davey did agree to his request that Satan leave her phallus in the wings whenever Christ was also on stage.

"In the year leading up to the play, the Church went through one or two paroxysms about whether or not they should do it at all," Constable told me. "And the day it happened, there was a huge thunderstorm half an hour before we opened." That might be taken as a bad omen at any theatre, but it threatened utter disaster for an open-air one like the Globe. In the end, though, it turned out that God was only teasing: "Virtually the whole cast came up to me and said, 'You see?' And then, five minutes before our start time, we got a rainbow." The play pulled in a packed house at both venues for this debut performance and was greeted with wild applause. Simon Hughes, the local MP, called it "the jewel in the crown" of Southwark's Millennium celebrations and called for it to be staged again every ten-years.

The *Sunday Telegraph*, as we've seen, was less impressed. "A religious play staged in an Anglican cathedral has provoked fury after it featured a swearing Jesus and Satan wearing a phallus," fumed the paper's Jonathan Petre. "Satan told scatological jokes and told Jesus to 'kiss my ass'." Petre managed to find one member of the audience who was prepared to call the play "disgustingly offensive", but also quoted Constable and Slee's robust defence. "The message is that even the worst sins are not beyond redemption," Slee told him. The play's producers, realising that an outraged howl from the *Sunday Telegraph* was the best publicity they could dream of, made sure to quote its verdict in all their promotions.

In April 2010, the anniversary production Hughes had suggested staged a three-night run, this time using Southwark Cathedral alone and playing to over a thousand people.

Zanna (right) with her assistant Natalie Boatfield.

11: Shakespeare's Bankside

It's fitting that Constable chose a stage play to celebrate Cross Bones' history, because Southwark's been a cornerstone of British theatre ever since the 16th century. Bankside can't claim either of London's first two purpose-built playhouses - those were both north of the river in Shoreditch - but it was home to the three most important theatres of the Elizabethan age and it's still one of London's liveliest districts for playgoers today. Within a mile of Redcross Way, either in Southwark itself or just across the boundary with Lambeth, drama is still staged every night at the National, the Old Vic, the Young Vic, the Globe, the Rose, the Menier Chocolate Factory, the Southwark Playhouse, the Bridge and the Union Theatre.

London's first two bespoke playhouses were the Theatre and the Curtain, opened in 1576 and 1577 respectively. The owners chose Shoreditch as their location because it was then just outside the city walls and so already the sort of disreputable area where lowlife scum like actors and theatre-goers might be expected to gather. Acting was considered a gutter pursuit in the 1500s - even a seditious one - so London's authorities wanted to segregate it just as they'd done with the city's licensed brothels.

For their own part, entrepreneurs wanted to build their new playhouses somewhere the law would leave them alone and where people were already in the mood to throw their money about a bit. Bankside answered everyone's requirements, so that's where the Rose (opened in 1587), the Swan (1595) and the Globe (1599) all made their home. It was the need to help supervise his company's construction of the Globe which persuaded a young playwright called William Shakespeare to abandon his rooms in Bishopsgate for new digs near the Clink prison. He was in his mid-thirties at that time and Bankside offered plenty of pleasures for a man of that age - particularly one who visited his wife and children back in Stratford so infrequently.

After confiscating the Church's Bankside land in his dissolution of the monasteries, Henry VIII had given it to Sir Ralph Sadler, who then sold it on to a property developer called Henry Polsted. In 1552, Polsted leased out stew-houses like the Barge and the Unicorn to new tenant-managers, who continued running them just as before. Henry's changes may have removed the stew-houses' legal status, but there was still plenty of demand for their services and money to be made. The ruling officials could always be bribed to turn a blind eye when necessary, so the question of whether you were trading legally or illegally was largely an academic one. The loss of the protection a licence had once afforded was inconvenient in some ways, but on the other hand it also swept away all the bureaucratic requirements maintaining that licence had demanded.

What little protection the 1161 rules had given the stews' customers was now swept away too. Robert Greene, who wrote a 16th century guide listing the dangers innocent country visitors would find in London, reminded them first about the perils of syphilis then warned against a scam he called "crossbiting".

The idea was that an appealing young Bankside woman would pick up a respectable man, take him to her room and lead him into a highly compromising position. At that point, her pimp would burst in pretending to be the girl's brother or husband, hurl the man to the floor and start threatening to drag him through the courts for defiling her. As he struggled into his pants, the client would become more and more terrified, finally throwing all his money and valuables at the two scamsters just so they'd let him flee. [89]

The Catholic Queen Mary came to the throne in 1553, restoring that religion's more pragmatic attitude to Bankside. The heavy policing imposed there eased back a little as a result. If Mary's reign had lasted more than just five years, she may even have agreed to her churchmen's suggestion that the area's old status be fully restored. "[They] were very likely to have gained their suit if she had lived a little longer," wrote the 16th century priest William Harrison. "The Stewes, saith one of them in a sermon at St Paul's Cross, are so necessary in a common wealth as a jaxe in a man's house." [90]

Mary's leniency toward the stews was reversed when the Protestant Elizabeth I took over in 1558. Elizabeth also set her face against new building in Southwark, which kicked the property speculation already rife there up a further gear and led to what houses it had being divided into smaller and smaller units. This made overcrowding in its tenement slums worse than ever.

It was hard for Southwark's residents to fight back against decisions like this because, unlike other London wards, they were not allowed to elect their own representatives. The London authorities, perhaps remembering the corrupt juries of Southwark's Liberty era, assumed its people were such a criminal, unruly bunch that they simply couldn't be trusted with electoral power. Instead, London summarily appointed a couple of aldermen of its own choosing to represent Southwark and told the Borough to lump it. "Southwark had become a kind of satrapy," Peter Ackroyd writes in *London: The Biography*. "Thus ensuring that, almost till the end of the 20th century, it remained a relatively undeveloped and ill-regarded place." [91]

The fact that London's laws rather than the Liberty's now applied on Bankside allowed the new Bridge Ward Without to treat its sex workers very harshly. Punishments included shaving the woman's head as a badge of shame, stripping her half-naked and whipping her through the streets, locking her in the pillory or a cage for public display, ducking her in raw sewage, and sometimes a sentence in the hellish Clink. For some observers, even this wasn't enough. "I would have some sharper law," Harrison wrote in 1577. "The dragging of some of them over the Thames between Lambeth and Westminster is a punishment that most terrifyeth them that are condemned thereto." [92]

Meanwhile, the poor of Southwark had lost the only scrap of help medieval society ever offered them. "The dissolution of the monasteries had the unintended effect of breaking the social safety net," the Southwark historian Patricia Dark told me. "If you needed a hot meal or a bed for the night and you had nowhere else to go, you could knock on the door of the local monastery. It wouldn't be fancy food and it wouldn't be a nice bed, but you would at least be kept from starvation or dying of exposure. When the monasteries closed, the bottom dropped out for a lot of people."

This change came just as England was beginning a century of rapid population growth (1550-1650), which threw more people on the streets than ever. One of the fastest-growing London wards was Southwark itself, where population trebled between 1555 and 1635, and much of this strain fell on the area around Redcross Way.

Records from 1603 show that Cross Bones's own St Saviour's

was the second most heavily populated parish in Southwark, with 37% of the Borough's people living there. Judging by the proportion of St Saviour's folks rich enough to pay "rates" - just 9.5% of the population against 28.9% in prosperous St Thomas' - it was also Southwark's poorest parish. Six years later, a survey of the Clink Liberty found that over a quarter of the households there were desperate enough to qualify for parish relief, a benefit then reserved only for the poorest of the poor. St Saviour's churchwardens began complaining that they were expected to deal with more poor people every day and one of their major concerns would have been the increasing burden of so many pauper burials. (93)

Figures from a 1567 accounts book show that over three-quarters of all the people receiving parish relief in St Saviour's that year were women, suggesting what Carlin calls "a pattern of heavily feminised poverty". Philip Stubbes' 1583 pamphlet *The Anatomie of Abuses* gives us a glimpse of what this meant in practice. "The poor lie in the streets upon pallets of straw, or else in the mire and dirt," he writes. "[They have] neither house to put in their heads, covering to keep them from the cold [...] nor penny to buy them sustenance."

This was the Bankside as Shakespeare found it when he moved there in the late 1590s: a broiling swamp of thievery, prostitution, drunkenness and rascality of all kinds. There were two theatres already operating there, two bear pits, a string of illegal brothels - some providing girls as young as seven - and countless pubs. Poverty and disease were rife in the Borough's middened streets and every now and again a deadly fight broke out, but nowhere else in London could offer such raucous, edgy thrills for the city's wild young men. (94)

I asked Patricia Dark to help me think my way back to 16th century Bankside by offering some sort of modern parallel. "Was it like Vegas in the 1970s?" I asked. "Soho in the 1950s? Pre-war Berlin?" But she had a better comparison. "It's Tijuana," she told me. "Tijuana in George Bush Jr's day was where you went if you wanted to have a wild, wild weekend - lots of underage boozing, lots of hookers, lots of blow. It's that kind of seediness, combined with the Wild West's saloons full of raucous card games. Everyone's having a great time, but then you lay the wrong card and someone pulls out a gun." (95, 96)

It wouldn't have been a gun in Shakespeare's day, of course but a sword. There's no doubt most revellers would have come to Southwark well-armed, as the British Museum's Neil MacGregor recently confirmed. Speaking on his BBC radio series *Shakespeare's Restless World*, MacGregor produced a dagger and a rapier, both Elizabethan and both recovered from the Thames just off Bankside. His guess was that they'd been accidentally dropped overboard (in separate incidents) by two of the drunken young men who stumbled nightly into the boatmen's crafts taking them back across the river after a good night out. "It's an impressive weapon," MacGregor said of the rapier. "The blade alone is well over a metre long and it's sharp on both sides and at the end. You can slash and pierce." [97]

Swords were partly a style accessory in those days, but any self-respecting young man would have felt obliged to arm himself for protection before setting foot on Bankside anyway. Once the drink started flowing, it was often these armed young men themselves who started the very mayhem they'd set out wanting to forestall. "Once swords become part of your dress as a gentleman, there is always the temptation to use them," the Wallace Collection's Toby Capwell told MacGregor. "If everyone is going to carry swords around all the time, they're going to come out pretty quick when there's some kind of argument."

Dark considered my suggested comparisons again. "There's possibly a veneer of Vegas in its heyday," she said. "But better, maybe, is Atlantic City during Prohibition. It's all shiny and glitzy and vaguely kind of glamorous, but there's always this undercurrent. If you're not careful, or if you're not lucky, or if you don't watch what you're doing, you won't make it back across the border." [98]

*****

The theatrical company Shakespeare belonged to was called the Lord Chamberlain's Men and they would not have been naïve about Bankside's dangers. In fact, they owed their whole move to Southwark and the glorious times they'd enjoy at the Globe there to a criminal enterprise. When their Puritan landlord Giles Allen refused to renew the Lord Chamberlain's Men's lease on the Shoreditch theatre which formed their base, the company simply turned up one day in the Christmas break and dismantled the building without his permission. They shipped the Theatre's old timbers across the river to Bankside and used these to build the Globe on a new site they'd just acquired there. (99)

Two years before helping to steal this wood, Shakespeare himself had a run-in with the law on Bankside. We don't know the full details, but the trouble seems to have started with a perjury row between Francis Langley, the man who built the Swan theatre in Paris Gardens, and William Gardiner, a corrupt Southwark judge. It's thought that the Lord Chamberlain's Men played a 1596 season at the Swan after their lease on the Theatre expired and that's probably how Shakespeare got swept up in Langley's dispute. The historian Leslie Hotson believes Gardiner escalated the feud by threatening to close the Swan and hence throw the Lord Chamberlain's Men out of work. (100)

Gardiner had a lackey called William Wayte, who complained in the summer of 1596 that four people had attacked him outside the Swan. He named his assailants as Francis Langley, Anne Lee, Dorothy Soer and William Shakespeare. When the case came to court, Wayte testified he'd been in real fear of his life. "By the standards of the day, it was a run-of-the-mill kind of brawl," MacGregor told his listeners. "The only remarkable thing about it is that we know Shakespeare was involved. The Shakespeare Four had to post bail and promise to keep the peace. They eventually settled out of court."

The first Shakespeare play premiered at the Globe is thought to be 1599's *Julius Caesar*. This ushered in a hugely creative period for our Bankside Bard, who wrote *Hamlet, Othello, King Lear, Macbeth, Coriolanus, The Tempest* and 11 other plays before the building burnt down in June 1613. That fire was started by a stray spark from the Globe's stage cannons, which set light to the building's thatch during the premiere of Shakespeare's *Henry VIII* there. Fittingly, this was his final play.

The company - now renamed the King's Men under James I's patronage - rebuilt their theatre on the same site a year later, where they continued staging plays for another 30 years. Shakespeare seems to have moved back north of the river in around 1604, but didn't finally leave London till 1613, when he returned to Stratford-on-Avon to retire. He died three years later.

Any writer living and working in an area as lively as Bankside was bound to find the neighbourhood's characters, history and atmosphere soaking into his work. In Shakespeare's case, he modelled Henry VI's Sir John Falstaff partly on an old soldier who'd once owned a Southwark inn. Sir John Fastolf, who lived from 1380 to 1459, really did fight with King Henry in France, but lost his reputation after the Battle of Patay in 1429. The English were heavily defeated on that day and many said Fastolf had survived only through cowardice. He was later charged with profiteering from the French wars, investing the proceeds in property such as Southwark's Boar's Head Inn. When Jack Cade's rebels arrived on Bankside in 1450, Fastolf fled rather than face them. "Who hath honour?" he may have asked himself as he ran. "He that died o' Wednesday." [101, 102]

Anyone who's seen Shakespeare's Falstaff in action will recognise this portrait. The playwright even named Falstaff's favourite tavern, the Boar's Head, after Fastolf's real Southwark inn - though he moves it across the river to Eastcheap. That's where the fictional Falstaff meets a sweet-hearted whore called Doll Tearsheet, who the Globe's Bankside audiences would have recognised as a familiar type. At any given performance, there would have been a handful of Doll's real-life sisters either working the crowd outside the Globe or dotted among the groundlings to cheer her on.

As far as the text of Shakespeare's plays is concerned, the most striking example of a Bankside reference is Gloucester's confrontation with Henry Beaufort, the Bishop of Winchester, in *Henry VI Part I*. Shakespeare based this scene on a real event of Henry VI's reign when those two men really were at war with one another. This happened in 1425 when the Duke of Gloucester was one of Henry's regents, ruling England on behalf of its child King. "In October, Gloucester persuaded the City authorities that Beaufort threatened an insurrection and London Bridge was barred at its southern end," the *Annals of London* explains. "The Bishop's men broke the chain and news of an impending fight spread like wildfire on the north bank. Forces soon confronted each other on opposite ends of the bridge, but the situation was defused by the mayor and aldermen." [103]

In Shakespeare's version of this face-off, Gloucester takes the opportunity to taunt Beaufort about his seamy duties on Bankside and slips in a punning reference to one of its biggest brothels:

Gloucester:
"Thou that givest whores indulgences to sin:
I'll canvass thee in thy broad cardinal's hat,

If thou proceed in this thy insolence."

[...]

"Under my feet I stamp thy cardinal's hat,
In spite of Pope or dignities of Church,
Here by thy cheeks I'll drag thee up and down."

Winchester:
"Gloucester, thou wilt answer this before the Pope."

Gloucester:
"Winchester goose, I cry, a rope, a rope!" (104)

There's another mention of Winchester Geese in 1602's *Troilus & Cressida* and this time Shakespeare is very explicit about the threat of disease associated with them. The speaker is a lecherous, degenerate old procurer, who looks the audience straight in the eye as the play ends and delivers this epilogue:

Pandarus:
"My fear is this,
Some galled goose of Winchester would hiss:
Till then I'll sweat and seek about for eases,
And at that time bequeathe you my diseases." (105)

"Galled" means "covered in sores", so the reference to Winchester Geese carrying syphilis is clear enough. Pandarus is teasing the audience here by saying he'd like to stay and continue the story, but dare not do so for fear they'll wheeze their filthy, diseased breath all over him. Instead, he'll get back to the stews and send a bit of his own infection the audience's way later.

Leave the Globe with an epilogue like that ringing in your ears and you could hardly help being hyper-sensitive to every cough and splutter in the crowd around you. Shakespeare's audience had more reason to be fearful than most, because plague was coming back to Southwark and this epidemic would put the Borough's graveyards under more pressure than ever before.

How to steal a theatre

"The Chamberlain's Men were in trouble and the only way out was to get in a bit deeper." That's James Shapiro, writing in his award-winning book *1599: A Day in the Life of William Shakespeare*. The theatrical company in question had Shakespeare as its resident writer, but that didn't save them from the crisis that hit as the 16th century drew to a close.

The company's six shareholders were Richard Burbage, John Heminges, Will Kemp, Augustine Phillips, Thomas Pope and Shakespeare himself. All worked on its plays in one way or another. Among the actors represented, Burbage was recognised as the leading tragic actor of his age and Kemp as its finest clown.

Shakespeare at this point was both writing for the company and acting in some smaller roles. When the 1599 crisis arose, he'd already written 20 of his 38 plays, including all eight plays of the histories cycle plus *Romeo & Juliet, The Merchant of Venice, A Midsummer Night's Dream* and *As You Like It*. You'd think an output like that would ensure his company a home for life, but now their Shoreditch base had locked its doors against them and they were reduced to ad hoc touring instead.

Burbage's father James had built the Theatre on a patch of Shoreditch land leased from a man called Giles Allen and given his son's company the residency there in 1594. The building's design had been inspired by London's large inns, placing the actors in a central open courtyard while spectators watched from covered galleries on all four sides. The English weather meant staging plays there in winter was almost impossible.

James Burbage's solution was to secure some land at Blackfriars and begin building an indoor theatre there, which he knew would be able to work all year round. There was some urgency to this, because Burbage knew the Theatre's lease was close to expiring and so far the Puritan Allen had refused to renew it.

Blackfriars, unlike Shoreditch, was inside London's city wall and this was a much more refined neighbourhood than any where a theatre had yet been built. Burbage hoped to turn this into a positive by pulling in a richer audience than he'd had available at Shoreditch, but in fact it proved to be the project's undoing. He'd already sunk £600 into building the new theatre - a sum which would be worth over £½m today - when Blackfriars residents blocked its licence. They were a rich, well-connected bunch and none of them wanted the noisy, drunken riff-raff a theatre was likely to attract coming anywhere near their homes.

Soon after this blow, James Burbage died, still without managing to renegotiate the Theatre's lease. Richard had no more luck with these negotiations than his father had done and now faced the additional problem that all the family's cash was tied up in the stalled Blackfriars project. Their lease on the Theatre duly expired and the Lord Chamberlain's Men found themselves homeless. Richard Burbage heard that Allen planned to demolish the Theatre and reuse its timbers for a less sinful building - and that's when he had an idea.

He gathered the other five LCM shareholders together and said he and his brother Cuthbert would supply £700 worth of the materials needed to build the company a new theatre if each of the others would agree to cover 10% of the construction costs, plus the expense of running the new place. This would be the first theatre designed, owned and run by its own actors and writers. Shakespeare and the rest agreed to borrow the money they'd need for their own stakes and told Burbage to go ahead. By December 1598, he had everyone on board and, a few weeks later, they'd rented the Bankside site where the Globe would stand.

Burbage's plan for obtaining the wood was simply to dismantle the Theatre and ship it across the Thames to the new site. His father had inserted a clause in the Shoreditch lease saying that all the materials he put into building the Theatre would remain his property for as long as the lease ran. But now that lease had expired, leaving Allen with the perfectly reasonable assumption that the building, like the land it stood on, now belonged to him.

Sorting this issue out in court would have taken months and eaten up any possible benefits in legal fees, so Burbage decided on direct action instead. On December 28, 1598, when he knew Allen was away celebrating Christmas at his Essex estate, Burbage and the rest gathered with a handful of carpenters and stagehands from the LCM crew. Heading the operation, they had a master builder called Peter Street. They armed themselves with a load of real swords, daggers and axes borrowed from the Curtain's prop department and marched to the Theatre's site on what's now Broadway Market.

"When the armed group arrived at the playhouse, they set to work immediately," Shapiro writes. "According to evidence submitted in the heated legal battle that followed, their appearance quickly drew a crowd - friends and tenants of Allen as well as supporters of the Chamberlain's Men, including Ellen Burbage, James's feisty widow." Allen's friends tried to block the demolition, but quickly found themselves out-numbered and had to retreat.

Keeping the crowd at bay with a mixture of lies and threats, Burbage and his crew had all the Theatre's timbers stacked on carts by nightfall and stored away in a secret Thames-side warehouse before midnight. The ice in the Thames that Christmas made boat crossings impossible and the tolls due if they'd tried to transport the timber across London Bridge were prohibitive, so they waited till the thaw of Spring 1599 before shipping the wood across the river and adding it to the foundations now dug at their new site.

"One can only imagine how furious Allen must have been when he returned to where the Theatre had stood and found it gone, the grass trampled, his field littered with mounds of plaster and shattered tile," Shapiro writes.

In the lawsuit that followed, Allen described the Lord Chamberlain's Men as armed thugs responsible for "pulling, breaking and throwing down the said Theatre in very outrageous, violent and riotous sort, to the great disturbance and terrifying [...] of your Majesty's loving subjects". Targeting Street as the man whose expertise had made the whole operation possible, he demanded £800 in compensation (worth about £200,000 today) plus punitive damages, but the court found against him. I like to think the decision went that way because the judge couldn't help admiring Burbage & Co's sheer cheek.

Ken Campbell's ribbon on the Cross Bones gates.

12: Going Underground

Cross Bones' modern era began around 1989, when plans were prepared to extend the Tube's Jubilee Line out to London's massive new office developments in Docklands and Canary Wharf. The site at Redcross Way, then seen as just a patch of derelict land, was one of the properties acquired in preparation for this work.

John Constable had moved to Southwark about three years earlier, not because he had any particular interest in the Borough, but simply because he'd happened to find an affordable flat to rent there. "It was regarded as a very run down and dubious area," he told me. "Taxi drivers would not bring you home here and policemen warned me about drawing out cash. On the other hand, although it was quite beat-up, it was also an amazingly atmospheric area, with loads of interesting little twists and turns in the back streets. It was full of derelict warehouses and some of those had been either taken on as short leases or squatted. As a result, you had lots of artists' studios, unusual spaces and clubs operating."

This was the era of London's first warehouse parties and the beginnings of an Ecstasy-driven dance culture which would dominate the coming decade. Matthew Collin's 1997 book *Altered State* gives us a glimpse of what Southwark was like as the warehouse parties began. He starts with the story of Paul Stone and Lu Vukovic, who had been among the dancers at West London's ground-breaking Hedonism club and decided to create a similar event of their own. "They booked some rooms in a recording studio on Clink Street in the shadow of London Bridge," Collin writes. "In 1988, that warren of streets was dark, dilapidated, desolate and sometimes rather frightening. The only sign of humanity was the nearby market, which would spring into life just before dawn, the lorry drivers and traders bemused at the danced-out, dishevelled clubbers wandering home sweaty and exhausted." [106]

Stone and Vukovic called their club RIP (for Revolution In

Progress) and created what Collin calls a "deliciously edgy" atmosphere there. Among the core DJs they used were Mr C and Eddie Richards, both of whom share their memories of the club in the book. "Every week, there were people trying to climb up drainpipes, giving backhanders of £20 to doormen to get in, doormen having to fight people off with baseball bats and dogs because they were going to rush the doors," Mr C recalls. "Complete madness." Richards confirms this picture, contrasting RIP with more respectable dance nights nearby. "Clink Street was slummier, dodgier," he tells Collin. "Dodgier characters on the door, dodgier characters inside, a dodgier feeling about it. I think it was a bit frightening - really frightening at times."

Among the villains and thugs Mr C remembers thronging the RIP dancefloor were an equal number of the stylish rich, hip enough to know this offered London's most intense night out, dressed to the nines and pestering the acid house kids for pills. Clink Street and its surrounding Liberty had hosted this unlikely mix of rich, poor and criminal pleasure-seekers for centuries and now the area was pulsing with that old anarchic energy once again.

Meanwhile, just a quarter-mile to the south, London Transport was surveying its new Redcross Way site. Excavations on the scale planned would inevitably disturb significant archaeological sites all along the extended route, so regulators had insisted the Museum of London be given a chance to mitigate any damage caused. When the museum's archaeological team heard one of the Tube's new electricity substations was going to be built at Redcross Way, that's when they stepped in.

"The site was known from documentary sources to be the location of a burial ground used during the post-medieval period," the MoL team wrote in its later report. "A small-scale investigation in 1990 was carried out by the Oxford Archaeology Unit, which showed the documentary evidence was correct." The museum won permission to carry out a dig on the footprint of the proposed substation, but was given just six weeks to get it done. [107]

The five-strong MoL team got to work on the site in February 1993. They worked only on the substation's footprint itself - an area equivalent to about two and a half tennis courts - and dug down just ten feet. In this single "box" of earth alone, they found 148 skeletons buried. The museum estimates this to be "less than 1%" of the total number of burials made at Cross Bones, suggesting the site as a whole provided a last resting place for at least 15,000 souls. All the human remains under the substation's footprint were removed at the conclusion of the six-week dig. Those in the rest of Cross Bones remain undisturbed.

"We are now standing on untouched burial ground," MoL's Adrian Miles told a BBC interviewer on the site in 2010. "There are several thousand burials beneath our feet. All the burials were in coffins, but they're of the poorest standard that I've ever seen. You're looking at re-used wood - it's probably cheap wood that's coming off the docks." [108, 109]

The whole of Cross Bones covers only about 2,000 square yards, as Patricia Dark reminded me when we discussed the MoL's estimates. "It's not big," she said. "It must be absolutely chock-full of bones." The MoL's photographs from its dig confirm this, showing coffins packed so closely together that their sides are almost touching. Layer after layer of dead were found crammed into the Cross Bones earth, with coffins sometimes stacked nine or ten deep. The top layer was just a few inches below the surface. Only a few of the coffins had nameplates attached and even those were of such poor quality that they'd long since become illegible. As with the ramshackle coffins themselves, the families who used Cross Bones simply hadn't been able to afford anything better.

All the bodies were buried on their backs, aligned east-west with their feet at the eastern end. This custom was observed in the belief that, when the Second Coming arrived, the dead would be able to sit bolt upright in their graves and immediately see the glory of the risen Christ in the east. As we'll see a little later, one unforeseen consequence of this practice was to tell grave robbers exactly where they should dig in any particular plot to get the body out with minimum fuss. [110]

The museum's analysis of the 148 skeletons it recovered gives us a fascinating picture of just who was buried at Cross Bones. Because these were the bodies closest to the surface and because they knew Cross Bones' graves were so regularly recycled, the team assumed all the burials concerned had been carried out in the site's final fifty years of use. That put the individuals' date of death at somewhere between 1800 and 1853, a period which takes in the first 16 years of Queen Victoria's reign. "[In the layer] we're excavating, it's very much the poor ground for the parish of St Saviour's," Myles told the BBC. "The people who would be buried here would be the poor of the parish, bodies found in the river, people from the workhouse, people who couldn't afford to pay for their own burials."

Just over two-thirds (70.2%) of the skeletons uncovered were those of children, this group representing 104 of the 148 skeletons in all. At least 98 of those 104 children had been six years old or under when they died, reflecting this part of Southwark's very high infant mortality in the first half of the 19th century. In London's poorest parishes - of which St Saviour's was definitely one - as many as one in three children then died before their fifth birthday.

The biggest single group of children were the perinatal ones, who died either in their mother's final three months of pregnancy or within a month of birth. There were 50 skeletons like this among the 148 MoL studied, representing a third of the grand total and nearly half of all the children involved. Next came those aged between one month and six years (48 people), aged from six to 11 (two people) and aged 12 to 17 (one person). There were another three skeletons which the museum was confident had belonged to children, but which were impossible to age beyond that. [111, 112]

The adult skeletons - 44 of them in all - were mostly aged between 36 and 45 (18 people), with the next most common groups being aged 46 or more (14 people), 26-35 (four people) and 18-25 (three people). There were five adult skeletons the team was not able to age any more precisely than that. Of the 39 adult skeletons it was possible to sex, 12 were male (31%) and 27 were female (69%). The biggest tranche of men were aged 36-45 at death (six people) and the biggest tranche of women were aged over 45 (12 people). Turning to the question of these people's medical history, the MoL's findings were these:

• **Periostitis was present in 89 of the 148 skeletons studied (60.1%).** This disease attacks the connective tissue coating human bones and causes severe pain. When a mother with syphilis passes that infection to the child in her womb, it can cause periostitis in the newborn baby. In a graveyard with as many infants in it as Cross Bones, that seems likely to be a major factor.

• **Fifty-nine skeletons (40%) showed signs of osteoarthritis.** Osteoarthritis is still very common in the UK, but today it normally hits people over 50. Only 14 of the 140 people it was possible to age at Cross Bones (10%) got to more than 45, suggesting the disease struck much earlier then.

• **Twenty-two of the skeletons (14.9%) had signs of scurvy.** Scurvy is caused by a lack of vitamin C and we know most of the people round Cross Bones had a very poor diet.

• **Eleven of the skeletons (7.4%) had signs of rickets.** Lack of calcium in the diet and a lack of sunshine cause rickets. People in the Southwark slums got precious little of either.

• **Twelve skeletons (8.1%) had healed fractures.** This category includes 50% of all the men and 14.8% of all the women. Industrial accidents and the violence of the streets may explain the high incidence of male injuries. No doubt Victorian Southwark had its share of wife-beaters too.

• **Nine skeletons (6.1%) showed evidence of treponemal infection, which is linked with syphilis.** Seven children and two women filled this category.

• **Three skeletons (2%) had evidence of surgery carried out at or very close to the point of death.** It's not clear whether the surgery killed them or whether they fell prey to Victorian anatomists.

• **Two skeletons (both children) showed evidence of histiocytosis-X, which can be caused by toxins in the atmosphere.** Southwark was full of very dirty factories by 1800, which made the air and the water supply filthy. This group represented 1.35% of the total sample.

• **One skeleton (a child's) showed evidence of smallpox**

112

infection. That's 0.7% of the total sample.

"The 19th century parish of St Saviour's, Southwark, teemed with people - the poor and destitute, living in overcrowded houses with bad hygiene, drainage and waste disposal and an inadequate and polluted water supply," the MoL's report sums up. "[This excavation provides] a window on a population struggling with harsh living conditions, who were poorly nourished and prone to infectious and deficiency diseases. Most were buried in cheap coffins and this heavily used, ill-kept and unconsecrated burial ground [...] contrasts with wealthy parishes elsewhere in London."

As the MoL team got on with the analysis that produced all this data, Constable was still exploring his new home. The National Lottery's Millennium Commission was pouring a fortune into this previously neglected stretch of the Thames' south bank and massive construction sites were springing up all around him. In 1993, building work started on Sam Wanamaker's replica Globe Theatre, in 1995 work began to convert the old Bankside Power Station into Tate Modern and in 1996 plans were announced for a stylish new footbridge linking Tate Modern to St Paul's Cathedral on the other side of the river.

"There was that real sense of things changing," Constable told me. "I knew Bankside was going to change out of all recognition, so one of my inspirations for writing *The Southwark Mysteries* was wanting to capture the moment that I was living here. On the 14th of November 1996, I got a group of friends together including Ken Campbell and John Joyce, one of his actors. There were about seven of us - we were actually a writers' group. I took them on a walk I called The Mysteries Pilgrimage and we visited Southwark Cathedral, Shakespeare's Globe, Winchester Palace, the site of the Tabard. These were already in my mind as kind of magical places. The one that was missing was Cross Bones." [113]

Nine nights after that, on November 23, 1996, Constable encountered the Goose for the first time and took down her puzzling verse: "And well we know how the carrion crow / doth feast in our Cross Bones graveyard". A month later, the MoL began briefing journalists about its analysts' conclusions from the Redcross Way dig, prompting one newspaper to warn that further development could obliterate this endangered "skull and crossbones cemetery" altogether.

113

That phrase made Constable think of the Goose again, so he went to the address the story had mentioned and instantly recognised it as one of his stops on that mad night with the Goose. "Told you so," she whispered in his ear.

As Constable got on with writing *The Southwark Mysteries*, Bankside's growing rave culture was gearing up for the millennium. One highlight planned was a new production of Neil Oram's legendary 24-hour play *The Warp*, which Ken Campbell had first staged back in the 1970s. The new production was to be directed by Campbell's daughter Daisy in a network of interlinked cellars underneath London Bridge station. Organised with the help of techno-hippy guru Fraser Clark and his Megatripolis club nights, the play was supplemented by a 24-hour rave in the same set of tunnels. The first event was held at the end of May 1999, with fortnightly repeats running well into 2000. Sensing a group of kindred souls, Constable was keen to get involved.

"I was in a very millennial mood," he told me. "I'd been writing all this stuff about the outlaws and the tantric tribe returning to Southwark and suddenly there's all these alternative people - old sixties hippies, people from the travellers' convoys, punks. They used to call it 'Glastonbury without the mud'. You'd have the whole of *The Warp* going on for 24 hours. You could either sit and watch the whole show or - what most people did - you could come and go. You had three dance floors, all with different music. You had a chill space and a main performance/gallery place. I used to perform in there a lot. I was doing *Southwark Mysteries* stuff, Goose stuff there."

The Megatripolis events had one more surprise in store too - this time a detail which linked millennial Southwark neatly back to the Medieval bath-houses which had given the stews their name. "For about five of the parties, they even had a giant hot tub, with everybody stark bollock naked," Constable told me. It was as though The Goose had never been away.

The best little whorehouse on Bankside

The biggest and best of the 17th century Bankside stew-houses was created and run by a woman named Elizabeth Holland. Holland's Leaguer, as this castle-like mansion in Paris Gardens was known, offered such fine levels of service and hygiene that even King James I was a regular customer.

Elizabeth Holland was this woman's married name, which may indicate she'd wed into the Holland family of gangsters who then ran much of Southwark's underworld. Her husband disappears from the story almost immediately, leaving the young Elizabeth to fend for herself at some point in the 1590s.

She made the mistake of setting up her first brothel inside London's city walls, which led to her being arrested in 1597 and sent to Newgate gaol. Fortunately, she'd already made enough money to ensure herself a reasonably comfortable life in Newgate until her fine was fully paid off, at which point she fled to Southwark before any physical punishment could follow. From that point onwards, she vowed, anyone hoping to arrest her again had better come with an army in tow.

By 1603, Holland had rented a large manor house in Paris Gardens and was ready to open for business again. The word "leaguer" at the time had connotations of both castles and brothels, which made it doubly appropriate for her new premises.

"The house itself was a grand mansion that stood by the river and was fortified with a moat, drawbridge and portcullis," says Melissa Hope Ditmore in her *Encyclopedia of Prostitution*. "What is striking about Holland's Leaguer is the way it was set up as a female community set apart from the rest of society - the drawbridge being the main means by which visitors could gain entrance to the establishment."

The Leaguer, like all Southwark's leading brothels at this time, modelled itself on a great inn, with the whole establishment arranged round a central courtyard. "The reception rooms were on the ground floor, facing on to the courtyard, which was entered through a great arch big enough to allow coaches to pass," Burford explains. "Next to the reception rooms would have been a restaurant and a bar - or perhaps several to cater for clients of different status and means. The women's chambers would have been upstairs." [114]

In her own book, *The Picara*, Anne Kaler adds that Elizabeth began using the professional name Madam Donna Britannica Hollandia. "This change of name allowed Elizabeth to follow the old custom that brothel madams were either Flemish or French and the tradition that continental harlots knew their business better than British ones," she writes. [115]

Its position in the slightly less built-up area of Paris Gardens gave Holland's Leaguer a measure of protection from the plague which periodically ravaged Southwark's poorer and more crowded parishes. Madam Hollandia also had the good sense to ensure a much higher standard of cleanliness than you'd find anywhere else on Bankside. She was running a classy operation here and neither the girls nor their clients were allowed to forget it. "Holland's Leaguer's popularity depended on the business-like atmosphere, its good food, luxurious surroundings, modern plumbing, medical inspections, clean linens and high-class prostitutes," Kaler writes.

Reports of the facilities on offer mention portraits of the establishment's most beautiful girls for gentlemen to choose among over a glass of wine, a summerhouse in the grounds for discrete assignations and a regular supply of plump new virgins shipped in from the Surrey countryside. It's even said Holland had a plaque made reading "James Stuart slept here", which she displayed in the main reception room. [116]

On the enforcement side, she employed an armed bouncer, said to be an enormous ex-con who was soppily devoted to her. When push came to shove, there was a spot on the riverbank where unwanted guests – or sometimes their bodies - could be unceremoniously thrown into the Thames.

Holland's Leaguer continued its happy prosperity till 1631, when Charles I decided to demonstrate his piety by ordering this notorious establishment must be shut down. "When a troop of soldiers arrived to enforce the closure, Holland enticed them on to the drawbridge, which she then let down [into the water], depositing the men in the moat," Ditmore writes. "The prostitutes then proceeded to empty the contents of their chamber pots over the soldiers, who swiftly retreated."

The women could keep up this resistance only so long, however, and the troops did eventually force them to close. Hollandia herself escaped and some accounts say her establishment enjoyed a brief resurgence in the Restoration, but its glory days were already over. The 1632 closure inspired both a stage play and a ballad, neither of which were inclined to take Charles I's censorious line. The road leading to the Leaguer's old spot on Bankside is still called

Holland Street today and can be found just behind Tate Modern.

Matt Wilcock's job includes managing the site's gardeners.

13: Puritans & Plagues

Even before the bubonic plague outbreak of 1603, St Saviour's parish graveyards were full to bursting. "The air must often have been reeking with pestilential vapours," William Rendle writes in his 1878 book *Old Southwark and its People*. "One little churchyard is filled, another spot close at hand is taken in and filled in its turn and so on, as the dead gradually become too many for the living. In 1573, the churchyard is enclosed with a substantial pale. 1594, 'the new churchyard'. 1620, 'the churchyard within the chain gate'. The vestry seems often to be looking about for burial places." [117]

The place names Rendle puts in quotation marks there are taken verbatim from the minutes of St Saviour's 16th and 17th century vestry meetings and some think 1594's "new churchyard" was the site we now call Cross Bones. That's certainly the phrase used to describe it in an August 1760 lease from the Bishop of Winchester granting one Edward Pearson access to "a place called the New Churchyard and situate in or near Red Cross Street in the parish of St Saviour, Southwark". It's by no means certain that the lease's new churchyard and Rendle's churchyard were the same place, but Pearson's document does confirm that Cross Bones was still owned by the Bishop of Winchester as late as 1760, and that's quite useful to know in itself. [118]

Our first reliable glimpse of Cross Bones in the historical record comes in John Stow's 1598 *Survey of London*, which mentions the 12 stew-houses dominating Bankside after 1506, then says:

> *"Ancient men of good credit report that these single women were forbidden the rites of the church, so long as they continued that sinful life, and were excluded from Christian burial if they were not reconciled before their death. And therefore there was a plot of ground, called the Single Woman's Churchyard, appointed for them far*

from the parish church. " (119-121)

The MoL believes it's our Redcross Way site Stow has in mind here. That conclusion's supported by both 1795's *Histories and Antiquities of the Parish of St Saviour's Southwark* and by 1833's *Annals of St Mary Overy.* "We are very much inclined to believe this was the spot," the first volume's authors write. "We find no other place answering the description given of a ground appropriated as a burial place for these women; circumstances therefore justify the supposition of this being the place." The *Annals* are even more unequivocal, saying: "There is an unconsecrated burial ground known as 'the Cross Bones' at the corner of Redcross Street, formerly called the Single Women's burial ground". (122)

It's fair to conclude from all this that Cross Bones was already in use as a burial ground by 1598, when Stow produced his survey, and that it was old enough even then for only "ancient men of good credit" to remember its beginnings. That seems to rule out 1594 as the date for the first burials of all there, though it may mark the date St Saviour's parish first took an interest in the site. Even by 1613, it was still not listed as an official parish burial ground, as we can see from a price list of burial costs St Saviour's published in that year. This mentions only the churchyard surrounding St Saviour's itself (now Southwark Cathedral) and the College churchyard on Park Street. The tariff includes a note that pauper burials can be conducted at the College ground, so my guess is that the parish didn't yet need Cross Bones for that purpose. (123)

"It became the parish poor ground in due course, though the exact date for the first parish interment in the cemetery is uncertain," the MoL report says. "[The St Saviour's price list] makes no mention of either the Cross Bones or the New Churchyard. This suggests that it was not in use as a parish burial ground at that time, though this does not rule out its usage as the earlier 'Single Women's burial ground'."

We know from the St Saviour's parish register covering 1538-1563 that the churchwardens there were already marking out the sex workers presented for burial, which suggests they were somehow segregating those particular graves long before 1594. As Carlin points out, this register "carefully notes the burials of prostitutes as, eg, 'Alys, a singlewoman' or 'Margaret Savage, common woman', while taking only rare note of the occupation of others buried". Perhaps it suited St Saviour's to let these women be interred at a quasi-official graveyard in the Bishop of Winchester's Clink Liberty? The Liberty governed every aspect of these women's lives in the early 16th century, after all, so why not let the Bishop's men bury them too and keep the parish's own grounds untainted?

Whatever the history of Cross Bones before St Saviour's got involved, it was surely the increasing pressure on all Southwark's burial grounds which led to the site being officially adopted. Plague took a heavy toll on the Borough throughout the 1600s and it was St Saviour's paupers who bore the brunt. In the plague year of 1625 alone, the parish had to find somewhere to bury 2,346 bodies, which Rendle estimates to be fully one third of St Saviour's population. This load was further increased by the 17th century's three exceptionally severe winters in London - those of 1608, 1615 and 1622 - which killed close to 300 people a week in the city and hit the poor hardest of all.

Taken together, these figures demonstrate both why Cross Bones has always been crammed so tightly with dead and why no skeletons from Stow's time remain there today. "A widespread response to the growing shortage of space, especially in the inner city, seems to have been to pack the maximum number of corpses into the available ground," Houlbrooke writes. "In so far as charnels [bone houses] were employed, it was in a more casual fashion than in medieval times. Where they did survive, their contents were probably treated with scant respect. 'Our bones in consecrated ground never lie quiet,' John Aubrey wrote. 'And in London, once in ten years the earth is carried to the dung-wharf'." [124]

It was also the 1625 plague outbreak which prompted one Southwark gravedigger to complain he was out of pocket by £11 and 15 shillings because of the huge number of poor people he'd been forced to bury without pay during those years. The 1613 St Saviour's price list I mentioned earlier shows that just the patch of earth for your loved one's burial could cost anywhere from twopence (with no coffin) in the parish's College ground to two shillings (for a coffin burial) in St Saviour's Churchyard itself.

On top of that must be added up to 16 pence for the Minister's services, another 16 pence for the gravedigger and fourpence each for bearers. Even if you picked the cheapest possible option in every category, it would be hard to bury your loved one for less than three shillings and sixpence and that was a sum far beyond what many in St Saviour's could pay.

"Burial fees often represent many days' wages for a labouring man or woman," Professor Boulton told me. "And that bill would come just as family finances might be tighter than normal following medical costs, loss of wages and possibly the loss of a main breadwinner." That's why so many families around Redcross Way had no choice but to opt for a pauper funeral instead and accept whatever godforsaken graveyard the parish might consign them to. [125, 126]

Charles I came to the throne in 1625 and immediately ordered a clean-up of the red light districts closest to London's walls. He left Southwark alone on that occasion, but attendances at its brothels, theatres and bear pits were already declining. Germ theory was still largely unknown, but people may already have intuited that the crowded, filthy streets of this very poor area offered more risk of infection than most. The prevailing idea at this time was that disease spread through foul air, so the stench of Southwark alone must have been enough to make many people fear visiting it. As with every outbreak of plague that century, anyone rich enough to flee London for the countryside did so with all possible speed. [127]

The plague returned more virulent than ever in 1630 and this time the authorities reacted by ordering Bankside's theatres, bear pits and other amusements to close down until the disease had retreated again. The idea seems to have been to discourage people from gathering in large crowds or - if they insisted on doing so – at least to choose a less disease-ridden borough than Southwark for their revels. The authorities had always viewed actors and playwrights as a potentially seditious lot, so silencing their voice may have also appealed for that reason.

Indirectly, these closures hit the brothels too. "If the pattern of previous outbreaks was followed, it could be expected that the normal 'let us be merry for tomorrow we die,' attitude would enable the prostitutes to carry on," Burford writes. "But on this occasion, the deaths from plague were very numerous and doubtless everybody who could get away did so. The Bankside never fully recovered from this blow." Another closure of the theatres followed in 1642 and then - the big one - in 1665. Before we get to that terrible year, though, there's the little matter of the English Civil War to deal with.

This war had been brewing ever since 1629, when Charles I dissolved the English Parliament for defying his financial and religious policies, then began an 11-year period of direct personal rule. He was forced to reconvene Parliament in April 1640 because he needed it to grant him money for his battles against the Scots, but once again MPs refused him and Charles dissolved their assembly after just three weeks. When he tried again that November, a zealous group of Protestant and Puritan MPs - many of whom suspected Charles was a secret Catholic - used the Parliament's gathering to voice angry complaints against him.

Relations between the King and his Parliament sank still further in January 1642, when Charles marched his men into the House of Commons and attempted to arrest five of its most troublesome MPs. They slipped away safely and Charles declared open hostilities in August that year by raising his standard at Nottingham Castle and inviting loyal subjects to rally behind him. The opposing Parliamentary army was led by Oliver Cromwell and the resulting conflict kept England at war with itself for the next nine years.

The same group of Puritan zealots who'd defied Charles in 1640 were keen to purge sinful pleasures from the land. They didn't limit themselves just to Southwark in this ambition, but naturally enough it was a major target. "In April 1644, Parliament closed all whorehouses, gambling houses and theatres," Burford writes. "The players were whipped at the cart-arse, fined for using oaths or sent to prison. Maypoles were pulled down wherever they could be found on grounds they incited the peasantry to lust. Nude statues, when not broken up, had their genitals covered with leaves and scrolls."

Southwark's taverns were left largely unmolested in this clean-up, if only because they were woven so tightly into people's everyday lives. Unlike every other policing body that had declared its intentions to clean up Bankside, the Puritans were fanatical enough to refuse the innkeepers' bribes, so any sexual trade that continued there had to move deep into the shadows.

The Puritan forces in Southwark were supported by the hundreds of Dutch and Flemish Protestants who'd emigrated there since 1575. Despite their countrywomen's reputation for supplying Bankside's most expert prostitutes, most of the new arrivals were sober artisans, who'd begun to industrialise large parts of the

Borough. They'd became more fiercely Protestant than ever when Charles I took the throne - blame those suspicions about his Catholic sympathies again - and helped to ensure that Southwark sided firmly with the Parliamentarian side when civil war began. And perhaps we shouldn't be surprised by this: no-one saw the violence and disease Bankside's seamy trade created more clearly than those who had to live with it on their doorstep.

Cromwell's army won a major victory at Preston in August 1648, charging the King with high treason and having him publicly executed in Whitehall five months later. His son, Charles II, who'd fled to Scotland, continued to fight Cromwell till September 1651, but his defeat that month at Worcester proved the war's last major battle. Two years later, in December 1653, Cromwell declared himself England's Lord Protector - a post that amounted to the monarchy in all but name.

Re-ordering Southwark under his new regime, Cromwell sold the old Clink Liberty's lands to a property developer called Thomas Walker. Walker added another chunk of real estate he'd bought from Southwark Manor and set about tearing down every building he found there to build tenements instead. This constant redivision of Southwark's housing into smaller and smaller units left the Borough a warren of packed tenements and dark, narrow alleyways strewn with both human and animal dung. Chamber pots were still the only form of indoor lavatory at this time and these were emptied from the tenement windows directly into the alley beneath. The rats which carried plague-bearing fleas to Bankside could hardly have asked for a better home.

When Oliver Cromwell died in 1658, his son Richard plunged the country into chaos by assuming he could simply inherit the Lord Protector's role as if it really were the hereditary Kingship. It was only after Richard had been overthrown and Charles II invited to return to England as monarch in 1660 that some semblance of order was restored. Five years later, we were back to the plague again.

It's the 1665 outbreak which we today call the Great Plague and there's no doubt that it deserves that name. Even the official Bills of Mortality admit that a total of 68,596 Londoners were killed by this outbreak during its 18-month run. That alone would make its toll equivalent to 15% of the city's population, but it's generally agreed today that these official figures seriously underestimate the true number of deaths. The more likely total in London over that period is 100,000 (or 22%) and, as always, it was in slum areas like Southwark that the infection spread fastest of all. [128]

In the midst of this outbreak, journalist Henry Muddiman wrote a letter from London to the Government minister Joseph Williamson. Muddiman reports that the city's burials in that week alone had reached 8,252, of which 6,978 were plague deaths. Samuel Pepys gives us similar figures in his diary entry for August 31, 1665. "This month ends with great sadness upon the public through the greatness of the plague," he writes. "In the City died this week 7,496 and, of them, 6,102 of the plague".

Both Muddiman and Pepys here were writing at something like the peak of plague deaths, but the fact that they're quoting the official Bill of Mortality's statistics means even these horrendous figures are likely to be an underestimate. Pepys acknowledges as much in the same day's entry, adding: "It is feared that the true number of the dead this week is near 10,000." [129, 130]

With so many bodies to be collected and disposed of, the parish authorities struggled to keep up, eventually resorting to stacking ripe corpses in the street until their overloaded carts could dump their cargo in the nearest plague pit and return for more. Collections and plague burials were first conducted at night to avoid public alarm, but this restriction soon proved impractical. "The people die so, that now it seems they are fain to carry the dead to be buried by day-light, the nights not sufficing to do it in," Pepys' August 12 entry tells us. Three weeks later, on September 6, he remarks how strange it is to see burials conducted in broad daylight on Bankside, "one at the very heels of another: doubtless all of the plague".

One plague pit in Aldgate housed over 1,100 bodies, which arrived with such relentless speed that they were being dumped in at one end while workmen still dug at the other. Daniel DeFoe, in his *Journal of the Plague Year*, tells us that in London "many if not all of the out-parishes were obliged to make new burying-grounds" and there's no reason to think St Saviour's would have been an exception. Lord Brabazon, writing to the *Times* in 1883, claims to have seen 17th century records showing that many victims of the 1665/66 plague were buried at Cross Bones itself, where "in one week upwards of 600 bodies were interred".

The combined effect of the Puritans' crackdown on Bankside,

the repeated closure of theatres and bear pits there and the unprecedented number of plague deaths in this latest outbreak was to end its status as London's Tijuana once and for all. A few entertainments, such as bear-baiting and prize fights, resumed there after the Great Plague, but Southwark would never again have the critical mass of theatres, brothels, taverns and gambling joints which fed one another's trade and made Bankside so much more than the sum of its parts. [131]

*****

The Great Fire of London in 1666 dealt another blow to Southwark's fortunes by making many of the shops and houses on London Bridge unstable, forcing their residents to abandon the area. Ten years later, Southwark had a disastrous fire of its own, which burnt down most of the remaining medieval inns on Bankside. By the time these could be rebuilt, whatever enthusiasm pleasure-seeking Londoners could still muster for Southwark had vanished. They turned instead to central areas like Covent Garden for their fun and the Borough began its grim transformation into a centre for "stink industries" such as vinegar making and leather works. [132]

The Thames gave these industries their power, their transport infrastructure and their means of waste disposal, but wealthy Londoners were keen to keep the noise and pollution they caused at arm's length. Just as with the stew-houses that had preceded them, the solution was to concentrate such filthy trades across the river in Southwark and let the slum-dwellers there endure the consequences.

As recently as the late 1500s, Southwark dye-house owners had been converting their premises into brothels because they knew there was more money to be made that way, but the 17th century saw this process jammed into reverse. In 1633, a Bankside stew-house called the Crane was transformed into a soap factory and 60 years later even the mighty Unicorn - once one of the two biggest licensed brothels in London - became a Southwark glassworks. [133]

"By the year 1700, the Bankside had lost almost every trace of its murky past," Burford writes. "It was turning into a bleak warehouse and wharf area, with a few dye-houses and a number of public houses serving mainly the watermen and labourers who loaded and unloaded barges and other vessels. A number of breweries had also been established in the immediate hinterland, surrounded by slums."

In 1750, London opened the newly built Westminster Bridge, about two miles upriver from Southwark, ending the lucrative 500-year monopoly London Bridge had enjoyed as the Thames' only permanent crossing. A new bridge in this far richer and safer part of the city gave people yet another reason to turn away from Southwark, speeding the deterioration there still further. One historian, writing in 1756, said the old Clink Liberty was now "a ruinous and filthy slum", adding that the Kent Street and Mint Street neighbourhoods surrounding Cross Bones were its worst areas of all. That was the state of the place when the Bishop of Winchester granted Edward Pearson his 1760 lease on Cross Bones, and it's very likely that Pearson was representing St Saviour's Parish when he signed it. [134]

The anarchic ghosts of old Bankside continued to surface in the Borough, first in 1772, when the Magdalen Hospital for Penitent Prostitutes moved from its old Whitechapel premises to a new site in what's now Blackfriars Road and then with the Gordon Riots of 1780. It was also in the 1780s that the radical campaigner Francis Place - then just a small boy - watched highwaymen setting off for their night's work from Southwark's Dog & Duck tavern on St George's Fields. "Flashy women come out to take leave of the thieves at dusk and wish them success," he later wrote. It was commonly assumed that the decaying taverns around St George's Fields were the favourite meeting places for radical insurrectionaries of every kinds and the breeding ground for all their plots.

The Gordon Riots burnt out two of Southwark's prisons - the Clink and the King's Bench - and the Clink was allowed to fall into disuse. Twenty years later, Horsemonger Lane Gaol opened in what's now Newington Gardens, adding a public gallows to Southwark's traditional glut of penal institutions. This hanged a total of 131 convicts before it was eventually closed in 1878, and appeared as a woodcut illustration on many gallows ballad sheets. [135]

Although the new factories brought jobs to Southwark, these were both dangerous and poorly paid. "Work in the soap factories or brick kilns meant a 12-hour day in steaming conditions, risking acid burn and injury," Kate Williams writes in her 2006 book *England's Mistress*. "Many women believed prostitution less dangerous than factory work and more bearable than domestic service. We might think nowadays that we would rather steal or beg. Beggars, however were usually attacked and crimes against property were so stringently punished that a girl who stole a handkerchief could be executed or deported." Prostitution, on the other hand, had been downgraded from a crime to a mere nuisance in 1640 and what laws remained against it were enforced intermittently at best. [136]

Williams quotes figures claiming one in eight of all the adult women in London worked as prostitutes in the late 18th century - I'm assuming this includes both full-timers and those who merely dabbled in the trade when needs must - and I've seen other estimates suggesting about a third of this total were former domestic servants. Street prostitution in any age is unlikely to match the soft-focus *Belle de Jour* fantasy, but we should remember also that health and safety was unknown in the hellish factories of the 18th century and that conditions for domestic servants weren't much better.

Girls as young as 12 could earn a living in the brothels of Georgian England, but housemaids that age received no more than a bare floor to sleep on and just enough table scraps to keep them alive. Even in adulthood, they were expected to work long hours for little pay and assumed to be fair game by their predatory male employers. When the alternatives were so utterly miserable, you can see how the move into prostitution may become a rational choice. [137]

At Cross Bones itself, it was now St Saviour's Parish which decided the site's future. Parish schools and graveyards have always tended to go together for the simple reason that both are generally built on Church land. In this case, a leasehold interest in the land proved close enough and that's how St Saviour's Charity School for Boys came to be erected at Cross Bones in 1791. Like the parish girls' school that followed 30 years later, the new building faced on to Union Street, but extended at the rear over a patch of Cross Bones' burial area that was already stuffed with dead.

"By the 1820s, the burial ground was completely surrounded by buildings," writes Dr David Green of King's College in London. "It was, like most urban churchyards, over-full and a serious cause for concern."

Crime in Redcross Way: 1709-1755

In 1865, the *Lancet* wrote that the area round Redcross Way hosted "a nest of thieves which has existed ever since the days of Edward III". Here's a few examples drawn from Old Bailey transcripts suggesting the magazine may have been right.

June 1709: Richard Hughes, hours before his execution at Tyburn, confesses to a string of robberies, including one at a Tobacconist's House in Redcross Way.

October 1730: Christopher Cornick, Edward Welsh and James Dickson go into the Golden Hind pub in Redcross Way and order a pint of beer. The barmaid, Jane Bordwell, serves it up to them in a silver tankard, then leaves the bar for a moment to take her child upstairs. As soon as she's out of the way, the three men leg it with the tankard. The landlady's son and a couple of Golden Hind staff chase them down the street, but Cornick is the only one they catch. He's tried at the Old Bailey, found guilty and sentenced to transportation. The tankard is never recovered.

September 1744: Patrick Askin, Luke Ryley and John MacEvoy hold up William Hall's coach in Frog Lane, Islington, then flee to Askin's lodgings in Redcross Way. Getting there about 11:00pm, they set about dividing their booty, which includes Hall's bright red coat and about ten guineas in cash. Edward Frost, another resident in the house, grows suspicious and peeps through the door of Askin's room, where he sees him trying on the stolen coat. Askin later confesses, agreeing to give evidence against his friends and so it's only Ryley and MacEvoy who hang at Tyburn the following month. Askin is sent into the army instead.

May 1745: Jeremiah Burton, a pickpocket living at Three Tuns Court in Redcross Way, is sentenced to death for stealing a silver watch.

February 1755: Elizabeth Williams steals a silk gown, two silver spoons and a handful of other small items from her employer's house in Hounsditch. Some of the stolen goods are later recovered at Armstead's pawnshop in Redcross Way, leading to Williams' conviction and transportation for a term of seven years.

Cross Bones' Mizuko Jizo statues guide stillborn babies to the afterlife.

14: Crossbones Girl

In May 2010, BBC television's *History Cold Case* aired an episode called *Crossbones Girl*, which gave us our best character sketch yet of a real individual we know was buried there. Starting from an unidentified skeleton excavated from the site in the MoL's 1993 dig, the BBC's team slowly constructed a portrait of the person those bones represented. By the time they'd finished, the skeleton was someone with a confirmed gender, age, diet, likely job, health record and - perhaps - even a name. All but the last of these conclusions were firmly rooted in strict scientific analysis of the bones themselves and the undeniable facts this analysis produced.

The two women who led this work were Professor Susan Black and Dr Xanthé Mallett, both of Dundee University's Centre for Anatomy & Human Identification. The most interesting part of their work for our purposes came in the programme's final stages, when skeleton CW1211 was finally given both a name and a face. In order to see how the team got there, though, we must first consider their forensic findings:

Date of Death.
The skeleton was found very close to the surface at Cross Bones, where the crowded conditions meant graves had to be emptied and re-used very frequently. This established the skeleton was interred there in the final few years before Cross Bones' closure in 1853. [138]

Gender.
Features of the skull like its brow ridges and its mastoid bones (which are found behind the ear canal) are much more pronounced in men. The team found no sign of such prominence here and so concluded that the skeleton was female.

Age at Death.

An examination with the naked eye was enough to tell Mallett and Black that the skeleton's arm and leg bones had not yet finished growing, which meant the woman must have been well under 30 when she died. A subsequent CAT scan showed she had very recent marks of fusion and childhood growth in her bones, allowing the team to refine their estimate to an age of between 15 and 19.

Height.

A simple measurement of the skeleton's leg bones put the girl's height at around four foot seven. "She's tiny," Black said. "Absolutely tiny." A report from Dr David Green of King's College in London, which provided much of the original research for *Crossbones Girl*, points out that even the average female convict in 1850 was nearly five inches taller than our girl. [139]

Social Status.

Short stature correlates strongly with poor diet and the low earnings and lack of education that implies. Mineral analysis of the bones confirmed the girl had eaten very little meat, but relied instead on whatever cheap bread and vegetables she could get hold of. This tells us CW1211 scraped a living on the bottom rung of Victorian society - just like everyone else who ended up buried at Cross Bones.

State of Health: Rickets.

The skeleton's leg bones showed the characteristic bowing caused by rickets, a bone-softening disease associated with lack of sunlight. "The rickets would have stunted her growth and made her susceptible to a host of infections, especially those of the respiratory tract," Green writes. "The smog that hung over London and often blocked sunlight from ever reaching street level meant that many children suffered from vitamin D deficiency, which accounted for the frequency of rickets."

State of Health: Syphilis.

The scars and pockmarks Black and Mallett could see all over the skeleton were textbook signs of advanced syphilis. The lack of telltale grooves in the skeleton's teeth ruled out the possibility that CW1211's mother had passed on syphilis while her child was still in the womb and this was confirmed by the fact that her skull had formed correctly in childhood. It follows that the disease must have been transmitted sexually. [140]

Age when Infected.

The tertiary (third stage) syphilis shown in the skeleton develops anywhere from three years to 15 years after the first infection, though Mallett assumed a maximum of ten years in CW1211's case. Combine that with the age data above and we see that she could have been infected as young as five. One possibility is that she fell victim to a particularly vile Victorian superstition insisting that a man could cure himself of syphilis by deflowering a virgin. In the underclass of Victorian London, that often meant raping a child. [141]

Appearance.

Part of the nasal bones on the skeleton's skull had been eaten away by syphilis, which would also have left fluid-filled boils and scar tissue on the girl's face. Dr Caroline Wilkinson was given the job of reconstructing the girl's face on a computer screen and her results shown later in the programme.

Likely Source of Earnings.

Dr Patrick French, an expert on sexually transmitted disease, was able to tell enough from the skeleton to diagnose gummatous syphilis, a condition that normally arises only after repeated infection. "The general view is that it's probably re-infection with syphilis that causes gummata," he said. "STDs, including syphilis, were strongly associated with prostitution at that time." As the programme pointed out, about 20% of women in Victorian London resorted to street prostitution at one time or another and now it began to look as if our girl was one of them.

Treatment Received.

The skeleton showed the extreme tooth decay associated with mercury treatment - then the only measure doctors could offer against syphilis. Further analysis of the bones revealed almost six times more mercury than the typical skeleton would have contained at that time, which strongly suggests CW1211 managed to get some treatment for her disease - probably at one of London's charity hospitals. "The pattern of healing suggests she was living with [the disease] for a long time and I think it's unlikely that it killed her," said archaeologist Fiona Tucker. [142]

*****

The next stage of the programme's investigation switched focus to historian David Green's research among the surviving documents. This is his summary of the forensic investigation's profile:

> *"Short in stature, bandy-legged and pigeon-chested, this poor young girl then contracted syphilis which, despite treatment with mercury, clung to her till her death.*
>
> *"Whether the disease or the treatment killed her remains unknown: perhaps she was one of the many who died of consumption in that period, or perhaps she succumbed to one of the cholera outbreaks that plagued the area. Either way, she was in poor health for most, if not all, of her young life.*
>
> *"This must have hampered her ability to earn a living and with her physical deformities and open sores, it would have been highly unlikely that she would have found work easily. If she turned to prostitution, she would have been one of many in the area who did so out of poverty rather than choice. Someone, however, paid for her treatment, so was she seen as a fitting object for charity, or did she have a benefactor who took pity on her situation?"*

The girl's bones had been found very close to the surface at

Cross Bones, so Green focused on deaths in the ground's final three years of use: 1851 to 1853. Only about 5% of the female deaths in London at that time occurred between the ages of 15 and 19 - our target group - and it was reasonable to assume that CW1211 had died in one of the five Southwark parishes surrounding Cross Bones. "Only 39 women aged between 15 and 20 were recorded in the death registers for the Southwark parishes of Christchurch, St Saviour's, St Olave, St Thomas and St John between 1851 and 1853," Green writes. "If the woman in question was buried in one of those years, then it is likely she is one of those 39 individuals."

Trawling though the surviving records from Southwark's parish burial registers, hospital death books and workhouse registers, Green drew up a shortlist of candidates which included the following women:

Amelia Hurley. Died age 16. Buried by Christchurch Parish on May 14, 1851, in an unknown location. Lived first in Southwark's Upper Swan Court and, later, in the parish workhouse. "She was from a very poor family, even by the standards of those living in the same court," Green writes. "Her family would have been hard-pressed to bury her."

Maria Leonard. Died age 20 in 1853. Recorded as a pupil at the School for the Indigent Blind in St George's Circus, Southwark, just two years before her death. Lived then in America Street, a slum area only 300 yards from Cross Bones. "Blindness was often associated with syphilis," Green points out.

In the end, Green plumped for a third candidate and updated Mallett on his conclusions as they sat together on-camera in the London Metropolitan Archives. "Here we have the Dead Book," he told her, opening a large Victorian ledger. "The burial registers of St Thomas' Hospital in Southwark. It's a charitable hospital, it takes a lot of poor patients and if she died in the hospital then it may be that she's in here." He turned the pages as he spoke. "We looked at the ages of the people who died and here we have this woman called Elizabeth Mitchell.

"She's aged 19," Green continued, pointing out the figures

column by column. "The date she was admitted: 5th of August, 1851. The date she died: 15th of August. She only lasted ten days there. She's in the hospital in Magdalen Ward - that was a ward for women with venereal disease. And on the right-hand side is a column for medical remarks, cause of death: 'Ask the physician. Came in for discharge and sores, died under physician's care with pneumonia'."

Keen to ensure we'd appreciated the significance of this find, the programme's narrator came in at this point. "Elizabeth Mitchell fits the profile of the skeleton," he said. "Aged 19, she came to St Thomas' Hospital ward for treatment of sores and discharge but died on the 15th of August 1851 of pneumonia. Next, David looks at the burial records of the parish of St Saviour's, where the Cross Bones cemetery was located."

Turning to St Thomas parish's register of burials, Green flipped the pages to August 22, 1851, then ran his finger down the column of names. He stopped at the name "Elizabeth Mitchell" and the note in its next-door column giving her last abode as St Thomas' Hospital. "There she is," Mallett exclaimed. "Number 2090, St Thomas' Hospital, 22nd of August 1851, 19 years."

"Mr Day, the minister, he buried her," Green continued. "So she went from the hospital and was buried by the parish. Her abode was St Thomas' Hospital, so they didn't know where she lived." The most Green was prepared to say on camera was that Mitchell was "a possibility" as the Crossbones Girl's identity and Mallett too was careful to acknowledge there was no certainty here. "Obviously, we'll never know," she told the team when next updating them. "But this does fit with her. She's in the right [hospital] ward, she's the right kind of age."

This was an impressive piece of work by all concerned, but there was one Columbo-style loose end which made me contact Green to see if he could shed any light. My question was this: Why would a woman who died in St Thomas's parish hospital, whose only known abode was in that hospital and whose interment is recorded in the St Thomas parish burial register not be buried there too? If CW1211 really was Elizabeth Mitchell, then how did she come to be buried instead in the next-door parish of St Saviour's, where Cross Bones lies?

"That bothered me too," he replied. "I wonder if somewhere between the entry in the burial register and the actual burial, a change in burial place occurred? Elizabeth Mitchell fitted closest, but without a very considerable amount of extra work, it would be difficult to prove anything more than a possible association."

It's a little odd to think of parish officials filling in a burial register before the burial itself rather than afterwards, but given the chaos prevailing in Southwark's poorest graveyards when Mitchell died, we can't rule it out. One possibility is that St Thomas parish discovered at the last moment that Mitchell had some sort of family connection or history of residence in St Saviour's, which meant the expense of a pauper burial could be dumped on them instead. "Local officials were always careful to enquire whether or not their parish had the responsibility to provide for a pauper," Green points out in his report to the BBC. "And to do so meant inquiring into the circumstances of an individual's settlement."

He cites the example of Joan Chick, a widow with five children who found herself in Hackney workhouse in March 1848. Hackney discovered that Chick's late husband Thomas, who'd died 15 years earlier, had once lived in St George's parish, Southwark. Joan and her children had lived in Hackney ever since Thomas's death, but the St George's link was enough for Hackney's parish authorities to unload the cost of feeding them on St George's workhouse instead.

If St Thomas Parish was able to discover Mitchell had some history making her St Saviour's responsibility rather than their own, then perhaps that would explain the sort of post-mortem transfer suggested here. Sadly, most of St Saviour's settlement records have been lost or destroyed, so there's no way of checking. But what does it really matter which name skeleton CW1211 answered to in life? We know quite enough about her from the forensic evidence alone to see the rotten hand life dealt her and none of that's going to change whatever her name was.

Murder in Redcross Way (1837): John Bryan

"I shall give them blood to drink or they shall give it to me," Thomas Bryan roared. It was Boxing Night, 1837, in Redcross Way and he was determined to fight his brothers. John, Jerry and Patrick Bryan all lodged in Redcross Way - Redcross Alley as it then was - with their families, and Thomas lived very nearby with his own wife in what's now St Margaret's Court. Everything that follows played out within 150 yards of Cross Bones. [143]

Thomas and Jerry had come to blows in the alley earlier that evening, but women from the family had separated them and dragged Jerry into their shared lodging house while Thomas stalked away. Neighbours later testified that both men had been drinking that night. Now Thomas was back, with his friend Patrick Mahoney and Patrick's son Daniel in tow. The Mahoneys, too, had their lodgings in Redcross Way. "I am not alone now," Thomas shouted at the window of the house where his brother had disappeared.

We don't know what the original quarrel was about, but it seems to have started with a row between the Bryan and the Mahoney women over some arrangement involving godparents.

Thomas got no response to his challenge, so he left again and the Mahoneys reluctantly followed. Seeing they'd gone, Jerry came out into Redcross Way again and asked with a show of bravado who was looking for him. Thomas had disappeared by now, but the Mahoneys hadn't retreated quite as far as Jerry thought and they rushed back to pin him against the wall. As the women clawed Jerry back inside the house again, John Bryan came out to try and calm everyone down. Nicknamed "John the Iron" for his work in a foundry, he seems to have been the man his neighbours came to when something in the street needed sorting out. But tonight the Mahoneys were in no mood to listen.

John Grant, a ten-year-old boy, watched what came next from his perch on a railing near the action. "I saw young Mahoney with a poker hitting John Bryan," he later testified. "I saw the youngest one [Daniel] hit him on the shoulder with the poker. It made him stagger a little and I saw him hit him twice more on the head with the poker. He then fell. He was close by the railing at that time. [...] Old Mahoney was standing by while [Bryan] was being knocked down and after he was down he came and kicked him. He kicked him twice after he was down. Then his wife, who was among the women, came and kicked him and kicked him again. I hallooed out 'Murder' and the Mahoneys ran away." [144]

Elizabeth Williams was watching the same scene play out from her upstairs window at 4 Redcross Way and confirmed Grant's account in every detail. One neighbour said Patrick had urged his son on in the attack by saying, "Will you see your mother struck?" But Grant, who'd watched the whole thing, insisted the Bryans had never laid a finger on Mrs Mahoney. [145]

Mary Bryan, John's daughter, was next to arrive. "I found my father laying on the ground," she said later. "I saw some people running and, suspecting them, I ran after them and found it was the two Mahoneys and his [Patrick's] wife. I called out after them and said, 'You murdering villains! You have murdered my father!' Young Mahoney turned round, lifted up a poker and attempted to strike me. But his mother said, 'Don't strike the child, whatever you do to the father' and he did not strike me. I went away into the Borough and called the policemen."

When the police arrived, John Bryan was able to stagger away with an officer supporting him on either side, but died a few days later in Guy's Hospital. Dr William Boyd, who examined him there, testified that he'd found a fractured skull and a ruptured artery in John Bryan's head, but that he could not be certain whether it was Daniel Mahoney's poker or Patrick's boot which killed him.

A week later, police had Patrick, Daniel and Thomas under arrest and an Old Bailey murder trial followed on January 29. Thomas was acquitted, but Daniel and Patrick both convicted of manslaughter and sentenced to transportation for life.

This La Catrina figure was a gift from the Mexican Embassy.

15: Resurrection Men

The records kept by St Thomas' Hospital tell us Elizabeth Mitchell was most likely born in 1832. That also proved an eventful year for those charged with managing London's graveyards, bringing not only the first of the four London cholera epidemics Green hints at above but also the legislation that ended a century of grave-robbing.

Doctors had always learned their trade by dissecting corpses, often using the bodies of executed criminals for this. No-one much cared what happened to bodies like that and, as long as students merely gathered to watch their teacher pick apart a single cadaver at the front of the room, Britain's hundred-odd hangings a year could supply the bulk of demand. Anatomists would still buy black-market corpses from corrupt sextons or gravediggers from time to time, but so far that trade remained small enough to be kept under some sort of control.

All that changed in the 1740s, when the Paris Manner of instruction became standard practice in London's teaching hospitals and private anatomy schools. This required each student to be given body parts of his own to work on, meaning every dissection session at every school now needed not just one corpse to work on, but many. It was clear the Paris Manner gave far superior results to the old system, so anatomy teachers had no choice but to adopt it - the teaching hospitals doing so because they knew it was essential to a proper training and the schools because students would desert them otherwise.

Most people still viewed the idea of dissection with extreme distaste, some even fearing that a sliced-up body might find itself inadequately re-assembled in Heaven, so no-one was going to volunteer their own dear departed for such treatment. That left no legal source of cadavers which could keep up with the huge increase in demand, forcing surgeons to turn to the black market en masse.

A whole new tribe of professional grave robbers were hard at work feeding this new demand in London as early as 1750 and their grisly trade grew rapidly as the city's reputation for surgical instruction pulled in more and more students from abroad. Even a surgeon as eminent as the Leicester Square anatomist John Hunter relied on purchasing fresh corpses from the so-called "resurrection men" at his back door and not asking too many questions about where those bodies had come from. Often, they'd simply been ripped from a nearby burial ground overnight. [146]

Grave-robbing in the capital peaked between 1800 and 1832, by which time as many as 200 students might be gathered in a large teaching hospital's dissecting room at any one session, each hacking inexpertly at the half-rotten limb or torso laid out before him. An accidental nick to their own finger or thumb could mean a fatal infection and yet still the pupils horsed around. Like all medical students, they affected a careless disregard for their work, treating the dissecting room like a senior common room where they felt free to eat and drink as the cadavers were wheeled in.

"On entering the room, the stink was most abominable," one lay visitor to William Osler's 19th century dissection room wrote. "About 20 chaps were at work, carving limbs and bodies in all stages of putrefaction and of all colours: black, green, yellow, blue. The pupils carved them, apparently with as much pleasure as they would carve their dinners. One was pouring [oil of turpentine] on his subject and amused himself by striking with his scalpel at the maggots as they issued from their retreats." [147]

The poet-to-be John Keats was an anatomy student at Guy's Hospital from 1815-1816, a period in his life which Donald Goellnicht addresses in his 1984 book *The Poet-Physician*. "While Keats was attending lectures on anatomy and physiology, he was also required to put his classroom knowledge into practice in the dissection room," Goellnicht writes. "The bodies for dissection were bought, for three or four guineas apiece, from body-snatchers, or 'resurrection men', who robbed local graves. This practice was carried on at night, the resurrection men delivering the bodies to the hospital naked, in sacks, since stealing a shroud was a criminal offence, whereas stealing a body was only a misdemeanour." [148, 149]

The fact that both Guy's and St Thomas' teaching hospitals were located so close to Redcross Way, combined with Cross Bones' poor security and the sheer number of bodies buried there at minimal depth, made it an ideal target for the grave-robbers. We have testimony from real resurrection men at the time confirming that poor people's bodies were always easier to steal because the rich were buried too deeply. It's no coincidence, then, that London's most notorious gang of bodysnatchers was based in Southwark and named themselves the Borough Boys in tribute to their favourite hunting ground. "There are records of corpses being taken from St Saviour's churchyards," the MoL's report confirms. "It is quite likely, given the vicinity, that bodies were obtained from the Cross Bones ground."

In fact, there's direct evidence they were. A report in the July 6, 1889 issue of *Guy's Hospital Gazette* records this incident from 1786:

> *"At the burying ground in Red Cross Street, named Cross-bones, belonging to St Saviour's Parish, four men, 'body snatchers' or resurrection men, were at work and dug up a body and proceeded to put it into a coach and got away."*

The same article mentions that St Saviour's had been forced to sack and prosecute one of its gravediggers, William Dodd, in 1717 for "carrying away the corpses of persons buried and disposing of them to surgeons for dissection". There's no indication which particular St Saviour's ground Dodd was using for his supply, but vestry minutes confirm the parish was already leasing Cross Bones from the Bishop of Winchester during the grave robbers' era. In 1788, the churchwardens there concluded that "the east side of the burial ground next to the common sewer" - a description fitting Cross Bones perfectly - was "open and easy of access to those who make an infamous and detested practice of stealing dead bodies". They responded by offering a reward of five guineas for any information leading to a bodysnatcher's conviction.

Two years later, St Saviour's replaced the broken-down brickwork surrounding Cross Bones with a new wall topped with broken glass. But, as Gillian Tindall points out in her 2007 book *The House by the Thames*, even this failed to do the trick. "In spite of these parish endeavours, it was reported [in 1803] that the Cross Bones ground had again been the target of grave-robbers, and that 'Mr Cooper the sexton has suffered the keys, at times, to go out of his hands'," she writes. "A door was to be blocked up and a new sexton appointed." In 1819, the new wall at Cross Bones was supplemented (or perhaps replaced) with a five-foot spiked-iron fence.

David Orme, who sets a grave-robbing scene at Cross Bones in his 2012 novel *The Bodysnatcher's Apprentice*, suspects neither the added walls and fences nor the fact that people lived so close by would have offered any real protection. "Most of the worst burial grounds in London were surrounded by tenements and yet body-snatching went on," he reminded me. "Many resurrectionists were in league with the gravediggers, so extensive noisy digging wasn't necessarily required." (150)

Knowing they could expect little help from the authorities, poor families sometimes tried to protect their own burial grounds by laying tripwires or even mantraps there to hinder unwary thieves. The worst of these were the spring-loaded traps normally used to combat poachers, which snapped their vicious spiked teeth into the leg of anyone who stepped inside. We've no record this was done at Cross Bones, but it would certainly have been a prime candidate for such traps. (151)

The custom that all bodies be buried on an east-west alignment with their feet at the eastern end told the thieves all they needed to know to extract a cadaver from the ground with minimum fuss. Any grave filled in the past day or two would still be visible as a patch of recently disturbed earth and the corpse's shoulders could always be found about 18 inches from that patch's western end. "They would dig down to the wider part of the coffin, get a crowbar under the lid and lever it until it split," Dorothy Davies writes in her 2007 essay *The Corpse King*. "The packed earth would hold the rest of the lid down. Then a rope was tied around the body under the armpits and it was pulled out." (152)

Orme has his own grave robber, Bill Baines, using exactly this technique during a nocturnal visit to Cross Bones in 1825. "The bodysnatcher's skill was to dig as little as possible and pull the corpse out through a small hole in the head end," he explains. "Feet first was harder, as hands and arms got jammed as you tried to wriggle it out." (153)

Refrigerated morgues were still unknown at this time, which meant there was no market for dead bodies in the hot summer months, when they simply rotted too quickly to be worth buying. This created what everyone called a grave-robbing "season" running from August till April. One former resurrectionist giving evidence to an 1828 House of Commons select committee testified that his gang alone had supplied 386 bodies to the anatomists in the 1809/1810 season and another 359 in 1810/1811. A second witness, this one a former parish officer, told the same committee that he thought there were around 200 professional bodysnatchers in London at the trade's height, creating fierce competition among rival gangs. "I have known them to fight in the graves," he testified. [154]

The resurrectionist here is not named in the committee's report, but the meticulous accounts he had to draw on suggest strongly that he was the Borough Boys' Joseph Naples, a former Clerkenwell gravedigger known to be the gang's bookkeeper. Naples is also thought to be the author of a genuine resurrectionist's diary later recovered and published by the Royal College of Surgeons. On one 1812 night alone, this diary records, the Borough Boys harvested a total of 13 adult corpses and two children:

> *"December 2, 1812: Met at Vicker's pub. Rectified our last account. The party sent out me and Ben to St Thomas's crib. Got one adult. Bill and Jack went to Guy's crib. Got two adults, but one of them opened. Took them to St Thomas's. Came home. Met at St Thomas's. Me and Jack went to Tottenham. Got four adults. Ben and Bill went to St Pancras. Got six adults, one small and one foetus. Took the Tottenham lot to Wilson, the St Pancras lot to Bart's."* [155]

The names there all match known members of the Borough Boys gang: Ben Crouch, Bill Hollis and Jack Harnett. St Thomas', Guy's and Bart's were three of the biggest hospitals in London, of course, the first two in Southwark itself and the third (St Bartholomew's) just across the river in Smithfield. Every hospital in London then had a graveyard of its own, known as a "crib" in underworld slang, so it's clear that Naples and his friends were selling these corpses straight back to the same hospitals that had buried them a day or two earlier. The "opened" corpse he mentions was one already operated on in hospital and hence of little (if any) value to the anatomists. "Wilson" was James Wilson, who ran a private anatomy school in Soho's Great Windmill Street.

It's interesting to note that the Guy's crib bodies were sold at St Thomas' - and perhaps vice-versa - presumably to ensure that dead individuals could not be recognised by the doctors who'd treated them in life. Turning a blind eye to the source of these bodies would have been one thing for the doctors involved, having it rubbed in their faces quite another.

It would obviously have made a lot more sense to let the hospitals simply pass unclaimed bodies from the wards where they died directly to the anatomy students in their own dissection room, but that would have required a change to the law, which public opinion still ruled out. For most people, the rational arguments in favour of dissection and the medical advances it brought were far outweighed by their instinctive disgust at the whole process. Even when surgeons reassured people that all the bodies they used in dissection sessions were later given a decent Christian burial, it didn't help.

This left successive governments unwilling to pass laws giving surgeons legitimate access to all the cadavers they needed - and so removing the body-snatchers' market at a stroke - but also reluctant to enforce the law as it stood. Crushing the body-snatchers' trade without putting a legitimate supply of corpses in its place would not only have destroyed Britain's reputation for continued medical innovation, but also have robbed London's economy of the hundreds of foreign students who went there every year to study anatomy. The result was deadlock, with the police taking action only when someone like the Borough Boys' ham-fisted Tom Light made himself impossible to ignore, or when a specific case was dropped directly in their laps.

That's exactly what happened in the case of anatomist Joshua Brookes, who repeatedly ran into trouble because he just couldn't get along with the resurrection men he used. One year Brookes, the owner of a private anatomy school in Mayfair, refused to give his regular gang of suppliers their traditional August gratuity, so they dumped one very ripe corpse in plain sight outside the door of his Blenheim Street school and another outside his home at the corner of Poland Street and Great Marlborough Street in the heart of Soho. When a couple of young women stumbled across the Soho body early next morning, their screams raised an angry mob outside Brookes' front door and it was only the quick intervention of coppers from the nearby Marlborough Police Court that saved him a beating.

On another occasion, Brookes used a rival gang, paying a hefty

16 guineas to buy a body they'd stolen from an undertaker in St Saviour's parish. His regular suppliers, angry at this lack of loyalty, shopped him at Union Street police station and suggested to PC James Glennon there that he might like to search Brookes' Blenheim Street premises. Brookes was part-way through cutting away the body's distinctive tattoo when Glennon arrived, identified the corpse with ease and ensured its return to Southwark for a proper burial. [156]

The St Saviour's undertaker was later found to have been complicit in this body's theft and served two years in prison for it. He'd taken a bribe from the resurrection men in return for agreeing to leave the body in an unlocked outhouse overnight, where they'd been able to collect it with minimum fuss. Brookes himself - who told police he believed the body was that of an executed criminal - faced no judicial punishment, but he did lose both the body and the money he'd paid for it. [157]

It's the gang's extreme reaction to Brookes' slights which tells us just how much they disliked him. More often, the resurrection men would punish disloyal customers by breaking into their premises overnight and severely mutilating any corpses purchased from their rivals. This rendered the bodies unusable for teaching purposes and so cost the surgeon they'd targeted a great deal of money. But for Brookes that clearly wasn't thought punishment enough - the gang wanted to be sure he got a good scare from the police too.

Brookes later complained that the same body he'd paid 16 guineas for in this affair could have been had for just two guineas back in his student days. New anatomy schools were opening in London every year at this time, their students were demanding ever-more practical experience as part of their training and it's this which explains the steep rise in price for every illicit corpse. As in any market where demand is growing faster than supply, the resurrection men were able to charge more or less what they liked.

One anatomy student writing in an October 1889 issue of *Guy's Hospital Gazette* recalled that some of his fellows had got so fed up with the bodysnatchers' arrogance that they decided to take drastic action of their own: "The students for a short time became their own resurrection men," he writes. "That, however, lasted but a very short time, as they were cheated and duped on every hand, and ran in much danger of very rough treatment at the hands of the law besides."

Initiatives like this were never more than a marginal part of the trade, and that left surgeons no choice but to keep their own full-time suppliers happy. Often, they agreed to pay any court fines the resurrection man might incur in his work, or even to support his family while their breadwinner was in jail. Sir Astley Cooper of Guy's Hospital was particularly careful to protect Naples and the other Borough Boys, boasting that he had such influence with them as a result that he could obtain the body of any dead man in England he cared to name. [158, 159]

Crouch's men had the contacts to pull it off too. In October 1819, his gang arranged for two packages to be delivered from Chatham in Kent to a Cheapside pub called the Cross Keys, just across the river from Southwark. One was a hamper addressed to Joseph Wright in Old Street and the other a heavy item of some kind, wrapped up in an old carpet and addressed to Oxford Street's William Simpson. The innkeeper accepted both these deliveries off the Chatham coach, the coachman telling him Wright and Simpson's agent would be there to collect their property soon. All seemed well, until the innkeeper noticed that the parcel wrapped in carpet had begun to stink and decided he'd better open it.

"He found the corpse of an old woman," Brian Bailey writes in his 1991 book *The Resurrection Men*. "The local beadle was called and he opened the hamper, which contained a man's corpse. The coroner was informed and the authorities waited for someone to collect the luggage. It turned out to be a man calling himself Williams who, having paid the innkeeper the bill for carriage, was arrested as he prepared to take the parcels away. He was, in fact, George Martin, one of Crouch's cronies, who was acting on this occasion on behalf of William Millard, the dissecting room superintendent of St Thomas' Hospital."

Richard Grainger, owner of the Borough's Webb Street anatomy school, told the Commons' 1828 committee that men like Crouch and Martin were "the very worst part of society", but said he was forced to meet their demands anyway. "For one resurrection man alone, I incurred an expense of £50, in consequence of allowing him a certain sum a week for two years while he was in prison," Grainger testified. "During the present season, I have expended several guineas supporting another man's family while he was in prison. These expenses fall not on the pupils, but on the lecturers, for if bodies are to be obtained, we must promise to take care of these men when they are in trouble."

Grainger was a surgeon himself and the solution he proposed for this whole mess was a new law stating that all cadavers not claimed by family or friends should be routinely offered to the anatomists before burial. He set this idea out for the committee then and there, but it would be another four years before MPs mustered the courage to act. In August 1832 - nearly a century after the body-snatching phenomenon began - Parliament finally passed the Anatomy Act. This ruled that all bodies deemed "unclaimed" or "friendless" should be given up for dissection.

The controversial changes proved difficult to enforce at first, partly because people felt they targeted only the poor and partly because of the religious fears about dissection that many people still harboured. Some parish workhouses took an obstructionist line, some crooked officials still found ways to scam the system and the illegal trade certainly didn't vanish overnight, but it was clear from 1832 onward that the bodysnatchers' days were numbered.

"The Act was successful in putting the resurrection men out of business," the MoL confirms. "It is estimated that 57,000 corpses were supplied during the first 100 years of the Act's operation. [Almost all] were from workhouses, asylums and hospitals, showing that the burden was indeed borne by the poorest. The Act left a long legacy of fear - that falling into poverty would mean the State claiming your body after death." [160]

Meet the Corpse King and his Borough Boys

London's most notorious grave robbers in the early 19th century were the Borough Boys, named for the fact that Southwark was both their base and their favourite hunting ground.

The core members of the gang - Ben Crouch, Tom Butler and Jack Harnett - had a background as scavengers in the Peninsular War, where they harvested teeth from dead soldiers after each battle was done. Some believe they killed any wounded soldiers they found and then looted their teeth and belongings too. [161]

Ben Crouch: A former carpenter and prizefighter who became a bodysnatcher after a spell working at Guy's Hospital. "He was a dandy, wearing sharp clothes, gold rings and frilled shirts," Dorothy Davies writes. "The surgeons knew him as an artful, impudent, bullying drunk [but that] did not stop them dealing with him."

The sheer scale of Crouch's grave-robbing operation, combined with his flamboyant personality, led to him being nicknamed The Corpse King. He handled the gang's negotiations with surgeons, charging two or three guineas for an adult corpse (that is to say, one taller than three feet) and up to a guinea for children. He's said to have secured upfront fees of as much 50 guineas at a single time for corpses to be delivered later. [162]

Crouch retired from the bodysnatching trade with enough money to buy himself a small seaside hotel. His reputation soon caught up with him, though: customers began avoiding the place and he died in poverty.

Tom Butler: Crouch's former partner in their Peninsular War activity. Doubled as a dealer in bones and teeth.

Tom Light: A former valet who, as Davies puts it, "didn't think too well". The gang must have found him something of a liability and he lasted only a few years in the bodysnatching business. "He was a clumsy worker and ended up in custody too often," Brian Bailey writes. [163]

I imagine Light as a Satanic version of Lenny from John Steinbeck's *Of Mice & Men*: strong on brawn, but with a very tiny brain. He was once caught while trying to drag three corpses over the wall of a graveyard into London's busy Pancras Road. On another occasion, he was arrested carting seven bodies up Holborn Hill in broad daylight.

Joseph Naples: a former seaman who served with Nelson's forces at Cape St Vincent. After his discharge, Naples took a job digging graves at Clerkenwell's Spa Fields, where he moonlighted selling the ground's corpses to the Guy's Hospital surgeon Sir Astley Cooper.

In 1802, Naples was caught, sacked and sentenced to a prison term, but by that time Sir Astley thought him too valuable a supplier to lose. He intervened with Lord Pelham, the Home Secretary, who ensured Naples was released. From that point on, he worked full-time with Crouch's gang.

Naples kept the accounts for the Borough Boys, meticulously noting down every body they stole. It's thought he also wrote the anonymous 1812 *Diary of a Resurrectionist* later recovered and published by the Royal College of Surgeons. After the Anatomy Act was passed in 1832, Naples retired from bodysnatching, trading his testimony to a House of Commons committee for immunity. He was later given a job in St Thomas' Hospital dissection room.

Bill Hollis: Another former gravedigger who moonlighted selling corpses direct to surgeons. The gangs didn't like gravediggers cutting them out of the loop like this and ensured Hollis got the sack by informing against him. He had no choice but to join Crouch's gang, where his old skills proved useful.

Patrick Murphy: Succeeded Crouch as the Borough Boys' leader. His greatest coup was netting £144 for 12 corpses in a single day, a sum worth over £10,000 today. One of the two surgeons who bought them was Naples' friend Sir Astley Cooper.

At various times the gang also included Bill Harnett and Jack Hutton. Ben Crouch, Patrick Murphy and Jack Harnett (Bill's nephew) seem to be the only three members who got out with any worthwhile amount of money. The rest spent it all as they went along and ended with nothing.

Jimmy Cauty's *Geese, Cathedral, Crossbones* **poster.**

16: John Crow's Megaphone

Zanna, a Southwark artist who's asked me not to use her surname here, has lived directly across the street from Cross Bones since 1995. She was one of the first Borough residents to understand the history and significance of the site, and has been campaigning on its behalf ever since.

"From the minute I discovered it was a graveyard, I thought what was needed was an opportunity for the local area to celebrate its dead – its alternative dead," she told me. "A garden, yes, but not a garden that erases it being a graveyard. John [Constable] knocked on my door because someone had pointed him towards me as a person who might know about the site. It must have been after his visitation from the Goose, because he was searching for some verification of what he'd experienced."

The first Halloween of Cross Bones followed a couple of years later, in 1998, and that's when another long-standing Cross Bones campaigner joined the fight. Jen Cooper, who we met in chapter 4, was drawn into the cause at an event run by the ecology group Green Angels.

"On to the stage came this man who recited poetry that had a really dirty beat," she told me. "The words he was saying just blew my mind." This was Constable, of course, and the poem in question was an extract from *The Southwark Mysteries*. "I didn't know he was connected to Cross Bones – I didn't know anything – but I got an inkling of John and his power as a poet," Cooper explains. "Because this is my part of town. I'm a South London girl. I met him and then I came to a vigil.

"Years ago, I'd had my own experience of the divine feminine rising within me. She was naked, with flaming eyes and blood on her body. I'm standing at the gate and I'm watching John recite what I call Goose Words. He throws himself up in the passion of what he's saying: "And Southwark shall arise naked in her Liberty!' I thought maybe it was the same vision I'd had. That was it for me! A South London goddess for a South London girl. What more could I ask?

"Every so often I'd get involved with the vigil. I became Gin Jen because I liked pouring the gin and singing us in. John's a great one for nicknames. Towards the end of the vigil, he'd say: 'Jen, do the gin'. And then it was 'Gin Jen'…"

In their battle to champion the burial ground's heritage, Zanna, Jen, John and his partner Katy gravitated together as core members of a loosely-knit group called the Friends of Cross Bones. "The Friends never existed as a formal organisation," Constable says. "Katy and I dreamed it up as a way of strengthening our hand in discussions with TfL and Southwark Council. In reality, it was just us and people who came to the Halloween of Cross Bones and the monthly vigils.

"We were a small group of dedicated and quite left-field people. At any one time, 20 or 30 people [would have been involved]. That's people who were coming to the vigils, who were contributing to the garden and publicising it. If we had a constitution, it was the original petition to protect the shrine and create a garden of remembrance. That was something we could all get behind."

When the Museum of London published its 1999 report on the remains recovered during its Cross Bones dig, Zanna repurposed its photographs of Elizabeth Mitchell's skull to make the first of her long series of protest posters for midnight pasting on the site's exterior fence. These have now appeared in about 20 clever and witty variations, all carrying the insistent reminder, "This is still the Cross Bones Graveyard".

"The local people who had been buried there – who had given their lives to the borough – deserved to be celebrated where they were buried in such large numbers," Zanna told me. "I wanted to inspire people to get active about their local history and realise things were changing: things that might not be in their interest. The campaign was always about protecting the land from further ravages. I'd put the posters up and they'd be torn down immediately. I'd put them back up during the night and they'd be ripped down again. At one point I went right along Southwark Street and down Redcross Way with posters.

"I'm very clear that without my work, John Constable would not have saved the Cross Bones Graveyard. It wouldn't have happened. He'd still be doing the vigil at the gates, but the ground itself would not be open to the public. It's not just the John Constable show - there are lots of other people that have got us to this point."

At this stage, the Cross Bones site was viewed by Southwark Council simply as "derelict land". Lumped together with the vacant plot immediately adjacent to Cross Bones, the combined site was christened Landmark Court and promoted to developers under that name. It was "land suitable for development," a TfL spokesman told *Property Week*. "Surplus to requirements". [164]

Slowly but surely, the Friends of Cross Bones' fightback began to have an effect. In 2002, Southwark Council refused planning permission for an office block at Landmark Court, citing community concern about the site's sensitive history. Six years later, it added a memorial garden to its list of potential projects for the site and hinted funds could be found if this ever went ahead. Friends of Cross Bones extracted a promise from Boris Johnson, then mayor of London, that there would be no commercial development work allowed at Cross Bones till at least 2015.

Still the developers persisted. In 2011 TfL press ads appeared touting Landmark Court as "a rare opportunity to acquire a largely cleared landmark development site" in "an area undergoing significant enhancement". Enquires were invited from any firm wishing to "comprehensively develop the site". There had been "dozens of expressions of interest", *Property Week* reported, including one from Pearson, the owner of the *Financial Times*, which was considering Landmark Court as a location for its planned new HQ. [165]

It's pressure like this that's always convinced Constable that demanding there be no changes at all to Cross Bones would be a pointlessly Quixotic gesture. "That's quite a big ask in the face of development, especially the way it's been happening so rampantly in Southwark," he told me. "I've had people tell me the land – just Cross Bones itself – was valued at £25m."

There has been a host of features recounting Cross Bones' story in British newspapers since 1998 - many of which I've already quoted here - and a fairly regular trickle of items on London's local TV news programmes too. The BBC's decision to build that 2010 episode of *History Cold Case* round the site kicked TV's contribution up to a national level. All this media activity, combined with John

Constable's tireless efforts to publicise the site's uncertain future, has ensured Cross Bones seeps a little further into the public consciousness with every passing year.

Novelists have also been quick to do their part. A simple search of Amazon UK's book pages turns up not only the David Orme novel I've already mentioned, but also Kathy Lynn Emerson's *Face Down Among the Winchester Geese* (2007), John Walsh's *Sunday at the Cross Bones* (2008), Kate Rhodes' *Cross Bones Yard* and Judith Arnopp's *The Winchester Goose* (both 2012). Orme's novel was published in 2012 too, suggesting the supply of these books is accelerating fast. Most seem to operate in the area where historical fiction intersects with either crime or romance novels.

For my money, Walsh's novel is the most intriguing of these, telling as it does the story of Father Harold Davidson, his self-styled "prostitutes' padre" of 1920s London. I particularly like this potted biography from the novel's frontispiece, which Walsh dates to about 1880:

The Working Girl's Life
Monday in the nursery ward,
Tuesday in the schoolyard,
Wednesday painting lipstick on,
Thursday going with George and John,
Friday at the Crown with Billy,
Saturday weeping down the 'Dilly,
Where will she rest from her tears and moans?
Sunday at the Cross Bones. [166]

Musicians have begun taking an interest in Cross Bones too, with the past four years alone producing songs about the place from Stuart Forester, John Crow, the Unbending Trees, Pillarcat, Gaggle and Cherry Choke. The KLF's multi-talented Jimmy Cauty chose a photo-montage poster called *Geese, Cathedral, Crossbones* for his own contribution, copies of which Constable found him pasting to the Cross Bones wall one night in June 2008. He invited Cauty inside to inspect the site for himself and the two men evidently hit it off. "Jimmy especially liked John Crow's Shrine for Dangerous Helpers with its broken gin bottle and cigar tin, its black feathers, its hairy Patron Saint of Addicts and verses giving thanks for being 'set free from mental slavery'," the Cross Bones website confides. [167]

It was also Cauty who suggested inviting Banksy - perhaps the most famous graffiti artist in the world - to paint a piece on Cross Bones' surface tarmac, "so they can't dig up the bones without destroying his work". This floor mural (or "floral" as Constable dubbed it), could make a fine replacement for Banksy's 2002 *Chequebook Vandalism* piece on the Clink's outside wall, which Southwark Council foolishly painted over. "Sorry, Banksy," Constable told the artist when he wrote to him with Cauty's suggestion. "Please can we have another one?" [168]

In 2007, Constable wrote to the Tate Modern on Bankside, playfully suggesting that it might want to buy the Cross Bones gates as part of its *Tate in the Community* project and then give them a permanent exhibition in the gallery. "Here is a unique, textured, living artwork, deeply rooted in the local community and the history of this site", he reminded the Tate's curators. "[This site's gates are] the manifestation of a deep creative response to it, constantly changing as new artists contribute."

The Tate replied politely that it could buy only works produced by a single identifiable artist - and preferably a recognised one at that. In May 2008, it put together an art trail through Southwark, inviting people to find the work of various Madrid artists sited along the way, but once again Cross Bones didn't get a mention.

And perhaps that's just as well. Rather than relying on the high art establishment, it feels much more fitting that Cross Bones should be immortalised by the ordinary people who find such inspiration and interest there. There are well over a dozen short amateur films about Cross Bones on YouTube, ranging from simple footage of the latest vigil to a cabbie's jokey ghost tour. As I write this in September 2013, the most popular of these has already racked up close to 17,000 views.

The effect of all this publicity can be clearly seen in the changing tone of developers' plans for the site. As recently as 2002, Transport for London's documents seemed keen to deny Cross Bones' significance altogether, stressing that "the site has been previously developed", that "there is no reason why development should not occur in the future" and quoting planning inspectors' remarks to that effect in TfL's 2002 Department of the Environment appeal. But any developers with an eye on Landmark Court now know they must spotlight their determination to treat the Cross Bones section of the site sensitively and be sure to include plans for a memorial garden there along with everything else.

Anyone hoping to get away with mere lip service to these ideas will find Constable and his fellow campaigners waiting to remind them of any promises they later break. Their ceaseless campaigning for Cross Bones has given John Crow a powerful megaphone - and everyone knows he won't be shy to use it on the Goose's behalf. "The only card we've got to play is public relations," Constable reminded me. "Ten years ago, when they talked about developing this site, they just talked about vacant land, derelict land - made it sound like it was just an eyesore with no significance at all. Now it's the Cross Bones Graveyard. That's a small, but very important achievement."

Promotional hoardings at the Liberty of Southwark site in 2022.

17: Seeking Closure

Cross Bones' final phase of use as an active graveyard began just as the resurrection men's era was drawing to a close. Throughout the 1830s and 1840s, St Saviour's churchwardens battled fiercely against health experts and poverty campaigners to keep the site open, despite clear evidence that it was spreading fatal disease through the nearby slums.

Realising in 1831 that the cholera epidemic already raging through Germany, Hungary and Russia was sure to reach London soon, the UK government issued St Saviour's authorities with a list of urgent measures required to clean up their notoriously filthy parish. At the top of this list was a demand to sort out the disgusting state of their pauper burial ground at Redcross Way.

"They didn't have germ theory really at that point, but they did know that dead bodies were not healthy and that it's not particularly great to have charity schools right in back of this heaving, enormous graveyard," the Souhwark historian Patricia Dark told me. In his report for the BBC's *Crossbones Girl* programme, David Green adds: "The dominant theory of the spread of disease was that it spread by 'miasmas' arising from putrefying bodies and rotting organic matter. The cholera outbreak heightened those fears."

Cross Bones was one big miasma by this point, so St Saviour's created a committee to report on just how bad the overcrowding there really was and suggest what practical measures could be taken to alleviate it. The committee, set up in November 1831, convened again to draft its response on March 17 the following year, and it's instructive to compare their hard-hitting conclusions at that meeting with the published report that later emerged.

As the MoL points out, this final version seems to have been arrived at by the simple expedient of St Saviour's churchwardens crossing out anything that looked too inconvenient or demanding in the draft. One measure quietly dropped, for example, was the committee's call for a corner of Cross Bones to be dug 12 feet deep so that the remaining area's shallow-buried coffins could all be moved there and their original spots cleared for new burials. Instead, the published report merely suggested that "it would be desirable" for future graves at Cross Bones to go down 12 feet. How this was to be achieved without the committee's clearance measures remained a mystery.

When cholera arrived in London in 1832, St Saviour's committee moved to alert the parish's churchwardens again – this time in a desperate letter. "Having viewed with much attention the Cross Bones Burial Ground, we find it so very full of coffins that it is necessary to bury within two feet of the surface, which we consider, especially under the alarming disease now raging, very improper," the letter warned. "We also find that, on a partial opening of the ground, the effluvium is so very offensive that we fear the consequences may be very injurious to the surrounding neighbourhood. We are therefore of the opinion under such circumstances and the expectation of close, warm weather that the Ground ought to be immediately closed." [169]

That seemed to hit home, producing a decision at the next vestry meeting empowering the committee to close Cross Bones down, raise the level of earth there by bringing in additional top soil and re-open the site only when it was restored to a fit state. It was only a few days, however, before the committee realised that it didn't have anything like enough money at its disposal to fund that amount of work, so it simply chained up the gates at Cross Bones instead. That lasted about a year, at which point the growing pressure from so many cholera and typhus deaths convinced the vestry to put Cross Bones back into use. By the end of 1833, it was once again as busy as ever. [170]

Although London's total cholera deaths retreated somewhat between the epidemic spikes of 1832, 1841, 1854 and 1866, both it and typhus remained a constant presence in the city's poorest boroughs. In 1837, the London Fever Hospital named St Saviour's as one of London's "constant seats of fever from which [typhus] is never absent". In the following year, we have figures showing the parish's population as 31,711, of whom 1,856 (or nearly six per cent) were registered paupers. Two hundred and ninety-four of those paupers (16 per cent) are reported as contracting either cholera or typhus in 1838 alone, of whom nearly one in four died.

Both cholera and typhus are commonly contracted from drinking dirty water, so these statistics should not surprise us. Seven years on from the government's order that St Saviour's must introduce some rudimentary hygiene to its slum neighbourhoods, the parish still had open sewers in every street and as many as 150 people sharing a single Mint Street lodging house. "The inhabitants of the area were unwilling or unable to pay for the proper disposal of sewage," the MoL says. "This led to waste being either directly dumped into the Thames, or in a cesspool beneath the floor of the house." [171]

As if all that weren't bad enough, diseased corpses in St Saviour's would often remain above ground for well over a week. Many of the poorest families in Southwark were Irish and wanted to observe that country's custom of holding open-casket wakes and having the family watch over a dead body for several days before burial. There was nowhere to lay out a dead relative except in the family's own very cramped living quarters, so that's the space they used. Lacking the money to provide anything but the most basic interment in the parish's foulest burial ground, what other way did they have to honour their dead?

Speaking at about this time, the undertaker John Wyld said he had known poor families to keep a corpse laid out at home for weeks. "In cases of rapid decomposition of persons dying in full habit, there is much liquid and the coffin is tapped to let it out," he told Sir Edwin Chadwick's inquiry into urban burial grounds. "I have known them to keep the corpse after the coffin had been tapped twice, which has of course produced a disagreeable effluvium." [172]

At the pauper graveyards in any major British city, Wyld added, there would be many funerals scheduled for every hour of the day. "During last Sunday, for example, there were 15 funerals all fixed during one hour at one church," he told the inquiry. "I have seen funerals kept waiting in the churchyard from 20 minutes to three-quarters of an hour." In cases like these, he said, the presiding minister would make everyone wait until the hour's full contingent of funerals had arrived, say a hurried service over the whole bunch of them in one go, then watch them buried in a single trench. Some pauper grounds managed this process better than others, I'm sure, but if Wyld's testimony represents the average state of affairs, it's probably safe to assume that Cross Bones was even worse.

Accounts differ on exactly what happened to the site between its 1833 re-opening and the vestry meeting of 1839 which I'm about to describe. Some say the whole ground was closed again around

1837, some that it was only the most crowded area of all - known as the "Irish Corner" - where new burials were banned. What we do know is that a two-year break in new burials in the Irish Corner allowed that area's remains to be cleared away around the end of 1838, making room for several hundred new corpses to be buried there in the future.

The sheer pressure of bodies requiring burial somewhere in St Saviour's remained as heavy as ever so, in February 1839, the parish churchwardens met to discuss getting Cross Bones back into full use. One of those attending this meeting was a surgeon called George Walker, who later described its proceedings in his book *Gatherings From Graveyards*.

"One gentleman argued that if the graves had been made deeper, hundreds more corpses might have been buried there," Walker writes. "Another admitted that it really was too bad to bury within 18 inches of the surface in such a crowded neighbourhood; and it was even hinted that 'the clearing', viz. the digging up of the decayed fragments of flesh and bones, with the pieces of coffin etc, would be the best course, were it not for the additional expense. The funds of the vestry and the health of the living were here placed in opposite scales: the former had its preponderance." [173, 174]

The vestry ended this meeting with a decision to pass formal responsibility for re-opening Cross Bones to the parish committee it had created eight years earlier, but left the committee in no doubt what decision it was expected to make. Clearing Cross Bones completely was far too expensive to consider, but it was imperative to get the site back to full operation immediately. The committee had no choice but to agree.

As a medical man, Walker was outraged to see St Saviour's parish finances put before its inhabitants' lives like this. He was equally disgusted by the state of non-conformist burial grounds in St Saviour's, including both the Quakers' graveyard in Ewer Street and the Congregationalists' ground (a former plague pit) in Deadman's Place. Both sites, he said, were "literally surcharged with dead" and "present a repulsive aspect".

Walker also reports a conversation with one Southwark gravedigger - he doesn't say from which particular ground - who admitted that new corpses could be buried in his graveyard only through "management" of those already interred. When asked what this management consisted of, the man became evasive. "He replied he would be a fool to tell anyone how he did it," Walker reports. "It was observed to him that the place appeared to be dreadfully crowded and it was feared there was not sufficient depth. 'Well,' observed the man, 'we can just give a covering to the body'."

Valentine Haycock, another Borough gravedigger, gave evidence to a Parliamentary Committee on the health of Britain's towns in 1847, where MPs asked him how his team had managed to cram 20,000 coffins into the bare acre of land at their disposal. "We dig ten feet and if we can get 12 feet we do," Haycock replied. "And then we pile them up, one upon another, as many as the grave will hold, perhaps six or eight or nine in it. Then, when that is full, we dig another grave close by the side of it and put another nine or ten in there. They are piled one on another, just as if you were piling up bricks." [175]

Haycock also told MPs that the worst moments of his job came when his shovel accidentally pierced the lid of an old coffin, releasing a stench which, he said, was "dreadful beyond all smells". In cases like that, he said, he was forced to clamber desperately back to the surface as best he could, fearing that his own death might come at any moment. "He told me that his eyes struck fire, his brain seemed a whirl and that he vomited large quantities of blood," Walker writes. "This man deserved a better fate." [176]

Walker tells us Haycock worked at "Martin's ground in the Kent Road", by which I think he means New Bunhill Fields, now the site of the Globe Academy school in Southwark's Harper Road. The surnames of the two men who owned this non-conformist burial ground just off the New Kent Road were Martin and Hoole. Haycock testified to MPs that Hoole had also rented out space in the site's bone vault, where bodies could be stacked for six months in return for a fee. He didn't say what Hoole did with the bodies when the six months was up, but the clear implication was that any flesh not dissolved by a good scattering of quicklime in the vault would simply be thrown into a quiet corner of the graveyard itself to fester on the surface.

A London newspaper got hold of this story, reporting that Hoole's vault was "over the shoes in human corruption" - meaning the slosh of half-liquidised human flesh there was deep enough to lap your ankles when you stepped inside. In his public lectures, Walker would delight in telling people about Hoole's panicked reaction: "The fear of the press inspired him with a sudden desire to set his house in order. He came in from the country, worked in his shirt sleeves at the piles of decaying matter heaped up in the vault, went home ill and died in a few days." [177]

London's cholera deaths reached epidemic levels again in 1848 and, once again, it was Southwark which bore the brunt. The Irish Potato Famine, which began in 1845, had brought even more poor immigrants to the Borough, where David Green's figures show 43% of housing was now in the slum category.

"Middle-class ratepayers - and there were a declining number of those in Southwark - often chose to move elsewhere, especially to the new suburbs that were increasingly linked by public transport to the central districts, leaving behind an increasingly impoverished population that came to depend in ever-greater numbers on hand-outs and poor relief," he writes. Board of Health statistics from this time show that cholera caused 19 deaths per thousand people in Southwark during the 1848/49 outbreak, and that's nearly six times the rate in more prosperous areas across the river.

Often, it was the disgusting state of Borough drinking water to blame. The two suppliers in this part of London were the Southwark & Vauxhall Waterworks Company and the Lambeth Waterworks Company, both of which took their intake directly from the most heavily polluted stretch of the Thames as it flowed through London.

Huge amounts of raw human sewage and all kinds of untreated industrial waste were dumped in the Thames near these intake pipes every day and the suppliers' only means of removing it before human consumption was to insert a few mesh filters in their pipes. In 1850, the doctor/scientist Arthur Hassall published the results of his microscope studies of London water, concluding that Southwark's supply was "in the worst condition in which it is possible to conceive any water to be" and "the most disgusting which I have ever examined". Lambeth Waterworks Company responded by shifting its intake pipe upstream to a cleaner stretch of the Thames, but the Southwark & Vauxhall Company couldn't be bothered. [178-180]

Southwark's graveyards made their own contribution to befouling the water too. "The subsoil of Southwark has always been porous, being made of earth, sand and gravel," the former health officer William Rendle writes in his 1878 memoir. "The effect is a more or less free passage for the contents of burial places, cesspools and the like to wells in the vicinity." Back in the 1850s, Rendle adds, he'd personally traced "evidence of the most offensive and dangerous percolation into the drinking water."

All this evidence made it clearer by the day that the filthiest areas of Southwark must be cleaned up if the area was ever to have a chance of getting disease under control. But there was a Catch-22 at work. "Unless you close Cross Bones, St Saviour's death rates will never decline," said the health authorities. "With death rates as high as they are, closing Cross Bones is out of the question," St Saviour's replied. It was that simple paradox which kept the two sides at war for 20 years.

On August 13, 1849, England's newly formed Board of Health forwarded two letters of complaint it had received about Cross Bones, telling St Saviour's churchwardens that, if these complaints were well-founded and immediate action not taken to correct them, the board would step in to close Cross Bones itself. The first of these two letters came from Mariane Gwilt, who lived with her husband George in one of the Union Street schoolhouses protruding into Cross Bones' land. Here's a few extracts from what she had to say:

> *"From the windows of the room called the school room, we have all this sickly Summer almost daily witnessed the most distressing sights. In the bone house with its open grating, which is not more than eight or ten yards from our windows, we have had sometimes from three to nine bodies lying in their shells for as many as ten days.* [181]

> *"On another occasion three or four weeks since, the body of a man who had drowned himself at Blackfriars Bridge was brought down here and allowed to lie in its shell ten days. Whilst he laid there, the bodies of two children who had died of the cholera were left in the dead house the chief of the time. Then the [suicide's] body was washed with a mop and pailfuls of water, the shell again washed out and all the filthy liquid, shavings and grass thrown under our windows. His clothes lie there at this time I am writing.*

> *"Several medical gentlemen have averred to me that this burial place is dangerous to the health of this densely-populated neighbourhood. [...] We are now both of us considerably advanced in years and my health has suffered materially these last five years. I have no doubt the impure air from this pestiferous locale injures the health also of the surrounding vicinity."* [182]

St Saviour's churchwardens fired back a feisty reply, picking holes in Mrs Gwilt's figures and saying the suicide's body had been left unburied (they said for three days rather than ten) only because of a delay in the coroner's inquest. His clothes had to be kept in case the family reclaimed them, St Saviour's added, and as for the other bodies left unattended in the bone house – an admitted seven over the past three weeks – surely Mrs Gwilt would not wish to see them stored in the families' homes instead? [183, 184]

The parish was equally defiant in tackling the board's second complaint, this one from a Dr Lever:

> *"Cholera has prevailed in this vicinity to a fearful extent. The Parochial Officers have been told of the danger incurred by their continuing to inter in the ground [but] still they will not discontinue, as they are afraid of losing their fees.*
>
> *"Upwards of 12 months since, the late Mr Callaway and myself signed a requisition as professional men, begging the churchwardens that no more burials might be permitted. To this requisition were appended the names of nearly every respectable inhabitant whose house is near the [graveyard], but the parish officers turned a deaf ear."*

St Saviour's replied that Cross Bones was "as well situate, as little offensive to health and public morals and as open as almost any ground in the Metropolis. From these facts, we are of the opinion that the burial grounds of this parish are not in a state to require special interference of the Board of Health."

Edwin Chadwick, the same man we met at the 1841 enquiry into urban burial grounds, was now heading the Board of Health - and he didn't agree with St Saviour's complacent view. On September 14, 1849, less than a month after the parish had responded to Gwilt's and Lever's complaints, *The London Gazette's* front page carried an official board announcement. Addressed to the St Saviour's churchwardens as a kind of open letter, it began by reminding them of the board's powers to inspect British burial grounds and demand action on any it found to be dangerous. The board's own inspector had now surveyed Cross Bones for himself, it said, and pronounced it a health hazard to anyone living nearby. Therefore, the board was ordering St Saviour's to stop burying people there immediately and not to resume doing so without its express permission. [185]

You'd have thought that would be the end of the matter, but still St Saviour's fought on. It replied that closing Cross Bones "would entail a serious inconvenience and great additional expense to the poorest inhabitants of this parish", arguing that the board's verdict was based "chiefly if not wholly on the false and exaggerated statements contained in a letter of Mrs Gwilt". When the board issued a legal summons against St Saviour's for failing to obey its closure order, the parish consulted its own lawyers and concluded the board had exceeded its powers by ordering Cross Bones' outright closure in the first place. [186]

Perhaps that's why the board's next ruling took a harder line. On October 16, it had *The London Gazette* carry another message to St Saviour's, this one preceded by an even longer list of the board's statutory powers. It then demanded that all the following changes must be made at Cross Bones before any further burials were considered:

- Entire surface (barring footpaths and any paved areas) to be covered with at least three inches depth of quicklime.
- Where this quicklime was disturbed for the purpose of digging a new grave, it must be replaced to a depth of three inches as soon as that grave was re-filled.
- All new graves on the site to be coated with at least three inches of quicklime at the bottom before the coffin goes in.
- One coffin per grave. No exceptions.

- All graves to be at least two feet six inches apart.
- All coffins to have at least five feet of dirt between the lid and surface ground.
- All coffins placed in vaults, brick-lined graves or catacombs on-site to be lined with lead and soldered air tight.
- If any bones or coffin parts should be unearthed, the earth disturbed must be replaced immediately and an extra three inches of quicklime deposited on that spot.
- No ground to be disturbed, or any new grave dug, on a spot where a burial's been made in the past ten years.

By this point in its long history, I doubt there was a single inch of Cross Bones where even half these conditions could be met, so you could argue the list amounted to another order that the ground must simply be closed down. By going through the formality of setting out necessary changes in this very public way, the board was ensuring it hobbled any legal challenge St Saviour's might care to launch in future.

*****

St Saviour's churchwardens met a week after this ultimatum appeared to hear the latest report from its Cross Bones committee. The chairman reported there'd been some cleaning up on the site and that a new path had been laid there. "It was found that the old path had no bodies under it and 'would afford ample accommodation for the wants of the poorer inhabitants for a long time to come'," says the MoL. We know St Saviour's approached the Board of Health after this meeting, asking if it could use the area under the old path for new burials, but not what the board said in reply. One way or another, though, as the MoL confirms, burials certainly did continue at Cross Bones well into the 1850s and there's good reason to believe nothing much changed in how the site was run.

As evidence for this, we have a November 1852 letter to Spencer Walpole, Britain's Home Secretary, from a group of residents in Union Street, Borough High Street and Redcross Way. These were the streets immediately surrounding Cross Bones, so people living there had more opportunity than most to observe what went on at the site and every reason to fear its effect on their health. Here's what they told Walpole:

> *"The gravedigger is daily seen with a long steel-pointed iron rod, sticking the ground here and there, spearing the top coffins until some wood gives way, whereupon the whole of the contents, sometimes many [coffins] in that particular grave, are turned out and remain several days above ground to the scandal of all Christian men. When each of these exhumations have taken place, there have been seen in such human remains a number of skulls too numerous to mention, lying like half-devoured turnips about a sheepfold and cared for as little."* [187]

The letter added that between ten and 13 people living at one of the underclass lodging houses in Redcross Way had died during a single month of the 1849 cholera outbreak and reminded Walpole that the Board of Health's closure order against Cross Bones had been allowed to go unenforced. "There has been no cessation in these scandalous outrages on the dead, nor the least abatement of the sickening and abominable effluvium emanating from this enormous heap of putrescence," it concludes. "We pray, Right Honourable Sir, and rely upon your kind interference to prevent the continuance of this great and most abominable nuisance to the safety of our families and the comfort of our homes."

Walpole responded by commissioning his own inspection of Cross Bones, this one carried out by a Dr Sutherland. The report he submitted to Walpole did not make happy reading:

> *"[Cross Bones] is evidently used for an inferior class of interments and can be considered only as a convenient place for getting rid of the dead. It bears no marks of ever having been set apart as a place of Christian Sepulchre. It is crowded with dead and many fragments of decayed bones, some even entire, are mixed up with the earth of the mounds over the graves."*

Sutherland's figures show that a total of 1,180 bodies were buried in Cross Bones' total area of 2,089 square yards between 1845 and 1851 alone, with the cholera years of 1849 and 1850 bringing the highest loads. "If proper regulations had been adopted for this ground [...] the whole area would have accommodated only 482 coffins, [and] it would have been full in somewhat less than three years," Sutherland writes. His figures demonstrate that even if Cross Bones had been completely empty in 1845 - which it very much wasn't - it would have already been packed with more than twice the number of dead it could safely carry by the end of 1850.

Burials at the College Ground had been abandoned by the time Sutherland inspected Cross Bones, leaving St Saviour's with just two parish grounds at its disposal: Cross Bones and the churchyard surrounding what's now Southwark Cathedral. Between the two, these gave St Saviour's a total burial area of just 3,583 square yards to serve a population of about 19,638. "The parish is a very unhealthy one and has an annual mortality of above 29 in the 1,000, [so] the annual deaths are 550," Sutherland continues. "Were the two grounds now opened for the first time and were all the parochial dead buried in them, they would be entirely filled in about 18 months." [188]

Sutherland's conclusions were that the area of parish burial ground provided in St Saviour's was "entirely inadequate" and that both remaining sites had "long been completely overcharged with dead". Further burials at either Cross Bones or the cathedral would be "inconsistent with a due regard for the public health", and so "should be wholly discontinued".

"This time the vestry was forced to act," the MoL says. "On 29 March 1853, the burial board reported that, after looking at alternative locations for burial, including parish land at Sydenham, the best solution was to approach one of the cemetery companies. This led to the offer of a piece of ground of between six and seven acres in the cemetery at Brookwood, near Woking, belonging to the London Necropolis Company." Four month's later, Lord Palmerston, Walpole's replacement as Home Secretary, ordered that Cross Bones must close no later than September 21, 1853. He rejected St Saviour's plea for a week's stay of execution while the LNC deal was finalised, forcing the vestry to make interim arrangements with the Victoria Park Cemetery Company in Hackney instead. [189, 190]

St Saviour's vestry minutes include a note made on October 24,

1853, confirming that Cross Bones had now been closed for good. In a letter to the *Times* 30 years later, Lord Brabazon, a campaigner for urban parks, claimed the last Cross Bones burials of all were those of Sarah Fleming, aged 36, who'd lived at St Margaret's Court in the Borough and a child named Sawday from Redcross Way itself. He dates these two final burials to October 31, 1853, suggesting the vestry minutes may have got a week ahead of themselves.

By November 1854, St Saviour's was ready to end its temporary arrangement with Victoria Park and switch to the ten acres it had leased at LNC's Woking cemetery instead. The parish charged 14 shillings for each adult funeral it arranged through LNC and 10 shillings for every child's funeral. This covered road transportation to LNC's Waterloo depot, one-way train passage for the body to Woking, two third-class return tickets for the mourners, plus minister and gravedigger's fees. St Saviour's added an extra shilling to the price if burial in consecrated ground was required, plus two shillings for every additional mourner who wanted to go along.

LNC's own third-class fares at about this time were set at two shillings (single) for every corpse and two shillings and sixpence (return) for each mourner, so all the ancillary services would have left St Saviour's little, if any, profit. Pauper funerals, of course, brought in no money at all and we have figures showing St Saviour's paid for 89 of these at Brookwood in 1858 alone.

Left with an inner-city graveyard it could no longer use, St Saviour's rented out Cross Bones to a Mr Stephens, who signed a 26½-year lease on the site in November 1854 at annual rent of £50. Stephens promptly sub-let the site to a local tradesman called Downs, who used it as a builder's yard.

In 1868, the Bishop of Winchester's rights to the old Clink Liberty's land were formally transferred to the Church of England's Ecclesiastical Commissioners, who duly passed Cross Bones' freehold on to St Saviour's parish. Given full ownership of the site at last, the churchwardens there waited till Stephens' lease completed its term in 1881, obtained the necessary Home Office development licences and offered Cross Bones as building land instead. This prompted an immediate protest from Lord Brabazon, who accused St Saviour's of desecrating Cross Bones merely to maximise its financial return. He quickly sketched out the site's history in a November 1883 letter to the *Times* and then issued this call for action:

"The ground is now being offered to the public, on lease, as an 'eligible building site'. It is with a view to save this ground from such desecration and to retain it as an open space for the use and enjoyment of the people, that I now address you.

"The trustees have under their consideration an application from a builder to acquire this ground for building purposes at a rental of £200 and at a meeting of the trustees held on [November 7], it was stated that, unless somebody came forward to purchase this space as a public garden, so that the dead might yet remain in peace, the trustees would be forced to let it for building purposes.

"The person making the offer has obtained the sanction of the Home Office, providing that he undertakes to excavate the ground to the level of the virgin soil and to remove all human remains. This he is apparently willing to do, but how it is likely to be done may be inferred from what happened in a similar case, where cartloads of earth mixed with human remains were seen leaving the ground for sale as garden soil.

"It is to be hoped the public will take this matter up and raise a sum - say, £6,000 - for [the site's] purchase to be maintained as an open space for the perpetual use and enjoyment of the people. This neighbourhood abounds in narrow courts and alleys, filled with the poor of both sexes, far removed from any open space."

Brabazon followed up this letter with a second one to the *Times* a few weeks later, saying St Saviour's was keen to maximise its income from Cross Bones now only because a recent change in legislation had abolished the church rates payments it previously received. The builder mentioned in his first letter, he added, was already drilling exploratory holes at Cross Bones to assess the amount of work need to clear the site of human remains and hence decide what final price he was prepared to offer. His plan was to erect "a block of industrial dwellings" on the site. [191]

In the end, it was not the prospect of this extra work which saved Cross Bones from the 1883 development deal, but Parliament's passing of 1884's Disused Burial Grounds Act, which made it illegal to build anything but a place of worship on any old burial ground. That legislation has been considerably weakened since, so it can't help Cross Bones now, but in the aftermath of Brabazon's letter it was enough to kibosh the whole deal. "The only thing that you could do with a piece of ground that had previously been used as a graveyard was build a church on it," Dark told me. "And you don't need a church there."

Returning to the option of short-term leases on the site, St Saviour's let it out to Charles Hart, a showman, who set up a full steam-driven fairground at Cross Bones in 1892. His nightly attractions there included a shooting range, a roundabout and a notoriously nerve-wracking new ride called the Razzle Dazzle. But residents nearby complained of the noise and Hart's fairground was closed down as a nuisance.

By 1928, the neighbourhood's collective memory had faded enough for developers to assume any human remains at Cross Bones must have been removed long ago and another team of builders excavating there were surprised to find themselves turning up human skulls. "A number of human remains was unearthed, skulls and limb bones predominating," the Borough's Medical Officer Horace Wilson wrote in his annual report. "They were found six feet below the surface and descended to a depth of ten feet. These bones were of considerable antiquity."

Wilson goes on to say that these particular bones were reburied at the LNC's ground in Brookwood, but that's no guarantee that the construction gang at Cross Bones was equally meticulous throughout the whole project. I wonder if their 1928 work went on to build the warehouse foundations the MoL found lined with bones in its own dig 65 years later?

Murder in Redcross Way (1898): Alice Lofthouse

William Gould had what we'd today call a portfolio career: at the age of just 26, he was already part market trader, part cellar man and part pimp. His half share in a market barrow selling fruit and flowers around Southwark never provided enough income on its own, so he moonlighted with occasional kitchen or cellar work in Redcross Way's lodging houses and the surrounding pubs. He was also a member of the area's most feared street gang, though whether the pimping was a gang venture or the young man's private initiative is unclear.

Gould got back to his own lodgings at 3 Redcross Way about 8:30pm on Saturday July 16, 1898, stowed his barrow away and went to the house's communal kitchen. For the past six months, he'd shared his bed in this building with Alice Lofthouse, a 23-year-old woman who'd left her soldier husband in August the previous year. She'd been "violent, bad-tempered and addicted to drink and promiscuous infidelity", the soldier later testified. [192, 193]

Lofthouse was there in the kitchen with several other residents when Gould walked in and began playing with the house's friendly dog. He'd no sooner sat down than she started berating him. Alfred Ford, one of the others sat in the kitchen that night, later testified that Lofthouse called Gould "a fucking ponce" and demanded that he give her the money she was owed. "She screamed out 'Where's my money, you bastard?' within minutes of Gould arriving home," Ford told a coroner's jury. "He said 'Give me time'. She kept on and he walked out and went to a public house." [194]

We use the word "ponce" much more loosely now, but its Victorian meaning was quite precise. Dictionaries agree that it began as a bit of thieves' slang meaning: "a harlot's bully" (Partridge); "one who lives off the earnings of prostitutes" (Cassell); or "another word for 'pimp'" (Collins). It's pretty clear what Lofthouse was accusing Gould of here and easy to imagine him sending her out to work the streets when times were hard.

Lofthouse stalked off after Gould when he left, following him to a pub called the One Distillery in nearby Borough High Street. Albert Gould, William's uncle, was already sitting at the bar there when his nephew and Lofthouse walked in. "She called him a foul name and started nagging him," Albert later testified. "She asked for a drink and he told her she could have what she liked." Another drinker present added: "He said, 'You can have a glass of ale,', so she had it. He paid for it. He then went out and she followed him."

By now, Eliza Bailey had joined the crowd in number three's kitchen. She'd called round hoping to find a room for her brother, who'd recently lost his job, and was sitting there with her baby when Gould and Lofthouse returned. "She and the prisoner [Gould] were quarrelling dreadfully," Bailey testified. "He said, 'Will you be quiet! You are drunk now!' I did not hear her answer, but she made an attempt to pick up a ginger beer bottle. She picked it up from the table and attempted to throw it, but did not do so.

"The prisoner then got on to the table and kicked her several times in the face and ribs. She was sitting down by the table and he had heavy boots. He kicked her with all his might. She said, 'Oh don't hurt me' and she ran to another table. He picked up a poker from the fireplace, got on to the table and he hit her with it twice. He hit her twice across the back of the neck and once across the back." Ford saw the attack too. "They were jawing together," he testified. "There was a bar of iron on the right-hand side of the fireplace and I saw him hit her with it - I think it was on the back of the neck - and she fell forward. I did not hear her speak again."

The other women in the kitchen gathered round Alice and concluded she was not dead, but only in a faint. Someone sent a boy to run for the doctor. "The prisoner came round to me and said, 'If you screen me, I will see you all right'," Bailey testified, adding that she did not reply. "I had never seen him or the woman before," she said.

No doctor appeared, so Gould and his uncle went to find help themselves. They returned with Dr Michael Burt, who'd had a quite different account of the attack from William on his way to the house. "He said he had pushed her off a form [a bench]," Burt testified. "When I got there, I saw the deceased lying on the floor between the form and the table. There was a frothy fluid proceeding from her nose, which was a sign that there was animation, but she never recovered consciousness. The prisoner came to see me at midnight, made a statement to me and I told him to go and report at the station."

Gould did so, pitching up at the local cop shop in the early hours of Sunday morning and speaking to Inspector Samuel Denham. The inspector summed up his statement like this: "I am living with a woman. I am not married to her. I have had a quarrel and pushed her over a table and she is dead". Gould was sober, he added, but seemed distressed. Police formally charged him with manslaughter and he appeared at Southwark Police Court next morning, where the *Sun* reported that Gould "entered the dock with a jaunty air and in no way seemed to appreciate the seriousness of his position". He was refused bail and returned to his cell. [195]

The next step was the Coroner's Inquest, scheduled to begin next day and that's where all Hell broke loose. Gould's friends - presumably other members of his gang - turned out in force whenever police had to move him. Their first opportunity to cause trouble came when the coroner granted Gould's request to view Lofthouse's body.

"The prisoner on his way to the mortuary to view the corpse was hailed with cries of 'Cheer up, Fatty' and 'You'll be all right, Bill'," the *Daily Mail* reported. "Immediately he got outside the Coroner's Court, the officers in charge of him were assailed by a savage mob, evidently bent on rescuing the prisoner. Six constables, three detectives and two inspectors were required to get him safely to the mortuary and back and five persons had to be removed to the police station, the officers being hooted all the way." [196, 197]

At the inquest itself, Bailey gave her testimony about Gould asking her to "screen him" and he burst out shouting in reply. "It's a lie," he yelled across the court. "That's what the detectives put into her head". Asked why she'd never mentioned Gould's approach earlier, Bailey said: "Because I was afraid. I had been threatened that if I said anything, I should be served the same as the deceased." Detective-sergeant Divall told the court he knew of another witness who "could entirely corroborate" Bailey's statement, but that this witness had also been threatened and refused to give evidence as a result.

William Lofthouse, the husband Alice had walked out on, gave evidence at the inquest hearing too – including the description of her character I've already quoted. He was a private in the Rifle Brigade and said he'd married her in September 1895. She'd walked out on him three times before their final break-up, but he'd always taken her back saying he didn't care who she'd been with in the interim. He'd come to the inquest, he added, because he wanted to "take a look" at the man who killed her. [198, 199]

After a long deliberation, the coroner's jury returned a verdict of wilful murder against Gould, adding that he'd acted "under great provocation". There was more tumult when police tried to get him out of the court and back to his cell. "As the prisoner was being moved, another ineffectual attempt was made to rescue him," the *Mail* reported. "The jurors were mobbed and had to be protected by police. Two female friends of Gould's named Burke and O'Connell were brought up at the Southwark Police Court later in the day and charged with creating a disturbance. The police stated that they had behaved like wild beasts. Burke was fined 20 shillings and O'Connell ordered to find a surety or go to prison for 14 days. [200]

"Thomas Edwards, a hulking match-seller, was then charged with savagely assaulting two constables who were on special duty in Redcross [Way] for the protection of witnesses. He was sentenced to two months' hard labour." [201]

Police upped the formal charge against Gould from manslaughter to murder on July 26, after the courageous Eliza Bailey helped them recover the bloody poker from 3 Redcross Way. His Old Bailey trial for murder began on September 13, by which time the gang seem to have briefed several witnesses of its own. One of these was Jane Page, who described herself in court as "a single woman" living "in the neighbourhood of Red Cross Court". She'd also been in number three's kitchen that night, she said, but offered a quite different version of events. Page's account agreed with Ford's and Bailey's up to the point where Lofthouse picked up the ginger beer bottle, but she claimed Lofthouse had actually thrown it at Gould.

"She went to go towards him and she staggered and fell over the table as she got on the form," Page claimed. "She got on the form and tried to jump on the table, but fell back off the form. I saw her fall. [...] She was very drunk. The prisoner was sober. I remained there till the doctor came. The prisoner was very kind to the deceased. [...] I did not see him strike her. I did not see him take the poker in his hands. He never struck her with it."

Under cross-examination, Page immediately changed her story, now saying that Gould had pushed Lofthouse off the bench rather than simply watching her fall. "She was standing on the form when he pushed her," Page said. "As she fell forward, she jumped and threw herself on her head backwards. She had got on the form, put her foot on the table and fell on the back of her head. She was on the table when he gave her the push."

Albert Gould told a similar story. "All I noticed him do was give her a push," he testified. "She fell against a form." Under cross-examination, he added: "I did not see the poker used, nor the woman kicked in the face". Both Albert Gould and Alfred Ford testified that William was "a teetotaller", who'd drunk only "a small lemon" at the One Distillery on the fatal night. So firmly were they agreed on this point that each used an identical form of words to convey it.

That's not the only reason to take all three of these witnesses' testimony with a pinch of salt. Page's account has the ring of someone who's set out to show Gould was entirely innocent and then been forced to amend her story as she went along. Albert Gould was William's uncle, liable to protect him for that reason alone, and Alfred

Ford looks to have been another member of the Redcross Way gang. Ford later admitted he'd been drunk himself both at the time of Lofthouse's death and while giving his first statement to police. He was 20 years old at the time and press reports called him as "a lad of the hooligan type". When Gould's trial began, Ford had just emerged from a month in jail for his drunken misbehaviour in Redcross Way and Borough High Street.

For more reliable evidence, the trial turned to Dr Burt, who'd carried out a post-mortem on Lofthouse, finding she had a fractured skull with shards of broken bone driven into the brain beneath. "It would have taken very considerable violence to cause that," he told the court. Shown the weapon found at Redcross Way, he added: "It was such a fracture as might be caused by this iron poker. In my opinion, a fall on the bare floor could not have done it."

Gould's defence relied on the fact that Ford and Bailey had described poker blows to Lofthouse's neck and back rather than her head, and pressed Burt on this point under cross examination. What of Page's account? Could it not be the accidental blow to the head she described which had killed Lofthouse? Burt was clearly sceptical, but had to admit he could not rule this out altogether. "If she had been thrown with great force, or if she had fallen from a considerable height on to a corner of the table or form, that might be possible," he replied. "[But] a fall from the form to the floor would not cause it."

That small seed of doubt - combined, perhaps with a bit more intimidation from the gang - was enough to save Gould from a murder charge and the hanging that would almost certainly have followed. Instead, the jury found him guilty of manslaughter and he was sentenced to 15 years penal servitude. The newspapers had a field day with the case, plastering every account with the newly-coined word "hooligan" to describe Gould and his friends. We can gauge the Cross Bones area's reputation in 1898 from the headline the *South London Chronicle* chose to sum it all up: "Notorious Red Cross Court Again".

Book Two
Cross Bones
2013-2023:
an oral history.

Cross Bones in June 2023.

The Interviewees

A few minor edits aside, the chapters you've just read remain unchanged from the *Outcast Dead* e-book I published in 2013. In this section, you'll find a brand new oral history covering events there in the very busy decade that followed.

In the course of that ten years, Cross Bones' appearance and way of doing things has gone through some pretty fundamental changes. Here you'll find all the major players discussing in their own words how those changes came about and why some proved so controversial. I've assembled this new material from a series of interviews conducted between November 2022 and July 2023. The people I spoke to, listed here in alphabetical order, are:

Polly Blake: Spokeswoman for Sex Worker Advocacy & Resistance Movement (SWARM).

Natalie Boatfield: Assistant to Zanna (see below) and a committed Cross Bones campaigner in her own right.

Joseph Bonner: A senior official at the Foreign Office and a Bankside Open Spaces Trust (BOST) trustee for about 12 years. Resigned from the charity in December 2020.

Isabela Nieto Castro: Political adviser at the Mexican Embassy in London.

Fernando Champion: Head of cultural affairs at the Mexican Embassy in London.

John Constable: Originator of the Cross Bones vigils and the site's highest profile champion for over 20 years.

Jen Cooper: Long-time Cross Bones campaigner. Took over running the gate vigils when Constable took a step back.

Charlotte Gilsenan: Chief executive officer of BOST since January 2019.

Helen John: The landscape architect and project manager who headed BOST's first phase of access work at Cross Bones.

Andrew Nunn: Dean of Southwark Cathedral from 2010 till 2023. Originator of Cross Bones' annual service of regret & reconciliation.

Laura Watson: Spokeswoman for the English Collective of Prostitutes (ECP).

Matt Wilcock: Joined BOST as Cross Bones' engagement manager in 2022. Also co-ordinates the site's volunteers.

Zanna: Another long-time Cross Bones campaigner. Among her work as an artist is the series of skull posters often found on Cross Bones' exterior wall.

*Thanks to everyone listed here for giving
me their time in the interviews.*

"I was starting to feel tired"

February 2013: A Southwark charity called Bankside Open Spaces Trust (BOST) takes over management of the Cross Bones site. It's a change that's been a long time coming.

John Constable: "In 2011, after the 13th Halloween of Cross Bones, I remember saying, 'The Goose is loose', by which I meant anybody could make a connection with the Goose and work with her in their own way. It didn't have to come through me. But it didn't work out. Within a month of me saying it, something huge would happen at Cross Bones and I'd find myself massively involved again.

"I was starting to feel tired and wanting a change. On a simple practical level, I was spending more and more of my life reading planning applications and making submissions, and less and less working on my own writing and performing. It had taken over my life. Katy was involved with me for the whole journey and did an awful lot in terms of creating the shrine and those things. We both had the strong feeling that if we just hung around Cross Bones indefinitely, we'd become the hungry ghosts.

"I started talking to BOST around 2012 or 2013, and somewhere around there BOST and I approached Transport for London."

Helen John: "I was employed by BOST at the time, building 27 community gardens across SE1. They got me involved [in Cross Bones] because I'm a trained landscape architect. John and Katy approached BOST and said, 'Look, we've got this connection. Is there any way that you would be willing to take on the garden as an open spaces trust?' BOST said, 'Oh, yes. We'd love to help.' It was a case of us putting forward the planning application.

"At that time, Cross Bones didn't even have a designation. It was just 'other land'. Friends of Cross Bones had been campaigning for a garden of remembrance there for many years, but they weren't getting anywhere with TfL because they were seen as this ramshackle group. Having had conversations with TfL, I think they were just a little bit fearful of the group because they didn't quite understand what they were. They'd been to a couple of the vigils and were a little bit challenged by what they saw. I think they were just frightened by the whole thing."

Jen Cooper: "[In TfL's eyes] we were outcasts. Nutters."

Joseph Bonner: "If you're a TfL manager dealing with this Cross Bones site, it's certainly something you go back and tell your wife or husband about. I was always saying, 'Celebrate Cross Bones and get them intrigued by it'. [...] I'm sure people in the construction world in London are used to coming across graveyards, but this is quite a special one."

John Constable: "Katy and I had been operating Friends of Cross Bones, but it was a very informal and often chaotic group. It was just us and the people who came to our events - the Halloween of Cross Bones, then the monthly vigils. Our alliance took in poets, mystics, sex workers, artists, musicians, people with mental health and substance use issues, people of all genders and proclivities, all faiths and none. We never had a formal meeting, though we took soundings during the gatherings at the gates.

"The Cross Bones forum was completely separate, started by BOST as a consultative forum for the management of the garden. Katy and I sometimes represented Friends of Cross Bones at the forum, though we always made it clear that we couldn't speak for 'the Friends', who sometimes disagreed with our approach or with one another."

Joseph Bonner: "That steering group, or forum as the members opted to call it, began in 2015. I chaired the group and Zanna, Natalie, Jennifer, John and Katy were all regulars - probably at almost every meeting. It was open to anyone with an interest in Cross Bones. We would meet four times a year and would usually have at least eight or nine people at each meeting. BOST would be represented by Helen John and myself as BOST trustees.

Our meetings would last about three hours, hopefully not because of my bad chairing but just because people were so passionate about the whole project. I am a civil servant, I work in the Foreign Office. I tried my best to use whatever experience I have of that to at least form the conversation, let everyone speak, and hopefully draw a conclusion and get some action points agreed."

John Constable: "From the outset, going to BOST represented a level of compromise. To me, Cross Bones at its heart was this wild, unregulated place, but it was a choice between just having that brief flowering – and it then being developed – or [finding a compromise]. As I saw it, getting TfL and a prospective developer to agree to protect the site was the only game in town.

"We weren't in the business of trying to manage a garden, so BOST with its established reputation for community gardening seemed the obvious choice. That meant a major transition for me, of course – from working in a very outlaw way to working with a local charity with a different set of contingencies."

Jen Cooper: "A lot of people fell away because a lot of people were ever so extreme. I'm aware that there has to be compromise. But it should always be a compromise on the side of protecting the ethos of Cross Bones and the vigils. We've got to defend against it becoming what the Goose prophesied: a heritage theme park."

Helen John: "Our Cross Bones forums, I have to say, were not easy. They really weren't. They were always constructive, but they were super-challenging. Sometimes me and the trustee who was there came away feeling completely bruised by it all saying, 'Do they not see that we're on their side?' There was a lot of suspicion about what BOST's interest in this was. At the same time, we were confused, because we thought, 'You came to us'."

Zanna: "Something about Cross Bones creates arguments, argy-bargy, disagreements among people who are all working ostensibly with the same aim. The ground is full of sad, angry, unhappy burials that have the energy of a difficult life – and that generates something in everyone that gets involved."

John Constable: "[Helen] became the focus of quite a lot of hostility. Some Friends of Cross Bones feel BOST is - I don't know what. I've stayed out of it, because an awful lot of it seems to be about personalities and territorial feelings.

"One reason Katy and I were keen to close our work there was the feeling that Cross Bones was into a whole new phase now. I always saw that, as Cross Bones moved into the mainstream, some of my special love affair with it would have to be let go, but that ultimately it would be worth it. It's always a complicated thing. It's a bit like when I first heard the Velvet Underground's *Venus in Furs* used to sell cars. It feels like, 'Is nothing allowed to be transgressive?' That was a big feeling I've had to navigate precisely because of the success of establishing the garden."

Andrew Nunn: "It's difficult when you've had someone as competent in what they're doing as John to then go to the next stage. He managed what could have been a very uncomfortable conjunction really well."

John Constable: "I know Andy [Hulme], the Invisible Gardener, was not happy. He had a different vision of it. I think he thought he could end up running the garden. It was territorial, but with very good intentions. I just didn't believe that was sustainable. That's partly because I'd had local councillors complaining to me about the state of the site. There was that danger of a backlash against Cross Bones, with people saying 'Oh, it's being used for drug dealing,' which was never actually true.

   "During that difficult period, when some of Cross Bones' neighbours were trying to get it developed, I'd go on site and there were these Ukrainian lads, who were getting drunk in there. They used to really get plastered. I was sweeping in there one day, and one came staggering over saying, 'Please let me out'. He'd been locked in when everyone left one day. Afterwards I wrote a message, which was partly for them, about respecting the dead: 'Don't dick with a goose's curse'. It was my way of saying, 'Yes, we may be a bit wild, but actually we know about respect as well'."

Zanna: "I think it was very sad that the Invisible Gardener's work was erased. You can't just come and erase someone else's vision with your own. There's always people with different views wanting to come in and impose their version on it. Everybody coming in needs to respect what was there before, and that isn't happening. Every new person that gets involved wants to imprint themselves on it and as a result of that there's a real danger that much of the ad hoc nature of Cross Bones will slowly just disappear. Because it's fragile.

"I think it was necessary to get an official organization involved with the land in order for it to have more public access. However, they've chosen, because they're a garden organization, to try to put less of an emphasis on it being a burial ground. You cannot call it a garden: it's a graveyard. The garden is secondary. Giving the important words power is an imperative."

Jen Cooper: "John had to find somebody who could hold the lease. The Friends of Cross Bones couldn't do it. We'd tried having meetings and being a proper group, four meetings a year. I think we managed two and then everybody just wiggled away. So of course everything had to be tidied up."

John Constable: "Helen became effectively the project manager. In the first couple of years, it was difficult because we were establishing our different attitudes on what Cross Bones needed to be, but we did genuinely form a very close friendship with Helen, and I hugely respect a lot of what she laid in place."

Helen John: "TfL had been trying to develop Cross Bones for years, but I think they realised by 2014 that it just wasn't going to happen because of the community's support for this space. Somebody from TfL has basically said that they did a cost analysis back in the '90s. They worked out that if they put £1 million on the table, they could exhume all the bones and develop Cross Bones. Of course, they didn't say that to the community, but the likes of Zanna, John and Katy knew what was afoot. That's why they campaigned so hard."

John Constable: "It was sometimes challenging work with BOST, but one of the things I'm pleased about is that we kept fighting to insist we mustn't lose the roots of Cross Bones – that it is dedicated to outcasts and specifically emphasising sex workers. That's an uncomfortable thing, and I think in the early days BOST found it quite difficult. I think they made an extraordinary journey actually. Since I've stopped being involved, they've continued to work with outsider groups, LGBT groups, sex worker groups, and that's really important.

"Friends of Cross Bones is where you find the awkward squad – and I count myself among them. I think our value to BOST was often to be their radical wing, if you like. Inevitably, TfL exerted a lot of pressure on BOST to limit its own commitments, and BOST could represent the Friends' proposals as pressure on them from the other side. It was good for BOST to be able to say, 'I don't think the Friends of Cross Bones would buy this'."

Helen John: "It's a very difficult line that BOST treads with all of our spaces, because we're working for the community, and for the council, and with developers. We didn't encourage the Friends of Cross Bones to object per se, but what we did do is make it very clear to the developer that the objection was coming via the Cross Bones forum. It showed the council the community support we have, and also gave us some teeth: 'Look we've got a community here. They're really serious about this. It's not BOST that you'll be seen to be working against - it'll be the community.'

"The Friends of Cross Bones weren't always keen on what I did, but at that stage it didn't matter. I said, 'Look, let's just get the Planning Commission to change this from derelict land to a private garden with access to the public, because that means we can ultimately open it to the public'. And that's what we did.

"The reason BOST exists is because there's massive social deprivation in the area, and also a massive shortage of open spaces for the people living in housing blocks and things there. Southwark Council was very keen that Cross Bones be open to the public, so they were hugely supportive of TfL and BOST collaborating in this way. Our lease with TfL began in November 2014. Cross Bones became a private garden with access to the public, which is what it remains today."

Matt Wilcock: "It's the creation of a new park, which is probably what Southwark will promote it as: 'We've got a new green space'."

"Compromise is dangerous"

August 2014: Cross Bones' ribbon-covered gates are moved about 40 yards down Redcross Way to clear access for TfL's Liberty of Southwark development site next door. This change does not go unnoticed by local residents.

Janef, London-se1.co.uk message board: "Walking past the burial ground earlier today it was a surprise to note the site gates and all the attached offerings have disappeared. Evidence of activity with heavy machinery inside the site. I'm not always the most observant, but those gates and their decorations were such a familiar part of that walk, and now there's just some wire screens there. Have I missed an announcement about development kicking off there?"

TfL statement: "It remains our ambition to bring forward a comprehensive redevelopment of the whole Landmark Court site and we are taking steps to identify a partner to progress a scheme on the site. In the meantime, we will be leasing the burial ground to BOST for the temporary garden, with managed public access. The burial ground will then form open space as part of a comprehensive scheme."
(202)

John Constable: "The reason for moving the gates was to move them away from the site they wanted to develop but, as so often with Cross Bones, that seemed to turn to our advantage. It aligned the gates with the garden itself and created a window into the graveyard before it was open. Up until then, it had been hidden behind hoardings.

"It was an amazing day when they moved them - Katy and I were there watching. They put them on a big sling attached to an earth digger, and then lifted them like that. Katy's got this wonderful photo of them floating in front of the shard: flying gates. It felt incredibly intense. It's that thing of people who leave something of themselves at the gates and a thought or an emotion. The gates start to get a life of their own."

Andrew Nunn: "The place where all the ribbons are and everything is very moving. Very touching and very powerful."

Joseph Bonner: "[The gates] are a living artwork. The fact that the ribbons are refreshed every month as a result of the vigils; Jennifer taking the old ribbons off to clean and wash them before putting them back. It's a labour of love."

Polly Blake: "I went down there for the first time last winter and I was very moved when I saw the gates. Having somewhere like that is really valuable – somewhere you can do something physical and material, like tie a ribbon, make an offering, put up a plaque. As humans, we need that physicality and that materiality in order to feel part of a tradition, part of a history. I think it's also a really valuable community thing."

Jen Cooper: "The gates are littered with my family. When my husband died, I put his picture up there – and his brother, his mum and his dad ..."

John Constable: "It works by example rather than by prescriptive commissioning of work. That's the distinction I make. It started with just ribbons from the vigils - from the Halloween of Cross Bones to begin with - and the odd totem. Then Katy started doing these spiderwebs and sun wheels and things and hanging them there. Then other people start to put things up, and it continues to develop."

Zanna: "I was very clear that compromise was dangerous. When we moved the gates and the boundary was established, I said the boundary was short of the point [where the graveyard really ends]. Every bit of compromise inches further and further away from the ideal. John's attitude was 'Better something than nothing', whereas my attitude was 'We must keep fighting for everything'.

"The point is, where was the boundary? I've always said I would want to question that. In the fighting over where the stopping point for the Liberty of Southwark site is and where Cross Bones went up to, we need to agree that they don't encroach. A middle ground section was agreed because they couldn't guarantee it wasn't part of the burial ground."

Joseph Bonner: "Zanna's been quite modest – perhaps too much so – about her contribution to saving the site and researching in the way that she did."

John Constable: "I've always felt Zanna and Natalie had a very different vision of Cross Bones [to my own]. I probably had the most disputation and outright arguments with them over the years. There were people who thought we should have gone for the entire site, including the area of the development – who were convinced the graveyard covered that whole site. For me, the point was to defend and protect what we could firmly establish as the Cross Bones Graveyard."

Jen Cooper: "There was a difference between John and Zanna in the way they would behave, because John would keep going gently, softly-softly. A lot of the time Zanna felt 'Grrr'.

"John's all spirit. With Zanna, it's spirit as well, but for her it's the physicality of the graveyard and campaigning for it to be owned by the people in perpetuity. John's thing is that the garden already exists in eternity. They're different people, but it's always struck me what a wonderful thing it was that a male and a female were doing so much work for Cross Bones – even though they didn't always agree and get on."

John Constable: "To me, the idea of Cross Bones has always been as important as its physical manifestation. If it had existed only for a single moment, that would've been enough in a way. Everything that's ever fully existed like that can influence people again and again. It can speak to people across time. To me, so much of Cross Bones is about time and eternity. My whole first experience [of the place] was exactly that, really, all these different times somehow being simultaneously present on a particular night during a particular, very enhanced walk."

"A symbol of transformation"
November 2014: BOST's short-term lease with TfL begins, giving it full access to Cross Bones for the first time and a chance to see what work's needed there.

Helen John: "When we first went on site, there were quite a few human remains strewn around the place. Not loads, but enough that you could see them very clearly when you went in. When the site was closed back in 1853, it stank to high heaven, so they poured limewater concrete all over it, which adhered to the bones. I'd been told about that, but it was only when I went there and saw these baby skulls encased in the concrete that I realised that's really what happened.

"When they pulled that all up, I had to do something with it. I

193

had to apply for permission from the Ministry of Justice. I sent off the application. Within 15 minutes of the e-mail, I had somebody quite high up on the phone saying, 'Is this Cross Bones ground in London?' I think, because they'd had run-ins with developers here in the past, they probably looked at my application and thought, 'Why is she asking for a burial licence? What's going on?' All I wanted to do is rebury the remains on site. I just thought, 'Wow, if anyone wanted to develop this place, they'd have a fight on their hands,' because I think the Ministry of Justice would resist.

"We didn't want to have these bones disturbed in the future anyway, just out of respect, but environmental health at Southwark insisted that we put in a buffer layer. We had a no-dig policy on site, so we put the bones down in one area and covered them with soil. Then we covered it with orange membrane, then more soil, then a layer of gravel, a second layer of membrane then more soil. What that means is that ,when our volunteers are on site, if they hit that first membrane, they stop. They know they mustn't go any further.

"After 2014, we were able to really start making the garden accessible. Before that, you could only access it from Redcross Way, and there was a step there. We needed to ensure you could get in even if you were disabled, or a wheelchair user, or someone with a pushchair or whatever. We established a new entrance on Union Street, which at the time was just a rubbly mess. We made massive changes in just a few months. The first thing we did was bury the bones, and then after that Arthur de Mowbray was in there for about three months building the Goosewing structure. That Goosewing is actually made of a lot of the debris that we found on site. We didn't throw anything away. (203)

"We introduced new raised beds and planted up everything, and we had to repair the old pond - we couldn't keep it as it was because it was lined with lead. Where we could, we repaired the surfacing, just curving off edges of concrete where there were trip hazards. Some of the Friends of Cross Bones didn't like the limestone we used [on the raised beds]. 'Oh, it's so bright. We can't bear that'. I said, 'I'll paint it with yogurt mixed with moss, and it'll go black'. Within months it was starting to darken. It's got some lovely mosses, and icons on it now.

"Gradually, we opened up the site. People say, 'Oh yes, Helen John, she designed the garden'. I didn't. All I did was tweak it enough to allow for public access."

John Constable: "It's interesting that BOST has kept some of the features, like our rackety old gate that we used to use to enter the Invisible Garden – the section with 'Touch 4 Love' on it. It was John Betjeman's grandson who wrote it up there for his brother, who was having a hard time. It's a lovely story."

Zanna: "[In the early days] one of the people living here was John Lycett Green, who was John Betjeman's grandson. He was the person who did 'Touch 4 Love'. That's what I mean about the fragility of the contributions that people make to that ground. They're very easily erased and gone forever unless there's some protection of them or they're documented."

John Constable: "One thing I really tried to pass on to BOST is the idea of DIY things that come very much from the grassroots, from the bottom up. Somebody places an object of significance to them, and somebody else respects it, adds to it. This is how so many of the shrines appeared. The suicide shrine started with somebody writing 'For the suicides', and leaving one ring."

Matt Wilcock: "That was completely unexpected. That was ground-up, and people have added to it. The odd thing disappears, which is part of the give and take of the place. It's a layered site and, just as decomposition happens under the ground, it happens above – this sort of churn.

"When something new pops up, it's such a lovely surprise. An enormous rabbit appeared a couple of months ago – about 1.2 metres tall, looks like the rabbit from Alice in Wonderland, done in mosaic. Someone must have squeezed it through the railings of the gates and placed it there. It rests just next to the suicide shrine at the end of the gates."

Jen Cooper: "In the main, I think [the work BOST did there] is lovely. The things that Helen designed were very good. Given that one of the Goose's guises is a medieval prostitute, I always think how delighted she'd be to be tarted up. When she goes out selling herself, she can fucking mix with anybody!

"As she says in the poetry, 'I traded hard at every yard'. Yes! Let's show this garden to be what I believe it is: two thousand years of history from the bottom up in a place that's no bigger than a postage stamp! If you're open to the spirit of things, Cross Bones will take you down into the deepest misery of the pain that has been there, and also lift you up into transformation. That's why the garden is important for us. The garden is a symbol of transformation being possible."

Helen John: "It was a case of proving to TfL we can run this space and stop the antisocial behaviour they were concerned about. 'We can allow public access, we can make it safe. Just give us a chance.' If we'd gone in all guns blazing and said, 'This is our space, we're going to take it over', they wouldn't have liked that. I think the term 'Meanwhile Garden' was very important too, both for the community to know we weren't making changes that were irreversible, and also to give TfL the confidence to let us have a go.

"I've got some really freaky stories. We had a water leak at Cross Bones one day, and I was just sitting there thinking, 'Oh, God, how are we going to get this bloody hose to work?'. My phone rang and it's Nicola, my colleague from BOST. She said, 'I'm standing outside Cross Bones with this contractor from up the road'. So I let this guy in, show him the problem and he immediately says, 'Yes, I can sort that for you'.

"I talked to him later and he said, 'I was walking along Southwark Bridge Road and Google Maps just suddenly came up. My phone buzzed, and it had this arrow on Cross Bones. I wasn't even looking for it.' It's so strange. I've had so many professionals who've got in contact over the years, and offered their services. Cross Bones really does pull people in. It massively does. I'm not a superstitious person, but it's really weird the way it attracts people."

PlanetSlade, Twitter (March 8, 2015): "Fundraising preview at Cross Bones. Some 70 or 80 of us toured the site with John Constable – perhaps the biggest crowd to gather there for 100 years. The work's coming along nicely."

Helen John: "The events started almost straight away, because we didn't do the burials ourselves - we invited the community in to do that. That would have been in January 2015, before the site was even open. That's the first thing we did. We invited a priest to bless the bones, there was incense and prayers, and we buried all the bones on site. Wherever we could use the community, we did - we'd have planting days as well. We had a series of workshops to build the raised beds."

"We needed to say sorry"

July 2015: Southwark Cathedral blesses Cross Bones in what Dean Andrew Nunn calls "a service of regret, restoration and reconciliation". This becomes part of an annual Cross Bones event called Bards & Blessings.

Andrew Nunn: "We chose the feast day of Mary Magdalene [July 22] partly because we were probably going to get better weather to do something outside, but principally because she is mixed up in people's imagination with fallen women. Anything that's slightly saucy in the gospels gets dumped on Mary Magdalene. And, of course, there was this association between the bishops of Winchester, the Liberty, the Winchester Geese and the place where, in unconsecrated ground, these women were buried.

"We needed to say sorry that the church could licence these women as prostitutes in the Liberty, yet not allow them to be buried in consecrated ground. That's the double-headed way the church can act at times, and it needs to be called out. The purpose is to make public atonement as far as one can. We're not going to go and consecrate the land now because it's no longer an active graveyard and that wouldn't be appropriate, but I can go and sprinkle some holy water, cast some smoke around and hallow that space.

"There's a longish introduction so I can set the scene. There are some prayers, and a reading from John's gospel about Jesus meeting Mary Magdalene in the garden after his resurrection, which seems appropriate there. There's a lovely sonnet called *Mary Magdalen* by Mark Malcolm Guite who is the chaplain at Girton College in Cambridge. He gave us permission to use that. After that, I take the holy water and sprinkle the congregation and the ground. We sing one or two hymns and it finishes with a general blessing."

Matt Wilcock: "Consecration is seen almost as a get-out-of-jail-free card for the Church that the local community doesn't want to give. There's almost a status now to being unconsecrated and requiring this annual ritual of atonement from the church. Some people love that Cross Bones has got this nickname of the Graveyard of the Outcast Dead, and it's a point of pride for many of the wardens. I think there might be some resistance to consecration. It's not necessarily an advantage."

Andrew Nunn: "The group of people who gather at the blessings, some of them would be very definitely Christian, some would tick that box on a form but take it no further than that, and some are quite definitely pagan. I haven't been involved with the vigils because I don't want to give the wrong message about this quite sensitive business. When we go on the 22nd, we do our thing, and then we gracefully withdraw. They can do whatever they want after that."

Jen Cooper: "You've been to a vigil. It's the most different thing that anybody could do because we create a space. We expand our time into eternity. Not in a church or a temple, but in the middle of the street."

Joseph Bonner: "Andrew's going to be a hard act to follow. He's got very much into the spirit of it [with his annual service]. I think that's been a very healing episode, even though it's not an act of repentance as such: it's regret, restoration and reconciliation. The words are very well put together, as you'd expect from Andrew.

"Of course, in the time of the Bishop of Winchester we weren't really talking about an Anglican Church per se – so it's not really for the Anglican Church to make an apology in any case."

Andrew Nunn: "Last time [I did the reconciliation service at Cross Bones], there were about 100 people there. It's really moving to be able to stand there and to lead that service with such a large gathering of people who are there for folk none of us have ever met. They come with a common feeling of respect for people who may have been deemed less than respectable in life.

"We can't undo the wrongs of the past, but we can learn lessons from them and commit ourselves to doing better in the future. The worst thing we do is either to criminalise sex work or to try and ignore it and push it away - because that then pushes women into really dangerous situations. There's something to be said for the bishops of Winchester trying to control that trade in the parish - to give the women a level of recognition and hopefully some kind of protection. Where they failed was not continuing to offer that protection from this life into the next. Those women deserve respect."

Jen Cooper: "The Union of Sex Workers hold Cross Bones as their kind of heart space. Every so often we still get sex workers, male and female, come along and offer something at the vigils."

Laura Watson: "In the last few years, we've had people getting in contact with us to say they wanted more visibility for sex workers at Cross Bones. The most recent was a member of the sex worker community who wanted to do more on making the issue visible there when you went to visit. Talks are still going on and as far as I know BOST has been sympathetic.

"We appreciate that the site is preserved out of respect for the sex workers there. It's just to have that history made more visible really - to think about what those women faced, and relate that to the situation now. What we're always trying to do is to say, 'Look, sex workers are no different from other people in society'. Women are trying to make a living, trying to put food on the table, shoes on their children's feet, and just get by.

"It's just a job that's the best choice out of a bad set of choices – which would also have been the situation for the women buried at Cross Bones. Under very different circumstances, obviously, because things would've been much harder. But it would've been, for a lot of those women, a decision: 'This, for me, right now, is the best of a bad set of choices'."

Polly Blake: "There's a huge amount of meaning in Cross Bones. It's somewhere that has a lot of weight of history for sex workers. It's really valuable to have places we can go where we can feel a sense of history and [know that] people who've done this work before us have also been.

"Being invited to take up space in central London is always important for groups who traditionally do not get invited to do so. If you're a sex worker, there aren't many places where you can go to feel part of a community or sit with your thoughts, sit with your memories. There's so few spaces like that."

Matt Wilcock: "We had a sex worker from Sydney visit Cross Bones the other day. She was in London for three or four days and specifically carved out half a day to come here. It was almost a pilgrimage [for her]."

2022 graffiti spotted on Cross Bones fence: "Shout out to everyone lost. Neverending love for witches and whores."

"We made it a problem for them"

July 2017: TfL names U+I as its "preferred bidder for a joint venture to deliver a mixed-use development on the Landmark Court site". They plan to build 80 flats there, plus 130,000 sq ft of new commercial space. [(204)]

TfL release: "The Cross Bones Graveyard, a historic graveyard for prostitutes and paupers adjoining the site, will be safeguarded with a view to support a high quality memorial garden.[…] TfL is keen to see Bankside Open Spaces Trust (BOST) continue their tenancy and are in discussions with them to arrange a new lease."

John Constable: "Early developers, I think, were confident they'd be able to build on Cross Bones – complete denial that it had ever existed. I think the change of attitude since shows the power of the campaign. TfL were influenced by that. Any development immediately to the north will inevitably change the whole feel of the garden, but at least these developers were making an effort to engage with the history, to take on board the cultural significance of the Outcasts' Graveyard and to respond as best they could to our vision of a wild sanctuary in the heart of London."

Zanna: "They have to [respond] because we've made it a problem for them. With Friends of Cross Bones and 'This is still the Cross Bones Graveyard', we've said No and we continue to say No. But compromises have been made. And with every compromise, we're pushing further and further into a lack of clarity about the future."

BOST newsletter: "We are negotiating a long term future for Cross Bones as the garden becomes part of a larger development known as Landmark Court. At present we have a short term interim lease for the space, but are asking for a lease of the same length as Landmark Court, 299 years."

Joseph Bonner: "There was a lot of anxiety about U+I - would they match the stereotypical image of a developer and only be interested in commercial advantage? [...] I was trying to look at things in an objective manner and hopefully come to a win/win scenario."

"Protectors of children & unborn babies"

May 2019: Cross Bones installs a group of Mizuko Jizo statues. These follow a Japanese Buddhist tradition for those grieving a child lost to stillbirth, miscarriage or abortion. They'll later win Cross Bones a cameo in the US TV series Better Things.

BOST newsletter: "Mizuko Jizo [Water Baby] statues offer a place of contemplation and are believed to be protectors of children and unborn babies. In Japan, offerings are made to the statues and stones may be laid next to them for the souls of children. Our statues were created by local Bermondsey stone craftsman Josh Locksmith and are based on a painting of the Buddhist deity Jizo, believed to be responsible for transporting unborn babies or children to the other world. '

John Constable: "That's an example of a BOST initiative. It was something Katy and I mentioned to them. Two friends of Cross Bones had had miscarriages, and one of them wrote [to us asking if there was some way Cross Bones could commemorate the children they'd lost.] I'd lived in Japan for a year and Jizo was everywhere, often with those bibs around his neck or little hat. He was perfect. Helen really took it up, commissioned those statues, and other people made hats and things like that."

Matt Wilcock: "[Some filming requests we turn down – they're] just not in keeping with what the site is. With *Better Things*, it was the final episode of the latest series. In episode 10, they made their own Mizuko Jizo statues and then came and saw Cross Bones. That was publicising the site in a very respectful way. That did go ahead." [205]

Andrew Nunn: "You need to consider whether some filming there would actually promote it in a positive way. It's very tempting to grab everything when money is on offer but you could regret it later. Then again, some things can be surprisingly wonderful and productive. I think you take each thing on its merits."

Matt Wilcock: "It has to fit within our ethical framework. We had someone who was contemplating bringing artwork for the walls, but they were making jokes about sex workers while I was showing them round and I thought, 'Maybe not'. It's very much about asking why people are doing it. Give and take is fine, but just take is not."

"Anyone can be John Crow"
Summer 2019: Constable begins training other Cross Bones supporters in the rituals and practices he's found most valuable when conducting vigils at the site's gates.

John Constable: "I held two workshops called Urban Magic in a beautiful old warehouse at the top of Redcross Way, then we processed to the graveyard. The aim of that was to give people a sense of how I worked with the Goose, and specifically a sense of how to conduct the vigils. What I'd learned is you have to get out of the way if you're going to channel the Goose. There is something quite wild and powerful that comes through and if you get in the way of that, you can get quite fucked up. If people start trying to use the Goose for their own power, well, that's at their own risk.

"I said one thing that later caused a bit of a stir. I said that anyone can be John Crow - that when you conduct the vigil you're John Crow channeling the Goose. It was said very playfully, but I think some people thought I was trying to impose John Crow on their personalities. These are the complexities of it."

Joseph Bonner: "I'm a fan of John. I love his passion and his creative talent – he's a great performer too. We miss him at the vigils, but Jen and others are doing an excellent job leading proceedings there now."

Jen Cooper: "John created what he called the Magical Collective: a shamanic work thing where he taught people how to run a vigil, what to do, ways to work. **It** was a group of about ten. Three of us were women, but the other two left very quickly. I became the only woman in there. Most of the others didn't want to stand at the gates and do the talking. They were happy being the Goose Samurai or doing other things, but they wanted to be in the background.

"[My role at the vigils is] not to be shy, that's all. I've got enough experience to know that whatever nerves I feel, that's just stage fright - it's not me. John would say 'As the voice, we are nothing. The Goose is speaking through us'. He used to say, 'Get yourself out of the way. Get yourself out the way'. He would say 'Get in touch with the John Crow spirit'. That's OK if you're a bloke, but to me the Goose and I are sisters. We're one: the Goddess and I are one. Instead of pushing myself out the way, I get bigger - and then down comes the Goose. We've all got slightly different approaches to it. We make space there for people to do whatever they want to do."

John Constable: "Jen, I suppose, was the nearest thing I had to a disciple. Not that I ever asked for disciples, but she's the only one who called me her shaman. She's been one of the prime movers in keeping the vigils going. Jen does it her way. It's very important to her.

"I never put it on anyone to say, 'You've got to keep the vigils going'. I feel 'Well, if they stop, that's fine. Something else will happen instead'. I like the idea that people learn the rituals I've passed down, because I do think they can hold you. But I also like the idea that people improvise. In a sense, that's what I always did when I was working with the Goose."

Jen Cooper: "During the Covid lockdown, I didn't go because I'm a bit older - but four or five people including Zanna kept up a human presence every single 23rd. When I say we've been standing at the gates every single month for 19 years, I'm telling the truth. When we started coming back after lockdown, I was the last woman standing so I became the Madam of Ceremonies. My thing is 'I might be too old to be a goose, mate, but you're never too old to be a madam!'."

Joseph Bonner: "The vigils can be very moving. I try to bring different people as often as I can. You never know who you might meet on the 23rd of each month: I was there once and there was a special adviser to the Prime Minister that I knew. I thought, 'What are you doing here?'" [206]

"I wouldn't have survived another winter"

November 2019: Constable leads a final Goose Night vigil at the gates, then takes a further step back from Cross Bones. Soon, he and Katy would relocate to Glastonbury.

Jen Cooper: "We had 250 people in the street for John's final Goose Night. We had the Dark Morris with Morris dancing. That was amazing."

John Constable: "I'd almost died on a visit to Ireland in 2019. In London I was living in a Georgian attic with one storage heater and draughty sash windows, climbing 46 steps every time I came home. I have COPD and asthma, and I wouldn't have survived another winter in that freezing garret. We got a big kick up the arse because the landlord's tanks in our flat burst on day two of [the UK's Covid] lockdown. Katy and I were looking to move out of London anyway. We'd saved Cross Bones but the rest of our neighbourhood was well and truly fucked.

"All those streets were so deeply interwoven with *The Southwark Mysteries* and with Cross Bones that [without the move] I would've continued to be involved. With hindsight, I think I'd have been dragged right into the middle of a whole bunch of contention. Even getting it at long distance wasn't helpful. It was very stressful, some of that. The trouble was often the requests for advice. I'd give advice and that would set off an argument, and then the arguments would get more and more vituperative. Eventually, I said, 'No, I'm not going to reply'. It was important to move because we couldn't have taken Cross Bones out of our daily life in Southwark.

"Everybody in Glastonbury has a magical story about how they come to be living here, and I certainly do. We came for my birthday, intending to stay a week, and by the time we left we'd actually taken a place here without really planning in advance to do that. What could have been a chaotic and very fraught period went incredibly smoothly, and we found ourselves living in a place we really love."

Matt Wilcock: "John Constable's story is a success story. He handed Cross Bones over to a large charity which has carried on looking after it, pretty much within his line of ethics and moral code for the site. It's a good succession story."

John Constable: "The other side of saying 'the Goose is loose' was the idea that I could then explore a different aspect of working with her in a new environment. She'll always be my spirit guide. In those early days when we moved here during lockdown, I'd walk the Goose around empty streets of Glastonbury: 'Let's introduce you to the locals, the spirits'.

"I'd always liked having the grit of inner London to ground me, so I was concerned that if I came to Glastonbury I'd just drift off into the ether. That hasn't actually happened. There is a lot of completely bonkers stuff – and some quite dark stuff - happening here, but you learn to navigate it. For someone who's always been inspired by myth and legend, it's a wonderful place to live.

"We didn't know it when we took the house, but we're actually on the corner of what used to be Gropecunt Lane and Cock Lane, so it's almost the same setup as Southwark. The Abbey is two minutes from where we live, literally just up the road. All this would once have been sacred ground but by about the 13th century they'd walled in the Abbey - so you get the sacred and then you get the very profane. [Where we live is the old] Red Light district, which seems a wonderful affirmation."

"Thirty years doesn't cut it"

January 2021: BOST announces that the details of its new lease with TfL are now agreed. The term set for the new arrangement is 30 years.

Helen John: "Cross Bones became a bargaining chip. They said to Southwark Council, 'If you give us permission for our housing/retail complex, we'll give you Cross Bones as a garden of remembrance. BOST said, 'That's lovely, but we want more than 30 years. We want it in perpetuity'. Essentially, what we were asking for is the same lease length [as TfL gave the developers], which is 299 years. We fought really hard for that at various planning meetings. The concession we did get was getting the lease under the 1954 Tenant's Act, which basically means that we've got an automatic right to renew."

Jen Cooper: "Thirty years is not long enough because they can so easily renege on that. It should be in perpetuity. It should be the same 299 years as the developers have got. That's my opinion."

Zanna: "Thirty years doesn't cut it. Part of our 'This is still the Cross Bones graveyard' campaign is about saying, 'This is not over'. That's the thing I kept saying to John: 'We've not won it yet. Thirty years has got very little meaning to the importance of protecting that ground for the future. Thirty years is not a win'."

John Constable: "I'd have liked a 299-year lease. That's what we pushed for. But I see Cross Bones existence as partly incremental. Twenty years ago, it didn't exist, then it existed as an idea, now it exists as something real. Who knows if London will be here in 30 years? It could all be underwater."

Matt Wilcock: "That 30-year lease was a compromise between us wanting 299 years and them offering, I think, 10 years initially. Thirty years isn't bad. It's long enough to be allowed to [continue our work on the site] and have the community put trust in a charity like BOST to fund larger works."

Helen John: "The fact that TfL were seriously looking at developing the site back in the '90s - that's not that long ago. That's 30 years ago, so add on another 30 years, it could still be under threat unless we keep going."

Jen Cooper: "I'm 72, so with a 30-year lease I'm going to be 102 when it finishes. On a very personal level, I've got it for life. But I'm also a grandmother and I am trying to defend the Earth for my grandchildren. For me to die with the reassurance that my grandchildren will be able to go there and visit their great uncle Gary and great grandad Chris and everybody, all of the outcasts …" [She trails away, becoming slightly tearful].

Guardian (February 22, 2022): "The largest expanse of Roman mosaic found in London for more than half a century has been unearthed at a site believed to have been a venue for high-ranking officials to lounge in while being served food and drink. Dating from the late second century to the early third century, the mosaic's flowers and geometric patterns were a thrilling, once-in-a-lifetime find, said Antonietta Lerz, of Museum of London Archaeology. […] The site is being redeveloped as The Liberty of Southwark, a complex of offices, homes and shops."

Charlotte Gilsenen: "The 30-year lease [won't start its term] until they've begun the actual development work at the Liberty site, so we've extended the interim lease. There's a delay due to the ruins that they've found. They're very rare and they need to protect them."

"La Catrina was part of social satire"
October 2021: Cross Bones installs a statue of La Catrina, the symbol of Mexico's annual Day of the Dead festival, for permanent display there. The statue is a gift from the Mexican Embassy.

BOST newsletter: "La Catrina is drawn from a sketch by Mexican illustrator Jose Guadalupe Poseda in around 1910. A satirical artist, the frequent use of skulls in his political cartoons suggested the message 'underneath, we are all the same'. […] Now La Catrina is synonymous with Day of the Dead celebrations, a reminder that the dead should be celebrated and not feared."

Fernando Champion: "[The ambassador] came across Cross Bones while walking in Southwark one day, fell in love with the place, then got to know the team and the history behind it. She said, 'I want to do something. I want to work with them.' Our current government in Mexico is very socially oriented. It's a very similar perspective to Cross Bones – the fact that so many people have been neglected for so long, not just in our country but everywhere, including London.

"Cross Bones is very emotionally charged, and that's why the ambassador wanted to do something there. Southwark's important to her because there's a big Mexican community living there, so it just felt natural. The first thing we were interested in was helping to make the site more visible. [We wanted] to start working on how we can bring those people's stories back, give them a voice and give future generations hope that things can change."

Isabela Nieto Castro: "The figure of La Catrina was part of social satire in the beginning. It's about how a lot of Mexican women were trying to adapt to European stereotypes, like the dresses and big hats. It started as Poseda's drawing making fun of this trait of wanting to deny your roots and go for the westernised world. Through time and tradition, she became a symbol that we're all going to die, so be true to yourself and don't take things so seriously."

Polly Blake: "I found La Catrina really interesting – I just was not expecting that at all. My brother used to live in Mexico. I went out and visited him and learned a tiny bit about Mexican culture. Cross Bones has the ability to be home to so many radically different groups and ideas - it's really fascinating.

"I love the little shrines to the Virgin Mary too. I love the idea of people being able to go and have quiet moments of reflection there. With a space that's meant for peace and reflection and meditation, it almost doesn't matter what the image is. It's more about the curation of a space [where people feel] able to do that."

Fernando Champion: "It's very linked emotionally and symbolically. For us, the Day of the Dead is a very special day, when our loved ones come back from the other side for one day and get to eat their favourite food and spend time with us. Cross Bones is a truly magical place. The work they've down to rescue this space and transform it is something the ambassador's very interested in. Transforming a space like that in order to transform lives is what really brought us together."

Helen John: "I worked with the Mexican embassy before I left the project. If we can build on those contacts going forward, that's the thing that will save Cross Bones. Not the fact that there are 15,000 bodies in there, because we know that a bulldozer could go in there, lift those bodies and move them. That's not going to save it. The only thing that will save it is to keep it politically really hot, and up there on the agenda."

Andrew Nunn: "It's fascinating how the Mexican ambassador is now involved. All of that high profile stuff would never have happened without making the site better and making it more accessible for people to move around there. So that's all to the good."

John Constable: "One thing I'm really delighted BOST has done is to develop this relationship with the Mexican embassy. Long before we really had any recognition, I used to talk about Cross Bones as a World Heritage site, because I'm a believer that if you say what something should be, sometimes it becomes it. That kind of affirmation does work magically."

"The forum? That's finished"

December 2020: Bonner resigns as a BOST trustee, citing concerns about the organisation's decision-making procedures. Now no longer chairing, he mentions his concerns in June 2021's forum meeting, which turns out to be quite a stormy affair. BOST closes down the forum a few weeks later.

Joseph Bonner: "I didn't go into the detail of anything, but I did raise the matter. […] It was Cornwall, the G7. It was not at all an ideal time for me to attend that meeting. I was walking up and down with the EU delegation, trying to deal with issues while [maintaining] a Zoom connection." [207]

John Constable: "After [Katy and I] moved on, several long-standing supporters staged a very public attack on BOST during a 'Jackie Weaver' style Zoom forum, after which BOST understandably wound it up. BOST is open to criticism for the way it handled the situation, but I still broadly support the way they are trying to manifest and embed the vision of the garden." [208]

Charlotte Gilsenan: "We had a significant amount of people complaining about the meeting and saying they didn't want to attend again, so we took the decision."

Natalie Boatfield: "The forum was shut down without explanation or justification. […] All community meetings are a lively discussion and it should be seen as a joy that the community has such strong views and ideas."

Joseph Bonner: "From a local point of view of democracy and consultation, the forum was a very good medium. […] To me, Cross Bones is so special it needs very careful handling, and I think the forum was allowing that to happen in a very positive way. I mean, even John and Katy were probably quite frustrated at some points, but they actually believed in it."

Jen Cooper: "That partnership between Friends of Cross Bones and BOST as expressed through the forum? That's finished. We had the forum and we were all in it together. Collectively, we decided on what was going on. Friends of Cross Bones and other people who are interested in Cross Bones could come together and communally decide on the future. To me, that was a perfect expression of how the community could own Cross Bones."

[Shortly after the June forum meeting there was a face-to-face encounter at Cross Bones itself, where one of the site's most committed campaigners lost their temper over BOST's unilateral

decision to close the forum. The campaigner involved admits shouting at one of BOST's staff during this incident, but says things went no further than that.]

"We have taken advice from the police"

October 2021: BOST e-mails Natalie Boatfield, Joseph Bonner, Jen Cooper and Zanna, banning them from entering Cross Bones' grounds and removing them from mail lists. One year on, when I conduct my new interviews, the anger and hurt sparked by this ban is still very evident.

The BOST letter (version 1): "Our staff, colleagues and partners have experienced a sustained pattern of aggressive and/or abusive behaviour in relation to Crossbones and the Liberty of Southwark site. This is unacceptable and potentially dangerous, and we have taken advice from our security team and the police.

"Accordingly, we are suspending your participation in all Crossbones related activities with immediate effect, including accessing Crossbones Graveyard and mailings.

"This suspension will continue until such time that we are confident that any future inclusion will be harmonious, productive, and not harmful to the future of Crossbones and all the Staff, Wardens, Volunteers, Friends, Contractors, Consultants and Visitors to the graveyard."

The BOST letter (version 2): "Our staff and colleagues have experienced a sustained pattern of disruptive and counter-productive behaviour, in relation to Crossbones." [209]

Zanna: "The fact is that Cross Bones is a public space fought for by the public, and the charity that's now running it sent out letters saying, 'You're no longer permitted to go on it'!. We're in the middle of trying to ascertain on what grounds they could do that – because, if they can do it to us, they can do it to anyone. The letter was very aggressive."

Natalie Boatfield replies to the BOST letter: "It is extremely insulting after 15 years of work to save the site – and Zanna's 25 years – to be accused and threatened in this way without any explanation, justification or [attempt] to resolve the situation. […] Let me clearly state, we feel discriminated against, we feel excluded and we feel like outsiders in our local community. I know I speak not only for Zanna and myself but also others such as Jen, Joseph and anyone else in the community who does not feel heard."

Joseph Bonner: "My own [e-mail] didn't give any specific reason for the ban, didn't give any rationale, didn't actually say under what authority BOST was acting to ban people."

Charlotte Gilsenan: "All I can say is that I need to protect the safety of my staff. […] "[The exclusions] were very much a temporary thing until everything settled down and we could bring people back in. Jen, for example has reapplied to be a warden and been accepted. It was a temporary thing so we could move on in a more fruitful manner than had previously happened." [210]

Joseph Bonner: "We've had communication from LandSec saying we are no longer banned. But I and others have said, 'Well, I think we need to have that from the organisation that banned us in the first place – and maybe some explanation, please'."

Zanna: "We put up a poster when we were banned [using BOST's exclusion letter as a gag across the skull's mouth]. We were amazed it didn't get ripped down, but I think it was too ironic for people."

"It's good advertising for them - a brand"

Spring 2022: Developer's boards appear round the Liberty of Southwark site aiming to exploit the area's outlaw reputation. How many "rebels and reformers" will be able to afford a flat there remains to be seen.

The Southwark Mysteries: "Come Heretic, Outlaw, / Jack Craw and Jack Daw, / Here shall ye all find Sanctuary, / Where the Actors and

Whores, / Are the Keepers of Doors, / That open into the Liberty."

Liberty of Southwark hoardings: "Come, Skylarkers & Square Pegs. Assemble, Rebels & Reformers. [...] Take your places, impresarios, creators and contraveners. The Liberty lives on."

John Constable: "I think any relationship with a developer is bound to be complicated for me and I certainly have mixed feelings when they paraphrase my poetry. I never wrote it to sell flats, but there it is. I've noticed the developers have piggy-backed on some of my ideas: 'Come Skylarkers and Square Pegs' is a clunky paraphrase of 'Come, heretic, outlaw...'. And they've even renamed the development The Liberty of Southwark. Iain Sinclair once observed that he'd opened up Shoreditch and Whitechapel to the developers by giving them a 'boho' glamour. My work has been used in a similar way in Southwark."

Matt Wilcock: "Cross Bones as a name and a brand is such a boon to a developer. I've heard developers say, 'We've got art students around the corner, we've got Cross Bones there'. They really hit the trendy area angle. It's good advertising for them – it's a brand. Some of our wardens grumble about it a bit: 'They've stolen our identity'. But everyone likes to be a bit of a rebel."

Joseph Bonner: "The fact that they now see Cross Bones as something to be celebrated rather than a group of 'awkward squad' neighbours means they can actually see the potential of it. When [the development] is completed, whether it's retail or residential or office, the people who are there will see Cross Bones as a great asset and be intrigued by its story."

Jen Cooper: "They're trying to make their living off Cross Bones' back. It's cynical."

"You've managed a graveyard before..."
June 2022: Matt Wilcock joins BOST to work as Cross Bones' engagement manager.

Matt Wilcock: "I'd just moved down from Hull, where I'd turned a graveyard that had become a dumping ground for rubbish into a functional garden again. I found it on the first day of lockdown when I'd just moved there, so I started litter-picking just to keep sane. That became a fully-fledged non-profit company which looked after that graveyard and other spaces in Hull. I applied for a community gardening job with BOST, but I was unaware of Cross Bones at the time. They said, 'Well, we've actually got this job coming up at Cross Bones. You've managed a graveyard before, so...'.

"Now I'm at BOST full time. I have two jobs there: I manage the garden at Cross Bones, but I also do the events, the communications, managing the volunteer warden and all that brings with it. We have a pool of 50 wardens, about ten of whom are active every week. Over the course of a month, we normally get 16, maybe 20 wardens in. We also have a team that's doing online promotion, but that's in its early days."

Helen John: "I wrote Matt's job description. Cross Bones didn't need a landscape architect anymore, because the work had been done to make it publicly accessible. What it needed was an engagement manager, to up those visitor numbers, get loads of people across the globe involved. Let's start making sure the books are written about it, that it appears on blogs, that it's really very well known locally and internationally. That's the only way you're going to protect it."

Matt Wilcock: "Once I was in post, John forwarded one of the requests that came in to his website and said, 'Could you deal with this? By the way, I'm John – you're always welcome to come and visit me in Glastonbury.' So I took him up on the offer and went to see him and Katy. I remember thinking from the very first email, 'This is a very different character to the shaman presented to me'. They were business emails."

John Constable: "I've met Matt a couple of times and he does seem to 'get' Cross Bones".

Charlotte Gilsenan: "Our vision is to make Cross Bones an inclusive space for everyone. That's the key objective. Since Matt's come along, he's got lots of different organizations and individuals involved in the space who are coming from quite a diverse background."

Matt Wilcock: "The key question to really ask volunteers is, 'What do you want to get out of this?'. Some don't find Cross Bones' history that interesting. Some just want to learn some horticulture. But we also get a lot of wardens who have been struck by the site's history and want to get something out of it in that sense. Some people want to make the site more public, some people feel moved by the history. Some just open the site and say, 'Welcome' quietly, but don't offer tours. Some like to take everyone by the hand and point out every nook and cranny. It's a slightly make-of-it-what-you-will activity.

"Another part of my job has been to welcome the local residents. We had a residents' morning just for people living in the local tower blocks with no green space to say, 'Look, this is your space'. We posted on all the local sites, social media, and so forth. We had 70 people come through the gates that morning. We're open on Wednesday, Thursday and Friday, but if you work on those days, you may have lived within 200 metres of the space for years and never been inside. This whole new audience, who had been so close by, were really moved [by the Cross Bones story]. That was nice. There was a flood of offers of volunteering from that group of people, because they're just round the corner: 'Of course I can do it'. That was a real success."

"A microcosm of Roman London"

June 2023: Archaeologists on the Liberty of Southwark site discover the ruins there to be a Roman mausoleum. The resulting preservation work means the next phase of access improvements at Cross Bones must wait till 2024/25.

Guardian (June 13, 2023): "The remains of a Roman mausoleum 'with an astonishing level of preservation' – believed to be the most intact structure of its kind discovered in Britain – have been unearthed in London. The 'incredibly rare' find has been excavated at the Liberty of Southwark development site, the Museum of London Archaeology has revealed.

215

"The level of preservation of the interior makes this the most intact Roman mausoleum ever to be discovered in Britain, according to MOLA, which led the archaeological investigations. Although the tomb was almost completely dismantled, probably during the medieval period, the signs are it was a substantial building, perhaps two storeys high, and would have been used by wealthier Romans, possibly as a family tomb."

Andrew Nunn: "The fact that they've been uncovering so much history on that site with the mosaic floors and all those kind of things shows that it's not just waste ground. It's ground that bears the marks of a complex history round here."

Polly Blake: "It's a place of real, urban historical importance. Somewhere that has a lot of really fascinating history."

Matt Wilcock: "The legal designation of Cross Bones is currently private land with controlled public opening hours, and it's going to become public land with controlled opening hours. It's going to be entering Southwark's green space plan more permanently [but] to become public land, it needs to be made safe in many areas.

"It's only ground-up work. We're getting a custom designed Cross Bones concrete layer put on top so it's all smooth and wheelchair accessible. We'll get a couple of ramps. We're getting a second entrance put in on the other side, which will link Cross Bones to a public green space. We'll be a closed site [for up to a year], but we're planning a couple of events and trails to keep the site in locals' minds. It will be closed, but activity doesn't fully stop."

Helen John: "Where we're putting in electricity for the new Cross Bones enhancements, we will put in trunking along the top if we can. If not, then there might be a little bit of digging, but we're hoping this can happen outside the boundary, on The Liberty of Southwark side."

Matt Wilcock: "The architect is talking about Victorian railings where the hoardings now are, with ivy growing on them. You'd be able to slightly see through [into the site]. No change to the gates. We're extending the flower beds. We're hoping for a cobblestone path which invites people to walk around, but also to have little cracks in it for what we call the Outcast Planting Plan. The idea is that weeds are essentially the outcasts of the natural world, so we get our volunteer gardeners to water all the cracks."

"Is Cross Bones' future now secure?"

That was my closing question to all the interviewees. These are the answers they gave.

John Constable: "I'm pretty sanguine actually. During the many setbacks and serious threats we've seen over the years, Katy and I would say to each other, 'Yes, but it's seen a lot worse than this'. This ground's been repeatedly raped. Now it's a garden. It's the flower of Southwark"

Joseph Bonner: "[If anyone tried to build over Cross Bones now] I think there would be a campaign. I don't know if people would chain themselves to the gates, but I wouldn't be at all surprised. I think the work that Friends of Cross Bones have done over the years, showing real tenacity, has been a fantastic example of how to square up to commercial interests."

Andrew Nunn: "I feel a lot more confident than I did, because the current developers seem so keen to draw on the history of the area. There is a real interest in the Cross Bones story. It's very much known out there. I doubt there could be something that would actually remove it. You can never tell, but I think there would be a very adverse reaction not just in London, not just in Southwark but [far beyond]. I think what would be a shame would be if it was sanitised by being made too beautiful – if it didn't have all that cracked concrete and all the homemade elements of it, you'd lose something."

Jen Cooper: "I think Cross Bones till needs fighting for."

Matt Wilcock: "I think it's 90% secure. This is why we're always inviting people who have sway over these decisions to build ties with us just in case - because until that 30-year lease is signed, I'll still occasionally feel tetchy."

Helen John: "Following Covid and everything else, people understand how important open spaces are as places for reflection, so I don't think they would ever get planning permission for Cross Bones now. It just wouldn't happen. There'd be so much community backlash. There've been plenty of other burial grounds around the UK where the bodies have been exhumed and development has happened [but] the difference is that Cross Bones endures in the memory of the people who live locally. I think that's the difference: it's not a forgotten burial ground."

Zanna: "The thing that's important to me is not a piece of poetry, it's not a play. It's that the land remains a piece of open land for people to enjoy forever. I don't see any reason why that aim is not achievable. The fight isn't over. Please get involved."

Sources & endnotes

Chapter 1: Roman Southwark

1) *The Bishop's Brothels,* by EJ Burford (Robert Hale Ltd, 1976). I've drawn very heavily on Burford's book for the first half of this narrative. For anyone with an interest in the seamier side of London history - Southwark's history in particular - it's an essential and hugely entertaining read.

2) Even bakers and cookshops had slaves for this purpose - known as the elicariae - who were sent out to the roadside selling cakes shaped like male and female genitalia. The understanding was that anyone selling these cakes would double as a prostitute when necessary. Competing with them were the independent sex workers Romans called noctiluces ("night moths") and those prepared to accept even the lowest copper coin in circulation for their services - the quadrantariae.

3) The stola, a long pleated dress, was seen as the mark of a respectable woman in Rome and for a prostitute to wear one would have been considered serious misrepresentation. This idea would return with the 12th century ban on sex workers wearing aprons.

4) *Underground London*, by Stephen Smith (Abacus, 2004).

5) Isis' son Horus – known to the Romans as Harpocrates – was worshipped in Southwark too. Here's Burford on the rites observed at his festivals: "Crowds of crazed women would dance and cavort, exposing themselves stark naked and copulating publicly with all comers. Females would hang garlands on the god's enormous penis, as many as they had had lovers the previous night. Often, the penis would be completely ringed and covered from sight with the offerings of a single woman."

Chapter 2: Arriving at the Vigil

6) The lights are a Southwark Council art project, unveiled in August 2008.

7) My notes from that night read: "*Guardian*-reading, cat-loving, vaguely mystical types, often quite mumsy. Kind-hearted and well-meaning. Not as nutty as you might imagine - no fancy dress. Handful of men only. One well-groomed hippy type with long hair and beard. A Japanese girl. Some quite young women: 20s rather than 30s."

8) Author's interview at Nelson's café, Southwark, November 2012.

9) Constable has since written that his early Goose visions – including this first encounter – were "triggered by huge doses of LSD" but warns others not to follow his example. "This was absolutely NOT a recreational drug trip," he stressed in one of our e-mail exchanges. "I'd spent more than a month planning it, and an entire day preparing

myself physically and psychically. [...] Without these disciplines, I may not have survived the experience."

10) *The Southwark Mysteries*, by John Constable (Oberon Books, 1999).

11) Cross Bones is, quite literally, just around the corner from an excellent little London theatre called the Menier. Whenever I went to a play there, I'd nip out to Redcross Way during the interval to see if anything interesting had been added to the gates since my last visit. The Menier's won a huge reputation for its staging of Stephen Sondheim musicals and Sondheim himself has visited the theatre several times. I often wonder if anyone there ever took this opportunity to show him Cross Bones, as I think the site would have appealed to him.

12) All the Guadalupe and Santa Muerte decorations were carefully removed and taken home after the night's celebrations, as they would certainly have been stolen otherwise. One of my favourite examples of the gentle humour often expressed at Cross Bones was the crocheted ornament attached to its gates in 2011, mounted on a cardboard surround warning: "Crochet thieves operate in this area".

Chapter 3: Laying Siege

13) If you're wondering how to pronounce "Southwark", just add a "k" to the end of "mother" and make it rhyme with that. It's "Suhth-erk", with a slight emphasis on the first syllable.

14) About half of William's army was made up of foreign mercenaries, most of them Flemish, and this may explain how Flemish women later gained such a strong hold over Southwark's brothels.

15) From the BBC website's *Christianity in Britain*.

16) Author's interview at Southwark's John Harvard Library, November 2012. This library's named after the founder of Harvard University, whose family once owned a Borough High Street coaching inn called the Queen's Head. He left Southwark for Boston in 1637 after the rest of his family was wiped out by plague.

17) The Church made this problem even worse in 1129 when it ruled that all priests must in future be celibate. Priests who were already married were told to evict their wives from the family home, putting yet another wave of destitute women on the streets.

Chapter 4: Samhain at the Gates

18) *Honouring The Outcast Dead: The Cross Bones Graveyard*, by Dr Adrian Harris (Fieldwork in Religion, Volume 8, number 2 (2013)..

19) Jen, I later discovered, was Jennifer Cooper, nick-named "Gin Jen" for another of her duties at the vigil. We'll meet her again later in the book.

---

20) Quote taken from JandBFrench's short YouTube film *Where The Prostitutes Were Buried in London*.

21) Some people never did find the right moment to read out their own ribbon, either because they were slightly embarrassed at the procedure or because they were reluctant to pipe up when others were talking. I think some people decided to take their ribbons home as souvenirs rather than attach them to the gates - something I was sorely tempted to do myself.

22) It was only after the ceremony ended that I noticed I'd been so intent on making sure the knot in Eliza's ribbon held firmly, that I'd managed to tie it right in the middle of her name. Fortunately, the age and date draped down nicely on either side of the knot, so I smoothed those into place instead.

23) The knots required often make it hard to read the full details on any Cross Bones ribbon, either in photographs or on the gates themselves. I have managed to transcribe a few though: "February 14th, 1785. Jane Jollif, a widow, aged 41 years"; "July 1840. Elizabeth Lade, Hart Inn, Age 1 year 6 months"; "Winter 1837, William Pearce"; "23rd October, 1833. Jane Stevens, Union Street, two years old"; "October 31st, 1728. Sarah Whitehead"; "December 25th, 1726. Mary, wife of George Wilson, a carpenter".

24) Letter to the *Times*, November 10, 1883. Brabazon was his own era's most doughty campaigner for Cross Bones – a Victorian John Constable, you could say. I like to imagine he might have had his own visitation from the Goose all those years ago.

25) One Friends of Cross Bones supporter has proposed a monument to Britain's prostitutes as part of any memorial garden that's eventually built there. His design shows Christine Keeler in her famous "backwards chair" pose.

26) A Book of Hours was a medieval volume collecting the particular prayers to be recited at each of the day's seven canonical hours: Matins, Prime, Terce, Sext, Nones, Vespers and Compline. The idea was that lay Christians could use these books to copy the daily routine of a monastery.

27) Cheap gin was one of the very few comforts available to the women destined for a Cross Bones burial and that's why it's become so central to the site's rituals. Gin's popularity among women later gave it the nickname "mother's ruin".

28) St Saviour's parish workhouse was in Mint Street, which lies just 300 yards from Cross Bones. This area was "surrounded with every possible nuisance, physical and moral," the *Lancet* wrote in 1865.

29) Posting in response to a 2008 Cross Bones video on YouTube, an archaeologist using the name Kuniklos reported finding a monastery well containing the bones of newborn babies. The team's conclusion

was that mothers whose illegitimate babies had died without baptism used the well to "bury" their bodies. "The well was on abbey property, so it's as close as the little ones would get to a proper burial," Kuniklos says.

30) Thomas Hardy's 1891 novel *Tess of the d'Urbervilles* has a scene showing just how much pain this issue could cause. When Tess's baby dies before it can be baptised, she refuses to accept the vicar's ruling that it must be buried in unconsecrated ground. "The baby was carried in a small deal box, under an ancient woman's shawl, to the churchyard that night and buried by lantern-light, at the cost of a shilling and a pint of beer to the sexton," Hardy writes. How many dead babies made their way to St Saviour's own churchyard under similar circumstances, I wonder?

31) Exchange of e-mails, November/December 2012. Boulton added that fully half of Newcastle's burials in the late 18th and early 19th centuries took place in the city's unconsecrated Ballast Hills graveyard for reasons of cost.

32) There's a scene is Charles Dickens' *Bleak House* where Lady Dedlock and Jo, a young crossing guard, visit a ramshackle pauper graveyard much like Cross Bones. When Lady Dedlock asks Jo if the ground is "blessed", he replies: "Blest? It ain't done it much good if it is. Blest? I should think it was t'othered myself."

Chapter 5: Birth of the Liberty

33) This principle gives us benefit of clergy and Psalm 51's role as the "neck verse". At a time when literacy was rare, simply showing you could read was taken as ample proof you were a member of the clergy. By reading Psalm 51 aloud in court ("Oh God, have mercy upon me."), a defendant could establish the secular courts had no right to try him and so escape a possible sentence of hanging. The principle was later extended to anyone who could read - clergy or not - and saved Ben Jonson's life when he was charged with manslaughter in 1598. Benefit of clergy's scope was steadily eroded over the following 200 years, but it wasn't finally abolished in Britain until 1827.

34) "These estates were later to become known as 'the Liberty of the Bishop of Winchester'," Burford continues. "Indeed, they may have been so designated even at this early date, but contemporary records are lost."

35) In the 225 years from 1330 to 1555, England had six Bishops of Winchester who were also Lord Chancellor, accounting for 29 years of the Chancellorship between them. Outside the royal family itself, only the Lord High Steward of England had more power than the Lord Chancellor.

36) When Burford's book was published in 1976, many scientists

thought syphilis may have been present (though unidentified) in Europe as early as the sixth century. But a 2011 study produced convincing evidence that the disease was brought to Europe by sailors returning from the Americas after Christopher Columbus's 1492 voyage. Atlanta's Emory University analysed 54 published reports identifying syphilis in skeletons from before 1492, but concluded that either the diagnosis or the bones' own dating was mistaken in every case.

37) Bishops had other ways of profiting from sexual desire in this era too. Priests at the time were technically celibate, but could pay the Bishop ruling their diocese a fee called a couillage which licensed them to keep a servant called a hearth girl living in their house. These girls, as Burford puts it, "kindled other fires as well". Rabelais, with his characteristic frankness, called these fees "bollock money".

38) Dr Johnson did much of the work on his 1755 dictionary while staying at the Anchor on Bankside, so he knew the area well. Defining a stew as "a brothel [or] house of prostitution", he adds: "This signification is by some imputed to this, that there were licensed brothels near the stews or fishponds in Southwark; but probably stew, like bagnio, took a bad signification from bad use." One of the sources Johnson cites for this is Act 5, Scene 1 of Shakespeare's *Measure for Measure*, where the punning Duke Vincentio says: "I have seen corruption boil and bubble / 'Till it o'er run the stew".

39) "Centuries later, Charles II was enraged to discover that his parliamentary supporters were in the brothels when they should have been [voting]," Burford says. "One of the King's vital measures was lost as a result."

40) *The Medieval Castle in England & Wales: A Political & Social History*, by Norman Pounds (Cambridge University Press, 1990).

41) The Bishop's court officials may also have been keen to crack down on low-level corruption among constables and bailiffs to prevent bribes being skimmed off at that stage. Only if a case came to trial could the court's officials hope to be bribed instead.

42) London's had many colourful street names which owe their origins to medieval prostitution. The most notorious example is Gropecunt Lane, an alleyway off Cheapside first recorded under that name in 1279. It was flanked by Bordhawe Lane (known for the sex workers who lodged there) and Puppekirty Lane (Poke-skirt Lane), but all three have since been obliterated by development. Oxford's Magpie Lane and Norwich's Opie Street were both once known as Gropecunt Lane too and for precisely the same reason. The name didn't finally fall out of use in Britain until 1561.

43) Fifteenth century Paris had Rue Grattecon, Rue Poilecon and Rue Trousse-Puteyne. Readers are cordially invited to translate these names for themselves.

44) *Encyclopedia of Prostitution & Sex Work Volume 1*, by Melissa Hope Ditmore (Greenwood Publishing, 2006).

45) Early forms of condom were available in England in the 1600s, but they never caught on in the Bankside brothels. Throughout the stew-house era, Bankside's girls relied on little more than a good hard piss and a wipe-cloth soaked in wine or vinegar to protect themselves from pregnancy and VD alike.

46) Southwark's Lock Hospital, located less than a mile from the Bankside stews, dealt with a great many VD patients. Its name entered the language as a generic term for any clinic specialising in sexually transmitted diseases, and can still be found in slang dictionaries today.

Chapter 6: Say Their Names

47) *South London Press*, November 6, 1998.

48) One of the most powerful moments I experienced at the theatre in 2011 came while watching Alecky Blythe's *London Road* at the National. Blythe tells the story of the Ipswich murders mostly from the point of view of people living in the town's red light district, but reserves one scene for the murdered women alone. Five actresses representing Gemma Adams, Anneli Alderton, Paula Clennell, Tania Nicol and Annette Nicholls stood stock-still on a silent stage, glaring out at the audience for what felt like a very long time. "Don't you *dare* leave us out of this story," they seemed to be saying. "Don't you fucking *dare!*"

49) *Financial Times*, December 27, 2008.

50) The Hop Cellars is still a pub, but its basement bar is now called The Sheaf.

51) *The Independent*, October 31, 2009.

Chapter 7: The Black Death

52) *Rosa Anglica*, by John of Gaddesden (1280-1361). Quoted in Burford, above. John hints his treatment will prevent unwanted pregnancy too.

53) John Wycliffe, the 14th century religious dissident, warned that monks and friars at this time were claiming medical knowledge in order to seduce local women. They targeted women whose men were away from home for some reason and told them no woman could remain healthy without regular sex. In *Of the Leaven of Pharisees* Wycliffe writes: "When Lords are away from home in wars or in justice or in parliament or in other lordships and when merchants do be in the country and when plowmen do be all day long in the fields, then these pharisees [lecherous ones] run fast to their wives under cover of holiness and fornicate with them."

54) Other streets in Southwark's red light districts, such as Maiden Lane and Love Lane, were named more ironically. The sarcastic wit

applied in christening these streets often ensures their names survive today where cruder ones do not.

55) Henry Harben's 1915 *Dictionary of London* tracks one alleyway's name changing from Shitteborwelane (1272) via Shitbourn Lane (1394) and Shetenborn Lane (1539) to the innocuous Sherborne Lane today. "Burn" is an old Scots word for stream and this alleyway seems once to have been a popular public convenience: Shitstream Lane.

56) Rick Powell from the UK's Federation of Burial & Cremation Authorities told me a buried adult body takes about 12 years to reduce itself to bones and that even a child's takes six. In times of plague, bodies were often disinterred much sooner.

57) *Death, Religion and the Family in England 1480-1750*, by Ralph Houlbrooke (Clarendon Press, 1998).

58) My understanding is that cases of murder in the Liberty went to the King's courts rather than the Bishop's. Perhaps the Bishop's court simply recorded these two cases before passing them to the King for trial?

59) This episode came as part of the Peasants' Revolt. Tyler's men were rebelling against a poll tax imposed by Richard II and demanding an end to the social structure that kept them in serfdom. Tyler was killed two days after the Southwark massacre when he confronted both the King and Walworth at Smithfield and some accounts say Walworth himself dealt the fatal blow. The revolt petered out at that point and Tyler's head was later displayed on London Bridge as a warning to anyone else who felt like making trouble.

60) *The Westminster Chronicle 1381-1394*, ed. LC Hector (Clarendon Press, 1982)

61) *Medieval Southwark*, by Martha Carlin (Hambledon Press, 1996). Stewholders were expected to be married men whose families did not live on the premises.

62) Among the single women who supported themselves without prostitution in Southwark, the most common trades were preparing food or peddling it through the streets (26%), textiles work such as spinning yarn (25%) or working as a seamstress (21%). "This suggests that most of the female householders of Southwark had slender economic resources, insufficient to keep a shop, a stock of goods or expensive tools," Carlin writes.

63) This was the raucous England of Geoffrey Chaucer, who wrote *The Canterbury Tales* at the end of the 1300s, using a real Southwark tavern called the Tabard as the book's first setting. In her own tale, the Wife of Bath reminds her grumpy husband that she could easily earn a living without him just by using what's between her legs: "If I would sell my pretty thing / I could walk as new-clothed as a rose / But I will keep it for your own pleasure".

---

64) I don't know how long Brenchesle and Osteler were kept in the Tower of London, or indeed if they ever emerged. Richard II, the man who'd sent them there, ended up in the Tower himself in 1399, where he was imprisoned before being taken to his death in Pontefract Castle.

65) By "canal dung" the report means filth from the sewer ditches.

66) In March 1543, the Earl of Surrey was brought to court for taking a row boat out on the Thames and using a catapult to fire stones at these women. He was punished with a stay in Fleet Prison, but it seems to have been damage to the windows rather than the women which sent him there.

67) In 1617, Bankside stewholders complained that innkeepers in the High Street had blocked an old alleyway which previously gave their customers a convenient short cut to the riverside brothels. The court ruled they'd been trying to make lazy punters spend money in the High Street's own establishments instead.

68) The British Museum's print room has a Bill Crook engraving showing this row of stew-houses as it appeared in 1547. He's helpfully labelled each one with its name and identifying symbol.

69) This joint gave its name to Rose Street in Southwark, which survives as Rose Alley today. "Plucking a rose" became an Elizabethan euphemism for sex.

Chapter 8: The Invisible Gardener

70) Calling our chat that day an interview makes my role sound far more important than it was. John's so passionate about Cross Bones that all I really had to do there was ask a single opening question, then sit back and let him talk. He scarcely paused for breath until about 40 minutes in and then only because he'd made a particularly expansive gesture which sent coffee flying everywhere!

71) For my account of William Kirwan's murder see *The Borough Mystery* on PlanetSlade.com.

72) The most interesting piece of recent graffiti on the door that day read: "RIP to the sket you used to beat! Her days are over. Devonport RIP". Sket is a slang term roughly equivalent to "slag" or "ho" and still current usage among British youth as recently as 2011. Whether you take the tone of this message as gleeful or mournful, it suggests that a whole new generation has discovered Cross Bones and understands its role.

73) John Constable maintains there was no such drug use at Cross Bones, saying that any vagrants who got in there seemed to prefer booze. "Clearing up there, I found plenty of Special Brew cans, but not a single needle," he told me.

74) Network Rail held a Transport for London lease allowing it to use this part of the site to store vehicles used in its Thameslink project.

---

75) *The Independent*, March 15, 2009. The 40-storey Swiss Re building, better known as the Gherkin, is clearly visible from Cross Bones.

76) *Sunday Times*, September 20, 2009.

77) This piece appears on **The Cross Bones Chronicles** website, but the writer's not credited by name. The Museum of London (MoL) excavation mentioned is their 1993 dig at Cross Bones, which we'll come to later.

78) Maxkollective has an excellent Flickr set of July 2008 photographs showing Andy and the other volunteers' gardening work at Cross Bones as it then stood.

Chapter 9: Farewell to the Stews

79) Syphilis takes its name from a 1530 poem by Girolamo Fracastoro. He invented a mythical shepherd called Syphilus who insults the god Apollo and is struck down with a hideous disease whose symptoms matched the new infection sweeping Europe.

80) Among the common people, syphilis was known either as "the great pox" (to distinguish it from smallpox) or named for whichever country the speaker's native land happened to dislike most. The English and the Italians called it The French Disease, the French called it The Spanish Disease, the Russians called it The Polish Disease, the Polish and the Persians called it The Turkish Disease, the Indians called it The Portuguese Disease and the Tahitians called it The British Disease. In Germany it was known as The French Evil, in Japan it was The Chinese Pox and in Muslim Turkey people called it The Christian Disease.

81) *The Guardian*, May 17, 2013.

82) The first recorded use of condoms as a measure against syphilis appears in a 1564 book by the Italian doctor Gabriele Falloppio, but it would be another century before the idea caught on in Britain. Until the early 1900s, when the first disposable condoms were introduced, the gentleman gave his sheath a quick rinse out after every encounter, then tucked it back in his wallet for next time.

83) Venice had a reputation for running Europe's most hygienic and best-organised brothels, where the girls were said to be both elegant and well-mannered. If syphilis couldn't be controlled even there, what chance did less punctilious cities have?

84) Winchester was then the wealthiest Bishopric in England, so there's no doubt Foxe was a very powerful man. Even today, the Lord Privy Seal is automatically given a place in the Cabinet of any British Government.

85) To understand what a vast sum £5 was at this time, consider the funeral accounts of Anne Fortesque, an Oxfordshire noblewoman who

died in 1518. Her elaborate funeral cost a total of only £39. The catering budget accounted for just over £10 of this, but still provided plenty of food and drink for all the 300 mourners attending.
86) Exchange of e-mails, August 2013.

Chapter 10: The Southwark Mysteries
87) *Sunday Telegraph*, May 14, 2000.
88) YouTube has footage of *The Southwark Mysteries* 2020 performance.

Chapter 11: Shakespeare's Bankside
89) *A Notable Discovery of Cozenage*, by Robert Greene (1591). An added refinement to crossbiting today is that the pimp starts taking smartphone photographs the moment he walks in and threatens to distribute them on the internet.
90) A jaxe of course (more usually spelt "jacks" or "jakes") is a lavatory, so the clergyman here was echoing Thomas Aquinas' 13th century remark about the palace cesspool.
91) *London: The Biography*, by Peter Ackroyd (Vintage, 2001). Ackroyd's view - and I think it's right - is that this attitude towards Southwark didn't change till the Jubilee Line extension became necessary in the late 1980s.
92) Published in *Holinshed's Chronicles*, 1577.
93) "From the late 16th century onwards, a growing number of parish overseers' accounts record disbursements for poor people's burials, especially the shroud and the grave," Houlbrooke writes. Coffins were seldom used for ordinary burials until about 1650. Until then, poorer people would simply be buried in a shroud or winding-sheet.
94) Thomas Platten, a Swiss traveller describing his visit to London in 1599, writes that he found prostitutes swarming around every tavern and playhouse in the city, as well as several child brothels in which girls aged from seven to 14 were supplied. He doesn't say where in London these brothels were, but every other taste was catered for on Bankside so I've no doubt this one was too.
95) I've only been to Tijuana once and even then it was just a day-trip from San Diego. The coach driver told us he'd taken another tourist group down there a few months earlier, but that one guy had failed to appear back at the bus for the return journey. They waited as long as they could, but eventually had to go back across the border without him. Two weeks later, this same driver was waiting at the Tijuana pick-up point again when the missing tourist staggered up. He'd lost his wallet and one of his shoes, his clothes were all over the place and he hadn't slept in days. Quite how the details were worked out at US immigration, I don't know, but they managed to get him back home in

the end - where he faced a rather awkward interview with his wife.

96) There's a 1992 episode of *The Simpsons* where Krusty the Clown refers to Tijuana as "the happiest place on Earth". Krusty would have loved Shakespeare's Bankside.

97) *Shakespeare's Restless World: Swordplay & Swagger* (Radio 4, April 2012).

98) After this tour-de-force explanation from Dark, I offered my own summing-up: "So it's *Boardwalk Empire* meets *Deadwood* with a touch of *Breaking Bad*?" She laughed. "Yes, exactly - plus bears!"

99) I've told the story a little more fully in this chapter's addendum.

100) Leslie Hotson's 1931 book *Shakespeare vs. Swallow* describes William Gardiner's life as one of "greed, usury, fraud, cruelty and perjury". I think it's safe to assume from this that he was related to the gangster clan of Gardiners involved in running so many Bankside brothels.

101) Shakespeare originally named his Falstaff character Sir John Oldcastle, perhaps with the idea of teasing the real Oldcastle's descendent Lord Cobham. Oldcastle was actually a protestant martyr of very sober habits, so Lord Cobham was not amused. He insisted that Shakespeare change the character's name, backed that demand up with various threats and duly got his way. The playwright was sufficiently shaken by this to add a disclaimer about Falstaff in his epilogue for *Henry IV Part 2*. "Oldcastle died a martyr and this is not the man," he has the play's final speaker say.

102) The remark about honour, of course, is Falstaff's own. It appears in *Henry IV Part 1*.

103) *The Annals of London*, compiled by John Richardson (Cassell & Co, 2000).

104) *Henry VI Part 1*: Act 1, scene 3.

105) *Troilus & Cressida*: Act 5, scene 10. *Cassell's Dictionary of Slang* cites a similar usage in 17th century popular speech: "No goose bit so sore as Bess Broughton's". Broughton was London's most famous courtesan at that time.

Chapter 12: Going Underground

106) *Altered State: The Story of Ecstasy Culture & Acid House*, by Matthew Collin (Serpent's Tail, 1997).

107) *The Cross Bones Burial Ground, Redcross Way, Southwark, London: Archaeological Excavations (1991-1998)*, by Megan Brickley, Adrian Miles and Hilary Stainer (Museum of London, 1999).

108) There had been warehouses occupying the footprint's ground until the 1980s and the MoL found foundations for these buildings as they dug. The builders who'd put those warehouses up had stacked the bones they disturbed neatly into the construction trenches lining the

foundations' walls.

109) *History Cold Case: Crossbones Girl* (BBC 2, first aired May 2010).

110) The idea of Christ rising in the east seems to be a mixture of sunrise symbolism and the fact that Jerusalem lies to the east of Britain. For corpses in the third or fourth layer down at Cross Bones, their first experience of resurrection would presumably be banging their head on the coffin above.

111) I'm using our modern understanding of the word "children" here as referring to anyone under 18 years of age. Infant burials in St Saviour's Parish spiked every summer, as the hot weather made children more susceptible to dysentery.

112) The MoL's sample was drawn from close to the surface at Cross Bones, which means its figures may over-represent the number of children buried there. Where not enough depth of earth remained to add another adult coffin to the stack you were burying, a child's one might just about fit – and that saved wasting precious space. It follows that the top layer of Cross Bones' earth may contain a higher proportion of children than the ground as a whole.

113) Ken Campbell was, in the words of Ian Shuttleworth, "one of Britain's premier theatrical fruitcakes". In addition to staging *The Warp's* first production and a Pidgin English *Macbeth*, he toured his own one-man shows on the history of ventriloquism and all kinds of Forteana. When Campbell died in 2008, Constable ensured he got a ribbon of his own on Cross Bones' gates.

114) At the other end of the spectrum were Southwark's cheapest, no-frills establishments. "In the lowest class of brothel, there would be no entertainment but plenty of liquor and the girls worked till they dropped," Burford writes.

115) *The Picara: From Hera to Fantasy Heroine*, by Anne Kaler (Popular Press, 1991).

116) "Under James' benevolent if drunken eyes, the Bankside amusement park flourished as never before," Burford writes.

Chapter 13: Puritans & Plagues

117) *Old Southwark & Its People*, by William Rendle (W Drewett, 1878).

118) The names "Redcross Way", "Redcross Alley", "Redcross Court" and "Redcross Street" were used interchangeably by the people living there in the 1800s. It's clear from context that they always have the same street in mind.

119) John Stow's *Survey of London* (1598).

120) By "excluded from Christian burial" here, I think Stow must mean they were buried in unconsecrated ground. Since the Reformation of

the 1530s, that issue was irrelevant in the church's official doctrine, but it may still have mattered to the common folk.

121) Houlbrooke thinks only an official condemnation by the Church would be enough to bar a woman from parish burial. "I think that only a known formal sentence of excommunication (in theory quite possible for a notorious prostitute) would have been sufficient to deny her churchyard burial," he told me. Other stew-house girls may have finished up at Cross Bones simply because they required a pauper burial.

122) *Histories and Antiquities of the Parish of St Saviour's Southwark,* by Matthew Concanen & Aaron Morgan (1795). Concanen was a poet, essayist and political pamphleteer who also spent 16 years as Jamaica's attorney general. His mischievous 1728 piece *An Essay Against Too Much Reading* was the first published article to claim Shakespeare hadn't written his own plays.

123) The MoL has found evidence of seven burial grounds in St Saviour's parish, only three of which were used by the parish authorities. The three parish grounds were St Saviour's own churchyard, the College Churchyard in Park Street (used by St Saviour's Almshouse) and Cross Bones (the parish poor ground). The other four sites were Deadman's Place (used first as a plague pit then by the adjacent chapel), the Baptist burial ground in Bandy Leg Walk (now part of Southwark Bridge Road) and two Quaker grounds (one on Ewer Street, the other on O'Meara Street).

124) John Aubrey (1626-1697) is best known as the author of *Brief Lives*. The dung wharf he mentions loaded cemetery bones on to waiting barges. These bones would later be ground into a phosphorous-rich power for use as agricultural fertiliser.

125) Boulton also quotes the accounts from Richard Bird, a Southwark vintner, whose family spent 15 shillings and twopence to bury him in 1626. This broke down to ten shillings and twopence for the ground, the funeral cloth and tolling of the church bell, three shillings paid to the minister, clerk and sexton (between them), fourpence each to the bearers and eightpence for the gravedigger. This would have been a relatively grand funeral by Southwark's standards at the time and far beyond what most people living there could expect.

126) Once coffins became obligatory for even pauper burials in around 1650, some parishes experimented with a re-usable model. This had a hinged underside which allowed the body to be dropped discretely into the grave without burying the coffin too. This was thought to be a step too far, however, and the practice was quickly abandoned.

127) The Clink Liberty's special status was briefly renewed under both Charles I and Charles II. I get the impression this was done purely as a courtesy to the Bishop of Winchester and that real power over the

Liberty's affairs remained outside his hands.

128) I checked with Patricia Dark to see exactly what geographical area these Bills of Mortality covered. "The City of London, the City of Westminster and the borough of Southwark were included in the Bills of Mortality, along with the parishes of Lambeth, Rotherhithe, Newington and Bermondsey," she told me. That means that the whole area covered by the modern boroughs of both Southwark and Bermondsey would have been counted in the Bills' 1665 plague deaths.

129) Muddiman also tells the story of a Newgate butcher declared dead of plague by the parish corpse collectors, but left laid out in his room overnight because their cart was already full. Next morning, the butcher's daughter went into that room and was startled to hear her father beckon her over to ask for a glass of ale. "The man took a pipe of tobacco, ate a rabbit and on Sunday went to church to give God thanks for his preservation," Muddiman writes. Many families preferred to keep their deceased laid out at home for a few days to guard against just this possibility, a practice which added still further to infection rates.

130) In the case of private burials, even quite wealthy families might delay interment by as much as two weeks. Houlbrooke quotes the instructions given to Dorothy Wood's coffin-maker in 1704: "Be pleased to take care of the inside, for the Gentlewoman is not design'd to be buried this fortnight." The writer is asking for the coffin's interior joints to be pitch-sealed with particular care to minimise any escaping smell.

131) Some of the Bankside girls opted for a trip to America, where they were sorely needed by the male settlers who'd followed the *Mayflower's* 1620 voyage there. "The great majority were enabled to start new lives, get married and become the mothers of many respected daughters of the American Revolution," Burford writes.

132) In 1757, Samuel Derrick compiled and published the first edition of *Harris's List of Covent Garden Ladies*, a highly explicit consumer's guide to the prices and specialities of the many working girls who kept rooms there. It was this area between Seven Dials and The Strand which formed the centre of Georgian London's sex trade now, entering the language in slang phrases like "Covent Garden gout" (meaning a dose of the pox).

133) The new factories also stretched into neighbouring Lambeth, where one 18th century press report claimed a local gang had been digging up bodies from the graveyards to harvest their fat for candles, their bones for alkali and their flesh for dog meat. As Peter Ackroyd points out, this report is both lurid enough and vague enough to suggest the story's apocryphal, but it does provide a chilling prophesy of the real grave-robbers who'd later target Cross Bones itself.

134) St Saviour's signed a lease for Cross Bones under the parish's own name in 1820 and finally acquired freehold of the site in 1863.

That was the year the Bishop of Winchester's remaining rights over the Clink Liberty passed to the Church of England's Ecclesiastical Commissioners, which is what made the transfer of freehold possible.
135) See PlanetSlade's *Jones and Harwood* essay for an example of a ballad sheet carrying this image.
136) *England's Mistress: The Infamous Life of Emma Hamilton*, by Kate Williams (Hutchinson, 2006).
137) That's certainly the view taken by Niki Adams, a spokeswoman for the English Collective of Prostitutes. "Why is it more degrading to work in the sex industry than skipping meals to feed our children, begging on the streets or working in low-wage jobs?" she asked a BBC journalist on Radio 4's *Today* programmne. (December 4, 2012.)

Chapter 14: Crossbones Girl

138) The MoL's archaeologists found this particular skeleton in a cheap, ramshackle coffin less than three feet below the surface. Other coffins were packed just an inch or two away on all sides, with eight or nine more layers stacked beneath.
139) Green's original report for the BBC contains a lot of information that never made it into the finished programme. That's where most of his quotes come from here.
140) The camera caught Black as she studied the skull's accumulation of distorted syphilitic bone. "That's just horrendous," she murmured. "That must have been so painful."
141) This is a belief still held in some parts of Africa, where it's held to be a cure for Aids. "You have huge HIV numbers and nobody is educated on how you get HIV," the actress and campaigner Charlize Theron said of her native South Africa in 2009. "Many think if they rape a child or virgin they will be cured of the disease." The 2011 Broadway musical *The Book of Mormon* mocks this superstition with an African character called Middala, who has to be talked out of finding a baby to pursue his own treatment.
142) The best you could hope for from mercury treatment was that it would slow the progress of your syphilis. It certainly didn't offer a cure and its side effects were hideous: vomiting, hair loss, amnesia, depression and extreme tooth decay. The programme compared it to chemotherapy today - a debilitating treatment people used only because there was nothing else.
143) Cross Bones lies in the stretch of Redcross Way between Southwark Street and Union Street, with the Boot & Flogger pub (10-20 Redcross Way) directly opposite its gates. Houses numbered 1-9 Redcross Way are just on the other side of Southwark Street, less than 150 yards from the burial ground itself.
144) Old Bailey trial transcripts: January 29, 1838.

145) Child witnesses like Grant (who'd never learnt to read) would take their oath in the Victorian courts by reciting *The Lord's Prayer* from memory. This was felt to show they knew the difference between right and wrong and so would not casually lie about what they'd seen. Grant had failed to clear this hurdle at the coroner's hearing, but a priest taught him the prayer in time for him to testify at the Old Bailey.

Chapter 15: Resurrection Men

146) However unsavoury this practice sounds to modern ears, we must remember that it laid the groundwork for every surgical procedure saving lives today.

147) William Osler was chief physician at Johns Hopkins Hospital in Baltimore and the visitor writing here was his uncle. Rectified oil of turpentine was known as "ol. Terebinth" at the time and seems to have been employed here as a disinfectant.

148) *Poet-Physician: Keats & Medical Science*, by Donald Goellnicht (University of Pittsburgh Press, 1984).

149) "Once Keats got used to the stink, maggots and livid colours of decaying flesh, no doubt he joined in the robust jokes that steadied them in their work," writes the poet's biographer Nicholas Roe. Distancing yourself in this way must surely be a necessary part of mastering such work.

150) Orme's comments here come from our exchange of e-mails in November 2012.

151) By 1822, people's fears about grave-robbing had become so great that undertakers started supplying metal coffins to those who could afford them. The extra weight of these coffins increased costs for every other aspect of the burial too and an 1822 St Saviour's price list shows such burials charged at over £12 for adults and nearly £10 for children. The result was to ensure metal coffins could be used only by the rich and hence left the poor more vulnerable than ever. If you could afford a metal coffin, you could afford a better burial ground than Cross Bones too, so I doubt they ever troubled the grave-robbers working there.

152) *The Corpse King*, by Dorothy Davies (2007) is available on Authorsden.com.

153) *The Bodysnatcher's Apprentice*, by David Orme (Kindle, 2012).

154) *Report From The House of Commons Select Committee on Anatomy, 1828*. The four resurrectionists who spoke before this committee were given immunity in return for their co-operation.

155) *The Diary of a Resurrectionist 1811-1812*, edited and commented upon by James Blake Bailey (Rarebooks.com, 2012).

156) The fact that the gang who shopped Brookes did so at Union Street police station (which is just around the corner from Cross Bones) suggests the undertaker was sited on that station's patch. It's possible

that the corpse was destined for Cross Bones when stolen and still ended up there after its recovery. One St Saviour's undertaker produced an 1838 price list showing he charged one pound, five shillings and eightpence to bury an adult at Cross Bones (equivalent to about £120 today), so the bribe must have been a lot more than that for our man to consider it worth the risk.

157) It saved the resurrectionists a lot of work when they could steal a body before its burial instead of having to dig it up later, so they often recruited accomplices like the undertaker here. Corrupt workhouse officials would fiddle the paperwork to make deaths in their own establishment disappear, then have the resurrectionist collect those bodies overnight.

158) By 1811, Crouch had grown so used to throwing his weight around that he actually called the Borough Boys out on strike, demanding still higher prices for the bodies they supplied. The surgeons managed to tough out this dispute by employing amateur body-snatchers instead, forcing Crouch and his men to resume work at their old rates. Many surgeons who'd dealt with the "scabs" during Crouch's strike later suffered the sort of revenge break-ins described in this chapter.

159) Sir Astley also pressurised Guy's Hospital into giving his incompetent nephew Bransby Cooper a surgeon's job there. In March 1828, the *Lancet* published a scathing account of a botched operation by Bransby which lasted over an hour and killed a patient whose life had not previously been in danger. "Not only did Cooper lose his way anatomically, he lost his head," the *Lancet* says. "His panicky use of multiple instruments and his barked and desperate orders to his assistants were observed by a number of his surgical colleagues."

160) Nothing that happens in Southwark remains consigned to the past for long and that turned out to be as true for the theft of human remains as anything else. In April 1998, Southwark Crown Court jailed Anthony-Noel Kelly, a local artist, for stealing body parts from the Royal College of Surgeons to use in making casts for his sculptures. A police search of his Southwark studio uncovered 30 stolen body parts, including three human heads, six arms, ten legs (with the feet still attached), three torsos and a brain.

161) Human teeth at this time could be sold to dentists, who assembled them into sets of dentures for their customers. These sets were later nicknamed Waterloo teeth, because so many of them came from the casualties of that 1815 battle.

162) Fifty guineas in 1815 would be worth about £4,000 today.

163) A valet – also known as a gentleman's gentleman - was the job Jeeves performed for Bertie Wooster. What on earth must Light have been like in that role?

Chapter 16: John Crow's Megaphone

164) *Property Week*, February 11, 2011.

165) *Property Week*, November 29, 2012.

166) I love this little verse for the way it condenses the girl's childhood, sexual awakening, working life and death into the passage of a single week. But Walsh may be pulling our legs when he labels it "old rhyme, c. 1880". *Cassell's Dictionary of Slang* dates "working girl" as a term for prostitute no earlier than the 1930s and as far as I've been able to discover, "lipstick" in the sense used here first appeared about 1920. If both these terms really were around in 1880, then the lexicographers have some re-writing to do.

167) Jimmy Cauty (aka Rockman Rock) is not only a musician, but also a witty and imaginative arts prankster. Google the K Foundation to find out more.

168) As far as I know, Banksy's never responded to this invitation. As we've seen with recent auction sales of his graffiti pieces (many of which have been chipped from the owner's walls under somewhat dubious circumstances), his prices have now risen to a point where any Cross Bones tarmac he decorated might well be worth removing intact for sale by the developers. It could even end up adding to their profits from the site.

Chapter 17: Seeking Closure

169) The minimum depth officially then allowed for burials at Cross Bones was four feet, or twice the minimum depth actually used. In patches where it was possible to dig much deeper, the sexton Mr Drewett explained, he buried the first coffin as deep as 16 feet, stacking later ones on top in the underground towers MoL archaeologists would later find there. "My system has invariably been to go to 14 or 16 feet where an opportunity offered, without respect to pay," Drewett wanted the vestry to understand. "The same has been done with parish and workhouse funerals, where I had no prospect of remuneration whatsoever."

170) In fairness to St Saviour's churchwardens, it was their responsibility to find *somewhere* in the parish where the huge influx of cholera victims could be buried. Quick as the vestry's critics were to condemn the state of Cross Bones, I doubt they offered much of an alternative.

171) You'd be in no hurry to empty an underfloor cesspool like the ones mentioned here, but the task had to be faced eventually. This was done using buckets carried in and out through the house, with all the casual spillage that implies.

172) Sir Edwin Chadwick, secretary of the Poor Law Commission,

produced his report from this enquiry in 1843. You can find Wyld's contribution extracted in the *Provincial Medical Journal* of January 13, 1844.

173) Take note of that "18 inches". Now even the two-foot minimum depth considered inadequate back in 1832 could no longer be maintained.

174) *Gatherings From Grave Yards*, by George Alfred Walker (Longman, 1839).

175) These 20,000 coffins stacked nine deep would make 2,222 "towers" altogether. Equally spaced in an acre's 4,840 square yards, each stack would get just over two square yards of surface area to itself. The depth would be even tighter, with each coffin given just 16 inches of the 12-foot hole Haycock mentions. It's a squeeze but, in an age when Londoners were rather smaller than they are today, just about possible. Photographs from the MoL's 1993 Cross Bones dig suggest a very similar density was achieved there.

176) This made me think of Christopher Hitchens describing the bloodstained dirt he found blowing into his own lungs as he stood next to an Iraqi mass grave in July 2003. "I hope never again to feel so utterly befouled," he writes in 2010's *Hitch-22*. "It was in the nostrils, in the eyes, on the tongue and in the mouth."

177) Thomas Hardy caught the horror of this bone house slop well in his 1882 poem *The Levelled Churchyard*: "We late-lamented, resting here / Are mixed to human jam / And each to each exclaims in fear / 'I know not which I am!'."

178) *A Microscopical Examination of the Water Supplied to the Inhabitants of London and the Suburban Districts*, by Arthur Hill Hassall (Samuel Highley, 1850).

179) The result of S&V's inaction was that, when cholera struck London again in 1854, Southwark once again showed the highest mortality in the city. That was also the year in which John Snow's epidemiology study of the neighbourhood served by a Soho water pump proved that cholera is primarily spread by dirty drinking water.

180) George Cruikshank, who illustrated many of Dickens' books, produced a scathing 1832 cartoon on the state of Southwark's drinking water. It shows S&V Water's owner John Edwards throned above a cesspool and toasting Southwark's citizens with raw sewerage.

181) The shells Gwilt mentions here were flimsy wooden containers used to transport a body before a real coffin could be found. Victorians used them rather as we use body bags today.

182) Like many Victorian letter-writers, Mrs Gwilt had a very verbose style. For the sake of both clarity and impact, I've made a lot of small cuts to her letter while transcribing it here, but you can find the full text in the MoL's Cross Bones report (see note 107). The same goes for

Lord Brabazon's letter below.

183) If anything, St Saviour's claimed, they'd gone above and beyond the call of duty with the suicide's remains. The parish chaplain had refused to wait any longer for the delayed coroner's warrant and buried the body anyway, thus "rendering himself liable to a penalty for doing so".

184) St Saviour's letter lists all the individuals involved here, giving us a reliable list of at least six people we can be sure were buried at Cross Bones. They were: Elizabeth Frances Lock (aged 4), died July 23, 1849 and buried next day; Harriet Horton and Mary Ann Priest (ages unknown), both taken to the dead house on July 24 and buried next day; Michael Leary (aged 8), died August 2 and buried next day; Mary Evans (aged 68), died August 6 and buried next day; Walter Cook (aged 14), found dead in the river on August 10 and buried next day. The seventh name mentioned is Charles Shooter (age unknown), the Blackfriars Bridge suicide, who was found dead in the river on July 22. St Saviour's would say only that he was buried "in one of the cemeteries" on July 25.

185) *The London Gazette*, launched in 1665, is the British Government's official journal of record. Its role is to print all manner of official government announcements to ensure they're available somewhere in the public record. It carried many warnings to overcrowded city graveyards at about this time.

186) It's at this point that any remaining sympathy I had for St Saviour's evaporates. Spending parish money on expensive legal advice to combat the Board of Health smacks more of hubris than any genuine concern for the people round Redcross Way.

187) Mariane Gwilt's husband George is among this letter's signatories. He was an architect, who drew up some plans of Cross Bones in 1821.

188) A year after Sutherland's report, St Saviour's was still showing some of the highest cholera deaths in London. Statistics published in the *Times* of November 9, 1853, show St Saviour's then accounted for 12% of all the cholera deaths in London and 20% of those south of the river.

189) Sydenham lies south of Southwark in the neighbouring borough of Lewisham.

190) The whole of London had a burial crisis on its hands at this time, which spawned a lot of private cemetery companies hoping to profit by making new land available. The London Necropolis Company ran corpse trains out of London's Waterloo Station to the new Brookwood Cemetery at Woking in Surrey, where bodies from St Saviour's Parish filled the first graves.

191) Brabazon was chairman of London's Metropolitan Public Garden, Boulevard & Playground Association. His two letters appeared in the

Times on November 10, 1883 and December 22, 1883, respectively.
192) We can get an idea of the living conditions at Redcross Way in Lofthouse's time from DrWot's YouTube interview with Joyce Newman, whose mother was born there in 1895. "It was old-fashioned buildings, with just one wash-house on the landing for three or four blocks and they were about five stories high," she says. "They were terrible places."
193) Lofthouse was Alice's married name, taken from her estranged husband, the soldier William Lofthouse. Some reports of the case call her Alice Fisher, which I assume was her maiden name. She was still married to William Lofthouse when she died.
194) Old Bailey trial transcripts: September 13, 1898.
195) *The Sun*, July 18, 1898.
196) *Daily Mail*, July 20, 1898.
197) "Fatty" was William Gould's nickname.
198) *Daily Mail*, July 27, 1898.
199) *Curing Hooliganism: Moral Panic, Juvenile Delinquency & The Political Culture of Moral Reform in Britain 1898-1908*, by Ian Livie (University of Southern California Phd dissertation, May 2010).
200) Burke's 20 shilling fine would translate to about £110 today.
201) *South London Chronicle*, July 23, 1898.

*****

Book Two: Cross Bones 2013 - 2023.

202) The Landmark Court site includes both Cross Bones and TfL's planned Liberty of Southwark development next door.
203) De Mowbray's Goosewing is a long, curved wooden canopy sheltering visitors as they move from Cross Bones' entrance to its central area.
204) U+I was acquired by Landsec in November 2021, which continued the Landmark Court project.
205) Max Fox, the *Better Things* character shown visiting the Mizuko Jizo statues at Cross Bones, had undergone an abortion earlier in the series.
206) This was during Boris Johnson's time as PM.
207) Covid precautions had moved the forum meetings online.
208) Constable's referring here to Handforth Parish Council's famously fractious Zoom meeting of December 2020. Jackie Weaver, the meeting's chairwoman, came under heavy attack there from participants challenging her authority.
209) I've seen two of the four BOST exclusion letters. Apart from this first paragraph, they're identical.
210) Shortly after my conversation with Gilsenan, BOST issued this

statement: "BOST, in the same way as every other Charity and Organisation that is responsible for looking after Public Open Space has policies in relation to anti-social behaviour in order to protect other users and those who look after our spaces."

Photo: Andy Porter Photography.

About the Author

Paul Slade is a London journalist. His work's appeared in *The Guardian, The Times, Mojo, Time Out, The Idler, fRoots* and many other publications. He's also made a handful of documentaries for BBC Radio 4 on popular music history and London's forgotten past. His previous book, *Black Swan Blues*, was adapted by Radiolab as an acclaimed podcast series called *The Vanishing of Harry Pace*.

Also available by Paul Slade

"A dauntingly complete and fascinating piece of work."
- *Greil Marcus.*

Also available by Paul Slade

"A fascinating account of the enterprise which preceded Motown by some 40 years." – *Mike Atherton,* Echoes *magazine.*

For more of Paul Slade's writing visit

www.PlanetSlade.com

Murder Ballads
Secret London
... and more

"A fantastic website." – *Dave Henderson,* Mojo.

Printed in Great Britain
by Amazon

46327623R00136